THE
PRIVATE
LIVES
OF
ENGLISH
WORDS

THE PRIVATE LIVES OF ENGLISH WORDS

LOUIS G. HELLER • ALEXANDER HUMEZ • MALCAH DROR

Wynwood® Press
Tarrytown, New York

WYNWOOD® PRESS EDITION 1991
*This edition published by special
arrangement with Gale Research, Inc.*

Library of Congress Cataloging-in-Publication Data

Heller, Louis G.
  The private lives of English words / by Louis G. Heller, Alexander
Humez and Malcah Dror. — 1st ed.
    p.   cm.
  Reprint. Originally published: Detroit, Mich. : Gale
Research Co., ©1984.
  Includes index.
  ISBN 0-922066-71-X :
  1. English language—Etymology—Dictionaries.   I. Humez,
Alexander.   II. Dror, Malcah.   III. Title.
[PE1580.H35   1991]
422'.03—dc20
                                                    91-14960
                                                    CIP

Copyright © 1984 by VERBATIM, The Language Quarterly
Published by Wynwood® Press
Tarrytown, New York
An Imprint of Gleneida Publishing Group
Printed in the United States of America

Contents

List of Headwords

v

Contents

vi

Contents

Contents

Contents

Contents

Contents

Contents

Contents

xv

Contents

Foreword

Geoffrey Leech

University of Lancaster

Man's interest in the history of words and their meanings dates at least from the time of the Stoics of Ancient Greece. For them, to trace the history of a word back to its origin was the best guide to its "true meaning" or *etymon*. This view still has power in arguments about words today. But the term *etymology*, derived from the Stoics' search for "the true and original meaning," is now understood simply as the search for a historical explanation of how a word came to have its present form and meaning. And the more successful and scholarly this search is, the more one becomes aware not only that the ultimate "origin" of a word can rarely be found but also that a determination to use a word in its oldest known sense would result in total confusion for one's hearers. For example, one could speak of friends *arriving* at one's house only if they came by boat (the Latin ancestor would mean 'arrive at a bank or shore'); one could speak of receiving a *fee* only if it were paid in the form of livestock (the Old English *feoh* is cognate with Latin *pecus*, 'cattle'); and one would speak of paying an employee a *salary* only if the payment were used for the purchase of salt. So the argument that a word means what it used to mean may be justly dubbed, for all its attraction, the "etymological fallacy."

This does not mean that tracing how a word came by its present meaning(s) is a futile enterprise; in fact, once one abandons the search for "ultimate truth" and concentrates on *how* meanings have evolved, the explanation becomes fascinating, if not stranger than the imagination could have foretold, as this book amply shows. Anyone who disbelieves should begin by looking up the words *buxom, nice,* and *treacle* in the following pages. The first impression may be that words change their meanings in unpredictable ways: but this will be corrected when one examines not the immense distance over which a word may have traveled in meaning through the centuries, but the various staging posts along the route. Here one begins to see a pattern of processes whereby one meaning gives rise to another. This Foreword will be concerned with a brief survey of these processes and their classification.

It is sometimes overlooked that a word typically has not one meaning, but a multiplicity of meanings. Between the varied current senses of a word like *bond* or *press* there is often a family resemblance which suggests that they have a common origin. Such similarities are the result of a phenomenon known as **radiation,** whereby from a common historical source a number of distinct senses have developed. Thus the idea of 'exerting pressure' in the Latin *pressāre* leads to both physical and abstract senses of the English verb *press*, to the denotation by the noun *press* of various implements for applying pressure, and then, via the *printing press*, to a transferred application of the term to the newspaper world. The image of radiation is that of a tree, in which various branches sprout from a common trunk, and often become themselves the basis for further subbranches.

But this metaphor has its limitations, for to the concept of radiation must be added the compensating negative principle of **fading,** whereby an old sense of a word—perhaps the "trunk" of our earlier derivation—dies away, so that it can be traced only through historical records, or more remotely, from historical reconstructions. When, as so often happens, the evolution of meaning is accompanied by changes in the form of the word, the earlier sense may become quite opaque to later generations, leaving the way open for further changes unconstrained by any memory of linguistic history. Most users of English today are unaware that, etymologically speaking, a *candidate* is a person dressed in white (after the practice of office-seekers in ancient Rome); that a *nice* person is *nescius* or 'ignorant' (in Latin); that *maudlin* sentimentality is that inspired by the image of the weeping penitent St. Mary *Magdalene*; that *joviality* and *panic* are states of mind respectively influenced by the Roman gods Jupiter and Pan.

The processes themselves of semantic change have been classified in various ways, but none of the classifications is all-compassing. We may start with the safe but rather unexciting observation that the development of one word sense from another may be seen as **extension** (widening) or **specialization** (narrowing) of meaning. An illustration of extension is *thing*, the meaning of which has become extremely wide and general compared with its Old English/Norse sense of 'public assembly.' Also, a special case of extension is the **generalization** of a proper name to a whole class of people, things, or events (see *derrick, dunce,* and *pander*). The opposite case of specialization is that of *deer, fowl,* and *meat,* whose ancestors in Old English meant 'wild animal,' 'bird,' and 'food,' respectively, and have thus moved from genus to species.

These classic instances are less characteristic of sense change, however, than a type of "sideways movement" which may be termed **denotative shift**, and which consists in a combination of extension and specialization. The word *gossip*, for example, comes from Old English *godsib*, meaning 'God-kin,' or people who were related to one another as godparents, etc., in baptism. It later lost the religious restriction (cf. the modern development of *holiday*) and extended its meaning to bosom friends in general. This extension accompanied a narrowing in another quarter: for the word could not, in this new sense, be applied to godparents with whom one was not on friendly terms. One way to recognize denotative shift is to observe that there is a missing link to be postulated between the older and newer senses. In this case, the missing link, or "bridge" between the two senses is the fact that sponsorship in baptism implies a friendly tie. Denotative shift may often be explained in terms of the related mechanism of **connotative extension**, which means that a connotation, or incidental association of the earlier sense, becomes a central part (or denotation) of the newer sense. In this way *timber* (earlier 'building material') came to mean 'wood,' the principal building material in the Middle Ages. In this way, too, *shambles* (earlier 'slaughterhouse') came to mean a 'place or scene of general mess and disarray.'

Some of the most surprising evolutions of meaning can be attributed to multiple shifts of this kind. *Restive*, which in its modern sense of 'impatiently active,' appears to have undergone a complete *volte face* in its derivation from Old French *restif* meaning 'reluctant to move.' But if one thinks of the intermediate stages 'obstinate' and 'headstrong,' the connection (which may have been helped by confusion with *restless*) is not too difficult to make.

Such changes of meaning may take place over the centuries by slow degrees. But we must now turn to a different kind of semantic change, which involves discontinuity, for example, in the switch from concrete to abstract meaning (as in the derivation of the meaning of *style* from 'writing implement' to 'manner of writing'), or from animal to human (as when a brave person is called a *lion*). This phenomenon of sense **transference** is supremely exemplified in **metaphor**, the term we generally use for transference based on a perception of similarity between the source and the resulting sense. Other types of transference, involving a connection other than similarity, tend to be brought together under the umbrella term **metonymy**. The transference of the Latin term *arena* from 'sand' to 'a place for sports/entertainments where the ground was covered with sand' is one example of metonymic transference. Another is the transference of *budget* from a French word meaning 'little bag' to the 'financial plans (which were kept in the bag).'

Cutting across the classifications of denotative shift and transference is another classification based on evaluative meaning. The categories of **pejoration** ('worsening' of meaning) and **amelioration** ('improvement' of meaning) are lamentably vague because they do not distinguish between different scales of value. Thus pejoration might be defined in moral terms: in this sense, *specious* as we use it today ('apparently good but basically bad') is a pejoration of Latin *speciosus* ('good to look at'). But in another context, pejoration might be applied to acquisition of an unpleasant social implication (e.g., *asylum* developing from a word meaning 'refuge') or of an unpleasant aesthetic implication (e.g., *grotesque* developing from a word meaning 'associated with caves or grottoes').

One point that seems to be generally agreed is that it is easier to find instances of pejoration than of amelioration. Ironically, this linguistic equivalent of the doctrine of original sin appears at least partially to result from a human tendency (which psychologists have dignified in the term "the Pollyanna Hypothesis") to look on the bright side, rather than on the black side of things. Euphemism, the use of terms of innocent meaning to denote what is unpleasant or indelicate, explains why, for example, *disease* ('lack of ease') and *indisposition* ('lack of order') have become terms for illness; why *lavatory* ('washing place') and *toilet* ('dressing room'—earlier 'little cloth') have become terms for a place for disposing of human excreta; and why *silly* (Old English 'blessed, happy'), *stupid* ('stunned'), and *simple* have become terms of signifying lack of sense or understanding. Of course, euphemism is self-defeating: the unpleasant associations persist and attach themselves to the new term, which then becomes tarred by the same brush as the old. The result, linguistically, is that whole series of words suffers pejoration.

Other cases of pejoration seem to result from other psychological causes. A worldly wise cynicism leads one to assume that if a person has some power or ability, it will be ill-used. Thus *crafty* and *cunning* have suffered pejorative development since they meant 'powerful' and 'wise.' *Officious*, from meaning 'obliging,' has come to mean 'too obliging'; and *obsequious*, from its earlier sense of 'obedient,' has taken on overtones of groveling servility.

Perhaps the psychological quality of snobbism can be invoked to account for a common semantic change whereby a term referring to lowly or rustic status comes to imply moral degradation: *villain* comes from Latin *villanus* ('farm-dweller'—later Middle English *villein* or 'serf'), and similar pejoration has befallen *churl, knave, boor,* and *peasant*.

The other side of the coin of snobbism is the amelioration of words such as *kind, noble,* and *gentle,* originally defining people as well-born or of high rank. A similar social bias lies behind the assumption that whoever attaches himself to the royal household, however humble his function, thereby becomes a person of importance. Hence the high positions designated by terms such as *chamberlain* (Old French 'room servant') and *marshal* (Old French 'groom, or horse servant'). Elsewhere, ameliorative change appears to be unusual and unsystematic—although, as a counterbalance to *crafty* and *cunning,* the more favorable synonym *shrewd* has improved on its earlier meaning 'malicious.'

Like pejoration, **weakening** is often regarded as a form of degeneration to which the meanings of words are prone. General tendencies to weaken the force of words have been observed, for example, in the reinterpretation of words meaning 'immediately' in the sense 'soon.' The word *soon* itself has undergone this development since Old English. Another familiar kind of weakening is that illustrated by words like *awfully* and *terribly* in their conversational role as intensifiers. The word *pest* (to quote a further example) has undergone considerable loss of force since its use in referring to plagues such as the Black Death.

We have already started to move from discussing "*how* do meanings change" to "*why* do meanings change." This second question is inviting, but of a higher order of difficulty than the "how" question, for to answer it fully would amount to predicting how words are likely to change their meanings in the future—something which few linguistic specialists would risk. But apart from noting the general psychological or social tendencies already mentioned, one may speculate on certain causes of change that seem to have operated in the past. **Subreption** is applied to a semantic change caused by change in what is signified rather than in the linguistic signifier. The word *pen*, for example, comes from a Latin word meaning 'feather,' and was literally appropriate when pens were made of quills. But when the term was retained for modern writing implements, it was plain that a denotative shift had taken place. This kind of change, owing to "linguistic conservatism," is also observed in the development of *horn* 'a musical instrument formerly made out of an animal's horn' and *straw* 'a thin cylindrical tube for drinking—formerly made from a straw.'

A factor that does not so much cause as facilitate semantic change is **folk etymology**—the remodeling of a word, often both in form and in meaning, on the basis of some imagined origin. The word now spelled *belfry* has no historical connection with bells, but in its earlier French form *berfrey* meant a 'protective tower.' The change in the form of the word has been accompanied by a corresponding shift of meaning, so that a *belfry* is now understood to be a bell tower. The opacity of the form of the word (through **fading**) lends itself to **phonetic restructuring**. This is illustrated by *prude*, which resulted from the merger of the two first words of the French phrase *Pr(e)u de femme* ('a woman of good character'), and which also illustrates, incidentally, the pejoration to which words of such meaning are prone.

Since we are now looking at *linguistic* causes of change, it is worth noticing that a common means of semantic transference is the loss of one or more words of a compound expression, as already seen with *prude*. This kind of development has been called **localization**, since the meaning that formerly belonged to the whole phrase becomes localized in the surviving part. An older instance is the derivation of *planet* and *comet* from Greek words meaning, respectively, 'wandering' and 'long-haired.' These derivations would be incomprehensible if we did not realize that the adjectives formed part of compound expressions meaning 'wandering (as opposed to fixed) stars' and 'long-haired stars'—the latter a metaphor drawn from the comet's appearance.

Other linguistic causes of change are coincident in form or meaning with other words in the language. It is argued that the word *quean* in the sense of 'whore' became obsolete because of its confusing **homonymy** with *queen*. **Synonymy,** on the other hand, is a cause not so much of obsolescence as of divergence of sense. When a large number of French words were borrowed into English in the Middle Ages, many Old English words which would otherwise have been their synonyms developed different, more specialized meanings. For example, *dōm* was replaced, in a general sense, by *judgment*; but *doom* lived on in the sense of 'fate' or 'condemnation.'

Yet one further cause of change, that of **contextualization**, may be mentioned. It has been ingeniously suggested that the transference of the word *bead* from the meaning of 'prayer' to that of 'small ball threaded on string' derived from the introduction of the rosary as an aid to prayer: "telling (i.e. counting) one's beads" could well be misinterpreted in context as the process of moving balls on a string.

Ultimately, explaining change of meaning requires full knowledge not only of relevant languages but of relevant civilizations and their history. While this is an unattainable ideal, to aim for it is to engage in a rewarding adventure. No other language, moreover, is more rewarding in this respect that English, which through the ages has borrowed its vocabulary from so many diverse sources.

Introduction

Louis G. Heller

City University of New York

The words of our language, the subject matter of this book, constitute an incredible heritage: they represent nothing less than a crystallization, a distillation, of the entire collective experience of countless speakers, transmitted in an unbroken chain from person to person, day by day, year by year, generation by generation, in a succession stretching backward through time to the most remote period of human antiquity. Wherever the speakers have traveled, whatever new artifacts or flora or fauna or customs they have encountered, whatever new beliefs or philosophies or sciences they have developed, whatever joys or tragedies they have undergone, their lexicon has accompanied them, growing steadily, adapting and accommodating itself to their ever-changing needs. New words have entered the language—new, that is, to our language, but often incredibly old in others; other words have fallen into disuse, grown obsolete and sometimes disappeared; many words have developed meanings that frequently diverge in startling ways from their earlier senses. Words, of course, serve as building blocks of communication, as tools of thought, and as outlets for our emotions; but they represent more than that: they are living vestiges of our past, and each bears the imprint of its passage through time. Every word in its own right is a souvenir of history with a unique story to tell. This book relates some of those tales.

The Private Lives of English Words relates the fascinating stories behind more than 400 English words: their diverse origins and the intricate ways in which their meanings and forms have developed through the centuries. Discussions of words in the entries, while based on the findings of linguistics, are written to interest the lover of words, particularly the nonspecialist. One can find history and fancy, mythology and religion, cultural influences and the manners of society, all contained in the information about the words. The general format of the text is that of a dictionary, i.e., alphabetical order is followed; but a quick glance within reveals that entries are written in an informal, yet nonetheless informative and factual style.

Several features have been included to increase the convenience with which users may find and compare information in the book. First, the Contents list the page number of every headword, including variant and related forms that are not given alphabetically. In addition, two appendices provide a handy index to the linguistic changes behind the words: in Appendix I, all headwords are listed with an indication of the linguistic processes at work in their individual histories; Appendix II lists the processes themselves, showing beneath each the words that illustrate them. Finally, the Index gathers together all cited headwords, forms, and glosses that appear in any part of the book, providing references to the entries and pages where such information can be found. We hope that these features, in conjunction with the text entries, will make *The Private Lives of English Words* a pleasant and easy-to-use resource for all who take interest in the vocabulary of English.

The nonspecialist rarely grasps the extent to which the vocabulary preserves the past, not just in the obvious sense that historians use words to tell what happened but also in the sense that the words themselves are artifacts. Just as the paleontologist can examine a single bone from a long-extinct species of animal and infer the nature of the beast, its habits, and all manner of other information not evident to the layman, so can the etymologist, or verbal detective, reconstruct a vanished history from a surviving linguistic fossil.

Every word has a form consisting of the sounds or letters that comprise it. Behind this form lies a meaning or, more frequently, a set

xxvii   **Introduction**

of meanings. The word *woman*, for example, contains as one part of its meaning the sense 'female,' as opposed to the sense 'male' found in the word *man*. It conveys the additional sense 'older,' or 'adult,' as opposed to the sense 'younger,' or 'nonadult,' found in the word *girl*. It also contains the sense 'human,' as opposed to 'nonhuman,' since the word *woman* contrasts semantically with words such as *mare*, *cow*, or *vixen*. (Linguists use the term *sememe* for these minimal contrastive meanings.) People using the word do not, of course, consciously run through a checklist of these or other semantic components. They grasp the entire set of meanings—the bundle of sememes—as a gestalt, an undifferentiated whole. This collective sense constitutes the *denotation*, which correlates loosely with the dictionary definition of a word.

Associated with each word is a set of one or more peripheral meanings or senses, sometimes called the *connotation* or *connotations*, which are less systematic and may shift from speaker to speaker and vary over time. These meanings often derive from the speaker's experience with either the person or thing to which the word alludes or from the context, linguistic or nonlinguistic, in which the word occurs. At one time, meanings associated with the word *woman* might have included 'wears skirts rather than trousers,' 'has long hair,' and so on. This part of the meaning is in constant flux, shifting with each change in the cultural scene. (E.g., many women now wear slacks rather than skirts; hair length has ceased to be a reliable indicator of gender.) Sometimes part of the peripheral meaning is purely idiosyncratic or personal. A man who has just been jilted may add 'fickle' to the connotative range associated with *woman*. When such peripheral associations become more systematic and regular, they may shift from the connotation to the denotation, becoming part of the central core of meaning. This is one common way which words change.

The history of *candidate* (which see) illustrates the three basic processes by which a word can change its sense: (1) it can add one or more meanings; (2) it can drop one or more meanings; and (3) it can both add and drop meanings. Starting with one meaning, 'wearer of whitened clothing,' *candidate* added another, 'aspirer to office,' kept both meanings for a while, and then dropped the initial meaning, at first irregularly, then completely, leaving the second as the one surviving. In other words, *candidate* underwent processes (1) and (2) in sequence, the cumulative result being process (3).

Interestingly, the adding of a meaning results in a **specialization** or **narrowing** in the use of a word (as in the restriction of meaning from 'anyone who wears a white toga' to 'one who does so to further his political ambitions'). The simple dropping of a meaning, on the other hand, extends the semantic range of a word resulting in **generalization**. The term *nausea*, for instance, once referred to those familiar unpleasant physical symptoms, but only as experienced by sailors. The dropping of that semantic limitation allowed the word to allude to any similar discomfort, even if felt by those who had never gone to sea.

There are numerous mechanisms by which such fundamental shifts in the sense of a word can occur. Among them is **localization**, a process that ultimately results in the addition of meanings to part of a phrase. First one or more words expand to a phrase group; then the phrase becomes so well recognized that part of the utterance becomes superfluous because the audience anticipates the entire meaning even without the added segments. This anticipation regularly accompanies very frequent use. Consider the modern phrase *in one ear* ... It isn't necessary to finish it, is it? The sense "localizes" in only part of the phrase, and speakers eventually drop the remainder. *Canter* from *Canterbury pace*, or *mile* ultimately from the Latin *milia passuum*, exemplify this process and also show that the stage varies at which localization occurs. In the former example, the change took place within the English language; in the latter, long before the word ever reached English. Often the etymologist can actually document the process with citations. Sometimes, as for the word *God* (which see), he can successfully reconstruct the original phrase on the evidence of cognates in other languages.

Another mechanism of change involves the **transference** of the word from one referent or object signified to another. *Chapel*, for example, once signified the object venerated within a particular building, not the edifice itself. Sometimes it is difficult to determine if the switch involves only one stage or if an intermediate stage intervenes during which the form stands simultaneously for both the old meaning and the new before it drops the latter.

On rare occasions the change of meaning rests on a deliberate bilingual pun, as seen in the word *tandem*, a Latin adverb usually translated from Latin by the phrase 'at length.' *Length* in English can be either temporal (the original Latin sense) or spatial (not the Latin sense, but one seized on by university wags to impart a new use to the old word). This device, of course, both drops and adds meaning.

Often the dropping of a meaning passes through two main stages: the first when the old sense becomes infrequent or inoperative but the speakers are still at least subliminally aware of it; the next when it has been so totally suppressed that no one—except perhaps professional lexicographers or others with special training—can recall its former existence. Many people today, and certainly most of those who were around during World War II, know that the word *quisling* as a term for 'one who betrays his country' derives from the name of the Norwegian general Vidkun Quisling, who assisted the Nazis in their conquest of his nation. But who remembers the connection between the words *dunce, derrick,* or *academy* and the people from whose names they derive? When the relationship between the meaning of a word and its origins is no longer functional or has been completely forgotten, we have a case of **fading**. Even when Romans used *candidatus* solely in the sense of 'office seekers,' they remained aware of the earlier signification, since they still used the versions of the same stem in the sense of 'whiten' or 'brighten.' Once the word passed beyond Latin into a language containing no such reminders of the original sense, the fading process reached its conclusion. When this deletion of a meaning occurs across linguistic boundaries, we call the process **linguistic filtering**. (See *boondocks* and *tattoo* for other examples.)

Subreption describes the semantic shift that occurs when a word continues in use while the thing it signifies undergoes some change. For instance, *artillery* once meant and still means 'a device for hurling destructive missiles.' In Middle English, however, the word (spelled *artillerie*) referred to 'bows' and 'catapults.' Today it signifies 'mortars' and 'howitzers.' The word *volume*, once a roll of parchment or papyrus with writing on it, still represents an artifact used for recording words; but the modern book is physically much different from the early *volume*, whose stem is related to that in *revolve*.

Words sometimes acquire new meanings solely from their functional use in a given context. *Shibboleth* (for a full discussion see the entry) occurs in a biblical context where the original Hebrew meaning was totally irrelevant. The word simply served as a convenient linguistic screening device: if soldiers knew how to pronounce it, they were friends; if not, they were enemies. Thus, *shibboleth* came to signify 'a word used as a test for detecting a foreigner or someone not a member of a particular group,' and its additional senses derive from that meaning.

Sometimes words start from a single semantic core and develop a variety of different meanings. The term **radiation** describes this process. For examples, see the entries under *dactyl* and *mackinaw*.

Another way of classifying semantic change is on a social scale, according to whether words have become more or less "respectable." Consider the **amelioration**, or improvements of words such as *constable*, once a 'stable attendant.' An extreme and highly ironic example of **pejoration**, or descent in respectability, is *dunce*, which derives from the name of one of the greatest scholars of the Middle Ages, John Duns Scotus, renowned for his learning, perspicuity, and subtlety of argumentation. Another example is *tawdry*, derived from the name of a queen who was once venerated as a saint.

Occasionally **folk etymology** plays a role in reshaping the meaning of a word. Typically, a partial phonological resemblance of segments of one word to another with which it has no historical relationship adds the meaning of the latter term to the semantic complex of the former. Thus, in the word *pester*, the sense of 'plague,' from a variant of the stem which appears in the English word *pestilence*, was added to a word that is historically related to the English *pasture*, through intermediated stages signifying 'to restrain within the bounds of a pasture,' then 'to restrain,' and eventually, with the added folk etymology, 'to plague or annoy.' Another example is *female*, a word that bears no historical relationship to the word *male*, the *m* of *female* being the same as that in *feminine*, and the *l* a diminutive suffix. The partial resemblance of the *m* and *l* of *male* caused both a phonological and semantic reshaping (the ancient sense of the original stem related to 'suckling'). *Crayfish*, a word related to *crab*, is another term reshaped by folk etymology. Historically, the second part of the word had nothing to do with *fish*, although, of course, both types of creature are aquatic.

Further discussion of the processes of semantic and phonetic change may be found in the Foreword by Geoffrey Leech. It is not the intent of this book, however, to teach the technical details of phonological analysis or comparative reconstruction. Such matters are the province of the historical linguist and will generally be avoided except in rare instances where a brief comment may clarify one or another point without overburdening the reader. Our purpose is simply to alert the reader to the kind of analysis that underlies the entries, which are closely akin to detective stories in their painstaking attention to detail—though some of them, perhaps, more closely resemble fairy tales. Indeed, it is amusing to note that the nineteenth-century scholar who first described in a structured way the phonological relationships between the Germanic and the other Indo-European-derived cognate words—a formulation still referred to as Grimm's Law—was Jacob Grimm, one of the brothers Grimm who collected fairy tales. It may be that the two genres are not so different after all.

THE PRIVATE LIVES OF ENGLISH WORDS

A

academy

Academus, the man reputed to have revealed to the brothers of Helen of Troy the place where she was hidden after being kidnapped by Theseus (an episode which occurred long before she departed for Troy with Paris, thus precipitating the most famous war of antiquity), lived in the country not far from Athens, and his estate, filled with plane and olive trees, adorned with statues, and watered by the river Cephissus, was the place, known as the *Akadēmeia*, where the philosopher Plato later met with his students.

Passing through Latin, the word *akadēmeia* entered English in the 15th century as *academy*, and was used as the proper name of the garden or grove where Plato taught. By the next century the relationship of an *academy* to either Plato or Academus was forgotten, and the term generally came to signify any 'place of higher learning.'

By the 17th century the word signified, as well, 'a society or group devoted to promoting learning or the pursuit of arts and sciences,' as in the contemporary American Academy of Arts and Letters, or the Academy of Motion Picture Arts and Sciences.

Alcatraz, albatross

In Arabic, *al qādūs* was 'the bucket attached to a water wheel used for irrigation.' This entered Spanish in two forms, *arcaduz*, meaning 'bucket' or 'conduit,' and *alcatraz*, meaning 'pelican.' The pelican, a tropical fish-eating bird with a bucketlike bill, was popularly supposed to bring water to its young in its bill—and indeed, the Arabs subsequently dubbed the pelican *al saggā* 'the water-carrier.' The island of Alcatraz, in San Francisco Bay, was so named by the Spaniards for its large pelican colony.

1

Alcatras entered English in the 16th century with the sense of 'pelican' and then underwent both a change of form and a change of meaning. The change in form involved the shift from *alca-* to *alba-* after the Latin word for 'white' (*albus*). The change in meaning resulted in the application of the term, as *albatross*, to the frigate-bird or petrel, a large sea bird quite different, both in habits and habitat, from the pelican.

alchemy, chemistry

As the *al-* of *alchemy* might suggest, this word comes to us from Arabic, although its ultimate origin is either Egyptian or Greek. Whichever the case, *alchemy* and its later derivative, *chemistry*, have taken a sufficiently circuitous linguistic route on their way to English that etymologists are still in disagreement as to its itinerary.

One theory has it that Arabic borrowed the *-chemy* part of *alchemy* (later adding the definite article *al*) from Greek, in which *Chēmia* meant 'Egypt.' This term was considered a plausible rendering of the Egyptian *Khmi* 'Black Earth,' an epithet applied by the Egyptians to that part of their country that bordered on the Nile, and by extension to the country as a whole. Through a process known to linguists as transference, *chēmia* came to designate the attempt to transmute base metals into gold, as well as the country where that dubious art was said to have originated. By the time of Diocletian (early 4th century A.D.), the word had acquired its Arabic article and lost its original sense of 'Egypt,' although the Romans were still quick to identify the 'black art' of *alchymia*, with its threatening economic implications, as an Egyptian invention.

Another theory has it that the *-chemy* of *alchemy* comes from the Greek verb *cheîn* 'to pour' and refers to Greek pharmacological arts with their heavy reliance on infusions. According to this derivation, the Arabs borrowed the Greek word *chymeîa* or *cheumeîa* 'mixture, mingling' and, prefixing it with the definite article *al*, used it to designate the art of mixing things together to make gold. Since this would probably have occurred during the Greek rule in Alexandria or shortly thereafter, the Egyptian flavor of the word would still have lingered.

In any event, the Arabs introduced *alchemy* to Europe through Spain, whence it made its way to England during the 14th century. There it acquired a number of largely pejorative extended senses, coming to mean, first, 'false gold,' that is, any metal masquerading as the real article, and then 'dross,' the waste product removed from molten metal.

By the 16th century the word was occurring without the redundant article *al*, thus making possible the creation *chemistry* and *chymist* (later, *chemist*). While at first used synonymously with *alchemy*, by the 17th century *chemistry* had come to designate the study of medicine as prescribed by Paracelsus. Today pharmacists and druggists are still known in England as *chemists*, and the science of mixing things together and analyzing their component parts is known as *chemistry*.

alcohol

Koh'l, a word found in Semitic as early as Biblical times, is the Arabic word for antimony sulfide, a cosmetic powder used as eye make-up by women of the Middle East. In some countries, such as Yemen and India, the powder is thrown directly into the eyes to increase their brilliance; in others, the traditional means of application involves making a paste or paint of the powder and rubbing it on the eyelids.

By the time the word entered English in the 16th century as *alcohol* (*koh'l* preceded by the definite article *al*), its meaning had broadened to include 'any fine powder, especially one derived by vaporizing a solid and then allowing the vapor to condense.' By the following century, liquid spirits derived by vaporization and condensation were also known as *alcohols*, the most notable being *alcohol of wine* (C_2H_5OH). By the 18th century *alcohol of wine* was commonly reduced to, simply, *alcohol*, and the original sense of the term as 'powder' disappeared. At about that time, *kohl* was reborrowed from Arabic, in its sense of 'powder used as eye make-up.'

Today, *alcohol* has been further broadened in chemical terminology to designate 'any compound consisting of a hydrocarbon group joined to a hydroxyl group.'

alcove

The Arabic *qobba* originally meant 'vaulted room.' It is from this form, preceded by the definite article *al*, that *alcove* derives. Like many other architectural, mathematical, and scientific terms, this one was first borrowed into Spanish during the Middle Ages, when the Arabs occupied Spain and were the acknowledged masters in these fields. It is speculated that since many vaulted rooms were small in those days, by the time the Spanish *alcoba* had traveled to France (where it underwent a few minor phonetic adjustments to produce the modern French *alcôve*) and then on to England, the meaning of the word had become specialized to 'an elaborately vaulted recess in a room, usually for a bed.'

By the 18th century, *alcove* had come to designate any recessed place (covered, though not necessarily vaulted) in a house or garden. It is possible that this most recent change was partly influenced by the phonetically similar, but etymologically unrelated word *cove* (which see), which had entered English centuries before, and survives as an architectural term.

algebra

Originally this derives from the Arabic *al*, the definite article, plus *jabr*, 'redintegration, restoration,' which became extended to mean 'the surgical treatment of fractures, the art of setting bones.' Its sense of 'putting things together' became further extended to refer to numerical operations. Thus when the 9th-century mathematician Abu Ja'far Muhammad ibn Mûsa Al-Khwârasmi wrote his treatise, he called it *Kitab al-jabr w'al muqabala* (*The Book about Redintegration and Equation*).

In a number of Arabic books of science, medicine, and mathematics which were translated into Late Latin, the term was used both in its sense of 'bone-setting' and 'number-manipulating.' By the 16th century, when the word had worked its way into English with the spelling *algeber*, its surgical sense had become 'bone-setter.' During the following century this usage was entirely displaced by the present-day mathematical meaning of *algebra*, 'that branch of mathematics which deals with the solution of equations and the general relations among numbers.'

algorism, algorithm

Like many other words that have come into English from Arabic, these emerged out of a series of confusions created by misinterpretations of what were originally transliterations from the Arabic to the Roman alphabet. The 9th-century mathematician known as Abu Ja'far Muhammad ibn Mûsa Al-Khwârasmi (the conclusion of his name, Al-Khwârasmi, simply means 'the man from Chorasmia,' then a town in Persia and today the Soviet city of Khiva) was the author of, among many other works, a treatise first published in Latin as *Algoritmi de numero indorum* (*Algoritmi* being another transliteration of Al-Khwârasmi). However, although the title should be literally translated as 'Remarks by the Chorasmian on the Indian Art of Reckoning,' it was soon interpreted as *Remarks on the Art of Reckoning with Indian Numerals—Algoritmi* being assumed to be a gloss on the kind of numerical reckoning under discussion, rather than as an epithet referring to the author.

By the 13th century, when *algorism* found its way into English, thanks to a consortium of souls who knew little Latin and a little less Arabic, the term had acquired the sense of 'the science of decimal numbers (of any provenance).' The decimal system, although we know its numerals as "Arabic," was originally Indian.

Algorithm, which first made its appearance in an English dictionary in 1957, is a corruption of *algorism* influenced less by the Latin rendering of Al-Khwârasmi's name than by the Greek word *arithmós* 'number,' itself of sturdy Indo-European stock. It has acquired a new, specialized sense in computer terminology: 'a set of rules or logical steps used to accomplish a given task.'

alibi

This word entered English in the 18th century in contexts in which it maintained the original Latin meaning 'in another place, elsewhere,' usually in legal passages where the accused tried "to prove himself alibi." Frequent employment in this sense resulted in the word itself becoming enough to evoke the complete thought 'proof, evidence, argument, or excuse that one was elsewhere.' Thus, the more limited sense of the word, an adverb, extended its meaning and underwent a functional shift to use as a noun and then later as a verb.

More recently, informal practice has even dropped the original significance of the word as 'elsewhere,' leaving only the connotation 'excuse' as its central meaning. The English cognate of the *al-* of *alibi* is the *el-* of *else* (or *elsewhere*).

The Greek cognate *allo-*, meaning 'other' has also entered English as a productive word element in scientific vocabulary (e.g., *allomorph*, *allomerism*).

aloof

The precise derivation of this word has occasioned much etymological speculation. The Old English *lōf* 'palm of the hand' or 'hand' probably preserves the earliest meaning of the root. The Middle Dutch cognate *loef* had come to mean 'a paddle or rudder used for steering a ship,' possibly from the resemblance of the paddle to a hand or perhaps from the use of the paddle as an extension of the hand. This sense survives in the Modern English nautical term *luff* or its variant *loof*.

The phrase *on loof*, which became *a loof*, literally 'on (the) rudder,' was a command to turn the ship, often with a view to steering away from shoals or other sources of danger. This notion of 'keeping away,' originally no more than a connotative extension of the meaning, became the primary significance when the expression was used in nonnautical contexts where there was no physical rudder, and eventually the earlier meaning was forgotten.

amethyst

From the Greek *améthustos*, *a-* 'not,' and **methustos* 'drunken,' thanks to the Greek belief that this clear purple quartz, with its winy color, could prevent drunkenness. The stem *méthu*, on which the cited form rests, meant 'wine' and is distantly related to the English *mead*, the beverage of fermented honey preferred by early Germanic tribes. In the course of the word's passage from Greek to Latin and then to the French from which English borrowed it, all memory of its original significance was lost, and *amethyst* remains as the name of the coarse crystal stone.

ammonia, ammine, amine, amino acid

From Åmen or Åmon 'the hidden one,' name of the chief deity (often associated with the sun god, as Åmen-Ra) of the ancient Egyptian state of Uast, whose capital was Thebes, in the Upper Kingdom, and of Kaset and Sambehutet in the Lower Kingdom. When the Theban princes conquered the Hyksos and established themselves as kings of both north and south, Åmen worshipers claimed preeminence for their previously local and comparatively unimportant deity. Some of the pharaohs incorporated his name into their own, as had earlier, pre-Hyksos rulers (Åmen-emhet I to IV). Before the religious reformer Ikhnaton (literally, 'it pleases Aton') changed his name, it was Åmen-hotep ('Amon is satisfied'); he was the fourth to bear that name. His son-in-law, the second to succeed him to the throne, born Tut-Ånkh-Åton, switched his name to Tut-Ånkh-Åmen, when the jealous priests of Åmon, who controlled the young ruler, reestablished the authority of their god.

The Greeks equated Ammon, as they spelled it, with their own Zeus, the Romans, with Jupiter. An adjectival extension of this word, ammoniakós 'pertaining to Ammon,' was applied to a type of rock salt found near a temple in Libya, whence comes halàs ammoniakós in Greek, sāl ammoniācum in Latin. This mineral, which served as an article of trade in antiquity, was useful for a number of purposes, among them the manufacture of certain dyes.

In 1774 Joseph Priestley prepared a type of gas (which he called "alkaline air") by heating sal ammoniac with lime. Seven years later, the Swedish chemist Torbern Olaf Bergman called this vapor ammonia, a shortening of the name of the principal ingredient. Subsequent compounding of the first syllable of this word gave ammine, amine, and the amino of amino acid. The meaning of the stem had begun to fade when the form passed from Egyptian to Greek, and even the source was lost when it passed from Latin into English. Thus 'the hidden one' now lies hidden in a number of common English words.

arena

The Latin harena, from which arena comes, originally meant 'sand' or 'sandy place' and often signified 'sandy desert' or 'sandy beach or shore.' When gladiatorial contests took place in the Colosseum or other amphitheaters, the bloodshed frequently caused the ground to become slippery, so sand was spread to cover the gore and give a firm footing. Thus, the word, by this time *arena* (having dropped the initial *h-*, which was very weakly articulated) extended its meaning to 'sandy place where the contest or struggle occurred.' Eventually, the word became generalized to mean any 'site of conflict or vigorous action,' regardless of whether or not the place was sandy.

English, however, has borrowed other words which rest on the same Latin stem and which continue to preserve the etymological sense, among them *arenose* 'sandy' and *arenilitic* 'pertaining to sandstone.'

arrive

Since the first settlers of the British Isles must have come by boat, as did the later marauding Romans, Norsemen, and Normans, it should come as no surprise that the word *arrive* comes from a Late Latin verb meaning 'to reach shore, to land a boat.' It comes to us through the Old French *ar(r)iver*, from the Late Latin **arrīpāre*, which derives from earlier Latin *adrīpāre* 'to bring to shore, come to shore,' where *ad* means 'to, toward, at,' and *rīpa* 'shore, bank' (from whose extended form, *rīpārius*, we derive *river*). (See also **rival**.)

Why the French chose a verb with the essential sense 'to reach shore, to beach a craft' as their all-purpose term to mean 'to reach one's destination' is not clear, since the Romans, who gave them the word, entered their country mainly by land. It is possible that the term was generalized from its original meaning by the rank and file of the conquering Roman army, who were often not native speakers of Latin. The Romans made it a general policy to impress into the military as many of the defeated as they thought they could handle, and, as a result, the Latin spoken by the lower ranks was often faulty.

Soon the verb *arrive* expanded its original nautical sense to embrace any means of reaching a destination, and so it has remained to the present day, when astronauts are seen to *arrive* on the moon by space ship.

arrowroot

Maranta arundinacea, a tuber called by the Arawakan natives *aru-aru* 'great meal, meal of meals,' served not only as a common source of food but as an antidote to wasp stings and wounds inflicted by poisoned arrows. It was this use that influenced the Englishing of the term to *arrowroot* when the plant was first encountered by European voyagers in the 17th century.

Arrow itself is derived from a Proto-Indo-European root, **ark^{w}*, which probably designated both 'bow' and 'arrow,' or so we might infer from the fact that the root appears in Latin as *arcus* 'bow' (from which come English *arc*, *arch*, and *archer*) and in Old English as *ar(h)we* 'arrow.' Presumably, Latin speakers focused on the 'bow,' while Germanic speakers focused on the 'arrow' meaning of the term.

assassin

The Arabic word for such dry vegetation as hay was *hashāsh*. One variation, unrelated but similar to that of the Modern English usage of *grass* for 'marijuana,' shifted the sense of *hashāsh* to 'hemp, cannabis.' Habitual users of this narcotic were called *hashāshīn*, the *-in* suffix a common Semitic plural ending.

During the Crusades, certain Ismaili fanatics of the Shiite branch of Muslims devoted themselves, under the leadership of a legendary sheik known as "The Old Man of the Mountains," to the murder of invading Christians. Since they fortified themselves for their holy, patriotic deeds by taking *hashish* (the English version of *hashāsh*) they also came to be called *hashāshīn*. This word, after passing through Medieval Greek, Medieval Latin, and the Romance languages, entered English in the 16th century and then again in the 17th in a form which came to be spelled *assassin*.

Both form and meaning ignored the plural ending. The original core of the meaning 'hemp users' had vanished, and the word had evolved two separate semantic lines. The 17th century transmission referred to the specific Ismailis who killed the Crusaders. The other, earlier transmission produced the meaning most commonly understood today, which refers to anyone who attempts to kill another—usually a public figure—by surprise or stealth.

atone

This word started out as a phrase, in combinations like *to bring at one accord* ('to bring to a single state of agreement') or *to set at one assent*. Gradually the *at one* part came to be enough to express the idea of the entire phrase, and by the beginning of the 14th century the final noun was often dropped. The remaining words occurred together so frequently that they came to be taken as a single word, written as such, with the meaning of 'unite, become reconciled.' With the establishment of the West Midland dialect of English, the word *one* with an initial *w*- sound became the standard English pronunciation when it appeared as an independent unit. This helped to obscure the historical connection between the -*one* of *atone* with the numerical *one*.

Sometimes the reconciliation or bringing into harmony required that one party give legal satisfaction or make amends to the other. When the reconciliation involved a coming to accord with the church or with the Lord, the satisfaction involved payment or penalty of some kind. At first this additional connotation was simply associated with the central meaning 'come to harmony or concord,' but by the late 17th century the sense had often become 'to make amends or expiate.'

attic

Attic with a capital *A* is an adjective referring to that part of Greece known as *Attica*, to *Athens*, or to residents thereof, while *attic* with a small *a* is a noun designating a 'room or whole story immediately beneath the roof of a house.' However tenuous the semantic connection between *Attic* and *attic* may appear at first glance, the noun is in fact derived from the adjective.

In some of the more impressive *Attic* buildings of antiquity, a small row of columns or pilasters was set on top of the uppermost story of the building, essentially as a decorative device. This architectural feature was known as an *Attic order*. When, in the 17th century, neo-Grecian architecture became fashionable in England, the top story of a building constructed in imitation of the *Attic* style was termed the *Attic story*, a slight misnomer, since the *Attic order* from which it took its name was a façade rather than an enclosed floor.

Subsequently, *Attic story* traded its upper-case *A* for a small *a* and became simply *attic* 'the top story of a house.'

auburn

As a set, color terms seem to have been among the least stable items of vocabulary among the Indo-Europeans, so it is perhaps not too surprising that *quburn* has come to designate a color quite different from that named by the Latin word *alburnus* from which it is derived. *Alburnus* is a Late Latin form meaning 'off-white, yellow-white, whitish' and is derived from *alba* 'white' (as in *albescent* 'becoming white, whitish,' *albumen* 'white of an egg,' and *albino* 'lacking pigmentation'). When the word first entered 15th-century English from Old French as *auborne*, it still retained its Latin sense of 'off-white, yellow-white.'

By the beginning of the 17th century, however, thanks in large measure to the existence of such variant forms as *abrune* or *abrown*, the sense of the term began to shift to 'brownish, golden brown' by association with the already well-established term *brown*. Today, while the spelling of *auburn* has reverted to its more nearly etymological form, the sense of the word has remained the same as that of the 17th-century *abrune/abrown*, and its association with the color white has been forgotten.

auction, nickname

The Proto-Indo-European stem **aug-*, meaning 'to increase,' and found in the Latin-derived word *augment*, reached English by various routes, sometimes with the original sense and sometimes with semantic changes. One variant, extended by *-tion*, the word-element used to form abstract nouns, became specialized in Latin as the ancestor of *auction* 'a sale characterized by successive increases of bids.' The focus of the term shifted from the idea of 'increase' to that of 'sale,' which the Romans had once expressed in such phrases as *vendere aliquid in auctiōne* 'to sell something by incremental bid,' and the word reached English in both senses. The etymologically primary sense, 'increase or growth,' became obsolete in the late 17th or early 18th century, although Greek variants of the stem, seen in words like *auxesis* 'growth process' and *auxin* 'chemical or hormone promoting growth,' retain the Indo-European significance.

Some Old English derivatives of the stem, such as *ēacian*, likewise meant 'to grow or increase,' but later came to mean 'to be (or become) pregnant.' Still later this usage became obsolete. A somewhat different shift acquired a negative connotation, 'to increase one's holdings with difficulty,' which turned into the modern verb *eke*, as in "to eke out a living."

Another variant in the Old English *ēac* served as an adverb, in the sense of 'also, in addition to.' This form became obsolete, but a corresponding adjective, meaning 'additional,' survived down to the 14th century in the combination *eke-name* 'additional name.' This was supplanted by *neke-name*, the initial *n* being acquired from the indefinite article in the phrase *an eke-name*. *Nickname* is the modern development of this compound.

auspices

The Roman *auspex* (literally 'bird-watcher,' from *avis* 'bird' and *spectāre* 'to watch, observe') had as his profession the art of divination by observing the patterns of birds in flight. His art was called *auspicium*, and it is from this word that the English *auspice* (more commonly found in the plural *auspices*) was derived, probably through French in the 16th century.

In Roman times, the sense of *auspicium* was already twofold: the word properly designated 'the activity of the *auspex*' but had also come to mean 'a sign or omen (discoverable by reading the flight pattern of birds).' *Auspice* had both these meanings in English. By the 17th century, it had come to mean any 'divine or prophetic sign or omen, especially one portending a favorable future.' It was during this century that *auspicious*, meaning 'favorable,' came into use.

A further extension of the meaning of *auspices* took place during the 17th century, to give the most common contemporary use of the word, now found almost exclusively in the expression *under the auspices of*. From 'favorable omen' the sense has been extended to 'favorable influence exerted by someone in an undertaking; patronage.'

average

The Arabic *'awārīya* meant 'damaged goods' and was borrowed into French as *avarie(s)* 'damaged or lost cargo.' In the late 15th century it passed into English as *averays* and, at some point during the first half of the following century, acquired the quasi-collective suffix *-age*, becoming *average*.

The earliest sense of *averays/average* seems to have been not 'damaged or lost cargo,' however, but 'duty, charge to the owner of shipped goods' as a form of surety against damage or loss in transport. This meaning eventually gave way to another which combined the notions of 'damaged or lost cargo' and 'payment for damage or loss'; by the middle of the 16th century *average* had come to mean 'financial loss incurred as a result of damage to or loss of cargo in transit and shared equitably among the interested parties, sellers, transporters, and receivers.'

It is from this latter sense of 'equitably shared loss' that the more general application of the word *average* evolved in the 17th century: the 'arithmetical mean derived by the division of N into a number or by the addition of N numbers and the division of their sum by N.' This is the mathematical sense of the term today. Further generalization has led to the use of the word to mean 'ordinary, run-of-the-mill,' as in *a person of average ability*, or *an average* (not outstanding) *job*.

B

basilisk

Basilískos is a diminutive form of the Greek word *basileús* 'hereditary king,' and thus meant 'princeling.' Possibly because their crested heads resembled the crowned heads of royalty, the term *basilískos* was also used to identify certain birds, fish, and lizards and was given to the mythological monster, perhaps based on the actual Egyptian cobra, which was said to have the ability to kill by its breath or glance.

When *basilískos* was borrowed into Latin, it was in the sense of 'serpent-dragon with lethal breath and glance.' Pliny advised his readers that the creature took its name from the crownlike protuberance on its head, which suggests that by Roman times enough of the original meaning of the word had faded as to make an explanatory etymology necessary.

Basilisk entered English from Late Latin *basiliscus*, again with the sense of 'serpent-dragon with deadly breath and glance,' but subsequently took on additional meanings. A particularly fearsome variety of catapult was called a *basilisk* in Medieval times, presumably because of its monstrous potential for dealing death and destruction at a distance, much in the manner of the mythical beast. Somewhat closer to their true etymological origins are the *basilisks* of the wren family (also known as kinglets) and the lizard members of the Linnaean genus *Basiliscus*, all of whom have crownlike crests.

bead

The Old English word *bedu*, the ancestor of the modern term *bead*, originally meant 'request' or 'entreaty.' The same root changed to a verb and, slightly modified in sound because of the verb-ending suffix that was once added (but which has since disappeared), became *bid*, as in "*Bid* him enter." Early in the Old English period the meaning became restricted to a request directed to the Deity, and then came to mean 'prayer'—any kind of prayer, even when it was not specifically a request.

A dramatic shift in meaning occurred with the introduction of the rosary in or about the 14th century as a device for counting or keeping track of prayers. To tell one's *beads* originally meant 'to count (or tally) one's prayers,' but the use of the word *bead* transferred from the prayers themselves to the round, perforated globules, threaded on a string, which were used as the counters. The meaning shifted accordingly, so that today a *bead* is any small, usually round object of glass, wood, stone, or metal, regardless of whether it is perforated or used in the religious function.

belfry

This word comes from a combination of two Proto-Indo-European roots, **bhergh* 'high (place)' and **priH* 'love.' The former appears in English *iceberg* (cf. German *Berg* 'mountain'), *burg*, and *borough*, the latter two apparently referring to the fact that early cities were built, where practical, on high, defensible ground. The root **priH* is found in a variety of English forms, *free, friend, Friday* (which see), *Frederick, Jeffrey*, and the now obsolete *frith* 'peace, security,' each representing a different extension of the original meaning.

In Middle English, a *berfrey* was a 'movable siege tower,' literally a 'high place of security or protection,' *ber-* being the reflex of **bhergh* 'high (place)' and *-frey* the reflex of **priH* in its sense of 'protection, security.' It is not clear whether the *berfrey* was, as its etymology suggests, a strictly defensive device which evolved into a piece of offensive military hardware, or if the tower so called was essentially offensive in function and was called something relatively innocent-sounding, in the manner of much modern weaponry. The question is complicated by the fact that by the 14th century the *berfrey* had come to be a 'fixed watch-tower,' whether as an extension of the meaning of 'movable siege tower' or as a continuation of its etymological sense of 'tower of protection.'

By the 15th century the term began to appear as *belfrey*, owing to a process linguists call dissimilation, a change reinforced by the existence of the word *bell*. Since bells were frequently hung in watchtowers to serve as an early warning device in case of attack, *belfrey* soon came to be thought of as a 'bell tower' rather than as a 'watchtower,' and the early meaning 'siege tower' disappeared altogether.

beriberi

The Singhalese word *beri* means 'weak,' and a reduplication of this form, *beriberi*, serves to intensify this sense, which once signified any extreme debilitation. In the late 19th century, malnutrition—particularly that associated with the lack of thiamine (vitamin B_1) which resulted from the milling and refining of rice—was endemic in Ceylon (now Sri Lanka) and other areas of the Orient, and *beriberi* entered English in 1879 in the restricted and specialized application to vitamin-deficiency disease. Since few English-speakers understood Singhalese, the original meaning, 'great weakness,' faded in the transmission.

bevy

The Modern French *buveur* 'drinker, toper' preserves the original sense of the root underlying the English word *bevy*, but the exact line of semantic development remains a matter of speculation. The Old French *buvee* or *bevee* meant 'drink' or 'drinking.' Some scholars believe there may have been a phrase like *assemblee bevee* or *companie bevee* 'drinking group,' which was later shortened, leaving the entire meaning located in the second word. Others see the semantic development as going directly from 'drinking' to 'group drinking' without any intermediate stage. In any case, the 'drinking' sense of the word disappeared, leaving only the meaning 'group,' applied, not unreasonably, to ladies (who may occasionally, but surely not necessarily, imbibe). By the 15th century the term was applied to groups of such birds as quail or larks, and, later, even to inanimate objects.

bizarre

This term seems to have originated in the Basque word for 'beard,' *bizar*, which was borrowed by Spanish as *bizarro*, acquiring the meaning of 'valiant, brave,' the sense of the word in that language today. The connection between 'beard' (or 'bearded person') and 'brave' is unclear, although possibly a beard was seen as a mark of virility and its wearer was assumed to be a virile, thus brave, man.

From Spanish, the word passed into French, retaining its sense of 'brave, valiant,' a meaning which was eventually replaced by the sense of 'unconventional, irregular.' Again, the shift is difficult to explain, although one may imagine that a 'brave' man was a 'nonordinary' one, and the nonordinary aspect of *bizarre* came to be emphasized at the expense of the earlier meaning.

When *bizarre* was borrowed from French by English in the 17th century, it was with the sense of 'unconventional, nonordinary,' a meaning which we retain today, when beards are no longer considered *bizarre*.

blackmail

The *-mail* of *blackmail* goes back to an Old English borrowing from the Old Norse or Old Icelandic *māl*, whose original meaning, 'speech' or 'talk,' remained in the cognate Old English form *mæl*, but which had evolved in Scandinavian to mean 'action-at-law, legal suit,' and then 'agreement, contract.' The particular agreement the Vikings had in mind was one by which the Old English peasants arranged to pay 'tribute or rent' in return for freedom from pillage or depredation at the hands of the invaders.

Modern Scottish dialects, the direct lineal descendants of the Northumbrian English spoken in those areas most subject to the Viking invasions of the 7th, 8th, 9th, and 10th centuries, still preserve *mail* in the sense of 'rent,' but only the compound *blackmail* retains the sense of 'payment extorted by threat of force or harm.' Originally a *black* payment was made in cattle, while a "white" payment was made in silver. (See also **mail**[1], **mail**[2].)

blanket

When the Old French word *blanket* first entered English around 1300, it referred to 'a white, undyed woolen fabric,' suitable for use in a variety of ways. Etymologically the meaning represents a specialization from an earlier sense, in which the focus was the whiteness. The stem *blank-*, on which the word rests, was an early Germanic loan into French, and an inherited Old English form of the same stem meant 'white, gray' or 'blank' in the Modern English sense. A variant, *blanca*, was applied to 'a white or gray horse.' The Dutch cognate *blank* 'white' or 'shining' suggests the more remote meaning, 'blazing, burning white hot,' which appears also in the cognate, *flagrant*, derived from Latin.

Some time in the first part of the 14th century first the 'white,' then the 'woolen' part of the meaning disappeared, and the term came to apply exclusively to 'a fabric used as a bed cover employed for warmth.'

bless

Old English *bletsian*, the direct ancestor of *bless*, rests on the same stem as that seen in the word *blood*, and the term originally signified 'to cause blood to flow.' Later it became 'to consecrate or invoke divine favor by means of blood sacrifice.' When religious practices stopped involving the offering of live victims, that element of the meaning disappeared, and the word persists in the sense of 'to consecrate, sanctify.'

bonfire

The first element of this word is a variant of the word *bone*, and, indeed, the spelling *bone-fire* survived into the 18th century. The fact that the Old English *bān* followed two different paths, depending on whether it appeared alone, *bone*, or as part of a compound, *bon-*, caused English speakers to lose the connection between the two forms. However, down to the 18th century the folk practice of gathering bones to be burned in a festive *bonfire* in midsummer persisted in parts of England and Scotland, preserving the primal tradition behind the meaning.

Citations of the 16th and 17th century attest a now obsolete use of the word as 'funeral pyre.' Strangely enough, although the suggestion is definitely speculative, there is a possibility that the English word *bone* may be distantly related to the Latin *funus*, *funer(is)* which underlies the word *funeral*, since the normal phonological development of the Proto-Indo-European *$b^h oin$- would produce the English and Latin forms. It is also interesting to note that the word *pyre*, derived from Greek via Latin transmission, is also the exact cognate of the English word *fire*.

boondocks

The source of a word frequently plays a role in its prestige, and this aura of social respectability affects the connotative meaning of the word. To this day, almost any English word of Latin or Greek origin carries credentials, thanks to the fact that throughout the Middle Ages Latin was the universal language of scholars throughout Europe. Greek entered English through Latin, or by way of the universities when it was recognized, during the Renaissance, as part of the classical heritage.

On the other hand, the few words that have come into English from Tagalog, now the basis of the indigenous national language of the Philippines, came by way of frequently illiterate or uneducated peasants. *Boondocks*—originally *bundok* 'mountain'—was one such word. When Philippine natives spoke of their distant homes or relatives in the mountains, English speakers understood the word as referring to remote rural regions quite unlike the more urbanized areas which they themselves inhabited. Thus the original meaning never passed through the semantic filter, and the word entered English as a slang term, in the garbled senses of a distant, backwoods, marshy, generally uninhabited place.

botulism

Toward the end of the 19th century it was remarked that a severe type of food poisoning was sometimes related to eating preserved meats, and the disorder was called *botulismus*, later simply *botulism*, from the Latin stem *botulus* 'sausage' plus the Greek-derived suffix often used in medical terminology to signify 'a condition.' The real culprit, later named *Clostridium botulinum* (from the Greek *klostr-* 'spindle,' owing to its shape), was a bacillus isolated by Van Ermengen in 1896, found in other foods as well as in sausage; but the name remained. Since few English speakers knew Latin, the connection with sausage was forgotten.

Ironically, *botellus*, a diminutive of the same word evolved through French, where it lost the *t*, entered English in the 13th century as the ancestor of the modern word *bowel*, possibly thanks to the similar appearance of intestines and sausages. The irony extends further, since sausages are traditionally made by stuffing animal intestines with spiced meats. Some etymologists have suggested that the

Latin word *botulus* itself goes back to an ancient root meaning 'intestine.' This, however, is highly speculative, and would require the assumption that Latin borrowed the stem from one of the neighboring Italic dialects, possibly Oscan or Umbrian, since the presumed reconstruction of the root starts with the Proto-Indo-European *g^w-, which normally became *b*- in those languages but *v*- in Latin.

bread

The earliest meaning of the Old English *bread* was 'piece' or 'fragment,' while *hlāf*, the ancestor of our *loaf*, had not yet come to signify 'an undivided unit of food.' The probable semantic path to the modern meaning may involve a phrase signifying 'a piece of the baked food,' which then dropped part of the phrase and kept that part which had originally referred only to the 'fragment,' now with the meaning 'baked food.' The phrase 'to break *bread*,' now signifying 'to eat,' preserves the early history of the word 'to break a piece,' seen in Old Irish *brúid* 'he breaks.'

Some Old English glossaries equate *bread* with the Latin *frustum* 'piece, bit', an exact cognate, representing the divergent phonological development of the same Indo-European form, through a different branch of the related family of languages.

bridal

The adjective *bridal* 'of or pertaining to a wedding or marriage' began life as a noun, the Old English *brýd-ealu* 'bride-ale,' a wedding celebration at which quantities of ale were customarily consumed. Through the increasing use of this compound as an attribute, *bridal(e)* came to be understood as an adjective ending in the familiar suffix *-al* (from Latin *-alis*) in the early 17th century, acquiring in the process the general sense associated with the word today.

Both components of the original compound, *bride* and *ale*, are Germanic in origin. While *ale* has maintained what was apparently its original sense of 'alcoholic beverage made from malt,' there is some question about *bride*. While most of the Germanic languages show a cognate for this form with the meaning 'woman about to be married or just married,' the Gothic form seems to have meant 'daughter-in-law,' as did the Late Latin borrowing *brūta*, which replaced the earlier Latin *nurus*, and which appears as Modern French *bru* 'daughter-in-law.' It is possible that the Gothic and borrowed Latin use of the term represent an extension of the original meaning, 'wife.'

broach, brooch, brochure, brocade

The Old Latin word *brocchus* 'the projecting teeth of animals' had a variant usually reconstructed as **brocca*, on the basis of derivatives in the Romance languages, which signified 'a spike, spit, or pointed rod' —probably anything that resembled a pointed tooth. This form served as a center of semantic radiation for a variety of words of quite different senses.

Broach entered English via French near the beginning of the 14th century, at which time it referred to 'any sharp-pointed implement,' including tools as dissimilar as pins, awls, skewers, and lances. This meaning survives today only in dialectal usage. Later specializations allowed it to signify 'a particular type of church spire that extends upward in four sides from the summit of a square tower,' and also 'a type of chisel employed by stonemasons.' Used as a verb, the word once meant 'to pierce or stab with a sharp point,' a sense now obsolete. Used to describe the 'tapping' of a cask of liquor in order to draw off the contents, the word acquired the connotation of initiating or beginning something, and it is in this sense that it has been generalized today: to *broach* a subject is to initiate it.

As *brooch*, the word became specialized from 'any pointed implement' to 'a sharp, pointed pin,' and added the connotation 'used to fasten something.' It was then further extended to include the entire item of jewelry, not only the pin used to fasten it. The term has even been applied to ornamental adornments that do not have pins.

Still another semantic line developed the sense from 'pin' to 'needle' and thence to 'items stitched or sewn with a needle.' A development of this specialization produced the word *brochure*, which rests on the same stem and is extended by a suffix meaning 'result of.' The early *brochures* were printed pages stitched together into a booklet. The 'stitching' sense has faded, and now the word describes pamphlets put together by any means, such as glue or staples.

An Italian specialization of the Latin *brocchus* gave the word for 'nail, stud, or tack,' and an extension of this produced the past participle *broccato*, 'studded with nails, embossed,' a description applied to a type of cloth of gold or silver threads woven into raised patterns resembling studding. This word entered French as *brocade*, either via Spanish, Portuguese, or Provençal or as a direct adaptation of the Italian based on analogous formations with the same suffix. It finally reached English in the 16th century as a general term for the richly wrought fabric.

bromide

When it was isolated from sea water and recognized as an element (atomic number 35) in 1826, *bromine* was so called because of its unpleasant odor, from the Greek stem *brômos* 'stink' plus the *-ine* that signifies a chemical substance. Normally, this element combines with other chemicals to form compounds known as *bromides*, for example, *ethylene bromide* (a major ingredient in anti-knock additives for fuels) and *potassium* and *sodium bromide*, used as sedatives. It is this connotation of 'having a soporific effect' that led to the usage of the term *bromide* to mean 'a boring person' or 'a platitude.'

buccaneer

While today we think of *buccaneers* as 'piratical sea-rovers,' the people to whom the term was first applied were the Tupi Indians of South America, who smoke-cured their meat by suspending it over a fire by a device called a *mukém*, borrowed by French explorers as *boucan* (cf. Portuguese *moquém*). When the French began to hunt, cure, and sell wild oxen and swine to other seafaring Europeans, they came to be known as *boucaniers* or *buccaneers* from the method, borrowed from the Indians, of curing the meat. The association of this meat and its purveyors with the privateers and pirates who were its main consumers led to the present-day use of the term.

Oddly enough, *boucan* never took hold in Haiti, the main French foothold in the Caribbean, although to this day the French Canadian word for 'smoke' is *boucane* (unlike the continental French *fumée*). Instead, the Haitians retained their local word for the smoking device, *barbacóa*, whence English *barbecue*.

bugle

The Latin word *būculus* 'a young bullock or steer,' a diminutive version of *bōs* 'ox, bull, or cow,' became the Old French *bugle*, which reached English by the end of the 13th century. The animal's horn, appropriately carved, served as a musical instrument, and, although the instrument was originally designated a *bugle horn*, the meaning became associated with the first element of the phrase, and the second element was dropped. Modern *bugles* are made of brass or copper, but the name remains as evidence of the instrument's ancestry.

The Latin *bōs* (*bovis* in the genitive case) itself represented a borrowing from either Oscan or Umbrian, the language most closely related to that of the Romans; the *g^w-* of the ancestral Proto-Indo-European *$g^w\bar{o}$-* 'cow' usually became *v-* in Latin, but *b-* in other branches. The indigenous Latin word, based on a variant of the same Indo-European root, was *vacca-*, an expansion of which passed through Spanish as *vaquero* 'cowboy,' and reached American English across the Mexican border as *buckaroo*. The Germanic treatment of the same *$g^w\bar{o}$-* gave Old English *cū*, which eventually became modern English *cow*.

bumpkin

A term which seems to have come from Dutch, and which nowadays refers to a 'rustic, simple person,' *bumpkin* was originally an epithet applied to a Dutchman, for reasons which remain unclear. For that matter, a number of English expressions refer to the Dutch in terms that are, to say the least, unflattering: a *Dutch uncle* is a 'stern critic,' *Dutch courage* is 'alcohol-induced bravery,' a *Dutch bargain* is a 'deal made under the influence of liquor,' a *Dutch auction* is a 'sale in which the auctioneer opens with a high price which is steadily lowered until a buyer appears,' a *Dutch treat* is an 'outing at which members of the party pay their own expenses'—that is, no treat at all—and to *take the Dutch route* is to 'commit suicide.' In the construction trade, a *dutchman* is a 'device for masking faulty work.'

One possible derivation for *bumpkin* is that it comes from the Dutch *boom* 'tree,' from which the English *boom* 'horizontal spar at the foot of a fore-and-aft sail' is derived, plus the diminutive suffix *-ken*. Another possibility is that the word comes from Middle Dutch *bomme* 'barrel,' plus the diminutive suffix *-kijn*. In either case, whether it be as a 'little tree' or a 'little barrel,' the connotation is that of a person both rustic and simple.

A third etymology that has been proposed derives the word from the English *bum* 'buttocks, rump' plus the diminutive suffix *-kin*. Given the original association of the word with the Dutch, this seems unlikely, although the meaning of *bumpkin* may have been reinforced by the English *bum* and *bumble*.

bust

The Latin word *bustum* 'place of burning and burial, tomb,' served to designate the final resting-place of the dead, whether they were cremated or simply buried. The term seems to have arisen as the result of a process etymologists call "back formation" from the verb *ambūrere* 'to burn around, to scorch' (from *ambi* 'around' and *ūrere* 'to burn'). Because the Romans commonly adorned the burial places of prominent people with statues in their likenesses, the sense of *bustum* gradually changed to 'place of statues' and then to 'statue, particularly of the human head and torso.' It was in this sense that the word entered Italian, passing into English in the 17th century.

A further extension of the meaning, found from the 18th century, allows *bust* to be used to designate 'the female bosom,' in this usage the bosom of a living woman.

buxom

The Proto-Indo-European root **bheug-* 'bend' gives us *bow, elbow* and *akimbo*, and *bog*, each in an extension of the original sense. To *bow* is to 'bend at the waist,' and a *bow* is a 'thing which is bent,' as a *rainbow*, a *bow and arrow*, or, by further extension, a *bow tie*. The *elbow* is that part of the arm which allows the arm to 'bend,' and if you stand with arms *akimbo*, your arms are 'bent.' A *bog* is 'pliable (bendable) earth.'

Buxom also comes from **bheug-*. It made its first appearance in English with the meaning 'pliable, compliant, obedient,' as attested in the 12th-century admonition to be *buhsum toward Gode*. Since then, *buxom* has undergone a series of successive extensions of meaning, 'obedient' itself being an extension of 'bend(ing).' From the sense of 'obedient' came 'flexible,' then 'happy, easy-going, jolly,' and then 'healthy, plump.' By the time this last extension of the meaning had taken hold, in the 16th century, the word had come to be used exclusively in connection with women, although earlier it had applied equally to 'humble or obedient' members of both sexes. Today, a *buxom* person is a 'woman of ample figure,' who may or may not be jolly or compliant.

C

cabal

This word comes originally from the Hebrew *qabbālāh* 'received, accepted,' a term which was first applied to the total of the learning which Moses is said to have received at Sinai. Later it came to designate a particular branch of that learning. Traditionally, Moses is held to have been given the Pentateuch (Five Books of Moses), known as the Written Law; a body of Oral Law that was written down centuries later; and an additional quantity of oral mystical teachings. As the Written Law came to be known as the *Torah* (from a word meaning 'teachings') and the Oral Law became known as the *Talmud* (from another word for 'teachings'), *qabbālāh* came to refer exclusively to that body of mystical literature not included in the other branches of received learning.

Traditionally, the *qabbālāh*, or *cabala* (also spelled *cabbala, kabala*, or *kabbala*), has had few students. Most Jewish subcultures prohibit its study until the scholar is 35 or 40 years old, and even then he is not encouraged. Because some cabalistic knowledge was considered to be a form of white magic, study groups were kept small to minimize the possibility of misuse of this esoteric learning. Thus, since students met clandestinely in small groups to pursue what some felt were "black arts," it was not long after the term *cabal* worked its way into English that it came to designate not the object of study, but the study group. By the 16th century a *cabal* was 'any clandestine, sinister-seeming group.' It was assumed that such a group was up to no good.

This sense was strengthened during the reign of Charles II, whose Privy Council included a group of political connivers whose names formed the acronym *cabal*: C(lifford), A(rlington), B(uck-

27

ingham), A(shley), and L(auderdale). Following the widespread use of the word in this connection, the word became fixed in its present meaning, 'a small group of secret plotters.'

cadet, caddie, cad

In Medieval Gascon French, a *capdet* was a 'little chief, little head,' from the Late Latin *capitellus*, a diminutive form of Latin *caput* 'head.' The term was originally applied specifically to a 'younger son of a nobleman, serving as a military officer at the French court,' since younger sons of the nobility were expected to make their careers in the military. The term passed into Standard French in this Gascon sense, but later was generalized to mean 'younger (son, brother).'

In the 17th century, while retaining both meanings, French *cadet* passed into English, which reworked the French meanings and, in the process, created the doublet form *caddie*. During the 17th and 18th centuries *cadet* was used to mean 'junior military officer,' while *caddie* meant 'military trainee.' The 18th century also saw the creation of the abbreviated form *cad*, which seems to have had a variety of senses, all of them suggesting assistant status: 'assistant to a coach-driver, wagoner's helper, bricklayer's mate,' and the like.

The following two centuries produced further semantic changes. A *cadet* came to be a 'military trainee,' while a *caddie* became an 'errand boy, porter,' and during the 19th century the term narrowed to mean a 'porter for a golfer,' the sense in which it is used today. *Cad*, in the meantime, came to mean, first, a 'youthful university hanger-on, a local who might run errands for the students'; then any 'local resident in a university town'; and, finally, a 'person of low breeding or disreputable habits,' the sense in which it is used in American English today.

cancel

The Latin word *cancer* (phonologically identical to, but not to be confused with, the word for 'crab' which underlies the name of the malignant condition) meant 'lattice.' Some scholars believe that it derives ultimately from a reduplicated form of a root meaning 'twist,' and that the *n* comes from an earlier *r*. The addition of a diminutive suffix produced **cancerlus*, whence came *cancellus*, which originally signified a 'small (or possibly a more closely twined) lattice.' A verbal variant of the stem meant 'to make a lattice (or something resembling one).' Romans who wished to annul some portion of a legal document made latticelike strokes through the section in question, and the verb came to be applied to this graphic act.

The term descended through the Romance languages, reaching English, probably through French, in the early 15th century, by which time the original meaning had started to fade, being replaced by the more general sense of 'to render void by drawing lines through it.' Further generalization continued, until the word simply meant 'to annul or repeal' without the physical act of defacing a document.

English borrowed other forms of this word, sometimes directly from Latin, among them *cancelli* (from the nominative plural of *cancellus*), which reverted to the earlier sense of a 'lattice or grating,' but took on a specialized connotation derived from its use to describe the screen or railing which separates the choir area from the rest of the church. A second specialization occurred when the word was used at the end of the 18th or beginning of the 19th century in the anatomical description of the latticelike spongy structure inside bones.

Another specialized use emerged from the 'lattice, railing' sense of a French variant, *chancel*, which became attached to the area separated, in a church or court, rather than to the screen that marks the separation. The officials who functioned in these areas were known as *chancellors*, a title applied at different times to people of diverse status and function.

cancer, carcinoma

The Proto-Indo-European root **ker*, preserved in the English word *hard*, in its doubled form, **ker-ker*, signified a 'hard-shelled animal.' In the course of time the original meaning faded and the word became restricted to a single species, the 'crab.' In the course of its phonological evolution to Latin, the first *r* of the word changed to *n*, giving *cancer*, while in the descent to Greek it was the second *r* which shifted, giving *karkinos*.

Galen, the Greek physician of the 2nd century, used both *karkinos* and *karkinōma* (a version extended by a suffix meaning 'swelling') to describe a malignant tumor, since he thought the enlarged veins in the afflicted area made the growth resemble a crab. Since Galen practiced in Rome for a number of years, eventually becoming physician to the Emperor Marcus Aurelius, the Latin word for 'crab' also became associated with the disease, and both *cancer* and *carcinoma* represent developments of the same root.

The Latin-derived variant has now extended its sense in popular usage to a more generalized, nonmedical meaning; "a *cancer* in the body politic" is 'any malignant or deadly element.' At the same time the earlier Latin sense of 'crab' also survives, since the ancients named one of the twelve signs of the zodiac *cancer*, and astrology preserves the 'crab' meaning, although certain fortune-telling columns in popular magazines and newspapers have replaced that sign, said to govern the period starting on June 21, with the moon, because of the negative connotations aroused by the medical sense of the term. (See also **lunatic**.)

candidate

In the Old Latin of the 2nd century B.C., *candidatus* meant 'clothed in white' or 'man clothed in white.' Since Romans seeking office wore white togas, the connotation of 'office seeker' became attached to the original meaning, and by the early days of the Republic the word had that specialized sense. Careful speakers, like Cicero and Horace, substituted *albatus* for *candidatus* when they wished to refer to a white-clad man who was not seeking office. Many terms with the *cand-* stem continued to exist in Latin with the original meaning, but once the word passed into English in the early 17th century all trace of that early sense disappeared, leaving it with its modern sense.

candy

The long line of transmission of this loan word began in the Indo-Iranian branch of Indo-European, where the stem meaning 'break' (Sanskrit $k^h and$) gave a word meaning 'piece' or 'fragment.' This came to be used as 'piece or lump of crystallized sugar,' and the Persian cognate *kand* dropped the original significance 'fragment,' retaining only the connotative extension of the term, 'sugar.'

Entering Arabic as *qandi* 'sugared' or 'candied,' the word traveled across the Mediterranean to the Romance languages, which, by the 15th century, had transmitted it to English in the generalized sense of 'confection.' The present word represents a shortening of the phrase *sugar candy*, the form which appears in all the earliest English citations.

cannibal

This word entered English in the 16th century in the sense of 'a maneating native of the New World,' through a misunderstanding. When Columbus arrived in the West Indies he asked the natives where he was, hoping to be told that he had reached India, his intended destination. Instead, he was told he had arrived in the land of the *Caniba* 'the Brave People,' which he took to mean that he had indeed reached the land of the Indian *Khāns*. As he found his way to other Caribbean islands he became aware that he had not, in fact, reached India, but a wild place inhabited by natives he called *canibales* 'natives of the *Canibe* (dialectally, Caribe).' The Caribbeans (*cannibals*) were believed by the Spaniards to eat human flesh. It is likely that this sense of the term was reinforced by the Latin *canis* 'dog,' the implication being that savages, like dogs, ate flesh.

The word was later applied by European explorers to natives who practiced cannibalism elsewhere in the world and lost its original connection with the Caribbeans.

cannon, cane, canal, canister, canyon

Etymologically, a *cannon* is 'a large reed,' the Latin *canna* (Greek *kánna*) 'reed' to which the augmentative suffix of the Romance languages *-(o)on* has been added. In fact, it is possible that both the Latin and the Greek forms derive from a Semitic word meaning 'reed, pipe.' It seems quite likely that the hollow, cylindrical *cannon* took its name from the reed, as did *cane*, a word which first appeared in print in English in the 14th century with the meaning 'a reed or reedlike stem'—a meaning which persists today. In the 16th century it took on the extended meaning of 'walkingstick.' *Canal* entered English in the 15th century with the sense of 'tube used for the conduction of fluid.' By the 16th century the term was used to designate both 'a tube for the conduction of bodily fluids' and 'a man-made watercourse.'

It was at about the same time that *canister* and *canyon*, the latter borrowed from the Spanish conquistadores, made their appearance in English. A *canister* was originally a 'wicker (*caned*) basket,' although today it has come to mean a 'container'; one of its specific applications is 'a container for powder and shot for a cannon.' A *canyon* is a long, tubular depression in the earth, so called by the Spaniards from the Latin *canna* plus the same augmentative suffix seen in *cannon*.

canopy

The word which underlies Modern English *canopy* entered Greek during the period of Greek rule in Egypt, when a *kōnopeîon* was 'an Egyptian couch covered with mosquito netting.' This word may have originated in *Kánōpos (Canopus)*, a city some fifteen miles from Alexandria, and then have been reshaped by analogy to the Greek *kônōps* 'mosquito'; or it may have taken its name from the mosquito itself, only later becoming associated with the Egyptian city.

In either case, the term for 'covered couch' is attested in Latin as *canapeum, canapium, conapeum*, and *conopeum*, which gives both English *canopy* 'covering' whether for a bed, throne, or public area, and French *canapé* 'couch; hors d'oeuvre (consisting of a cracker or piece of bread covered with a condiment or other food).' Thus the Latin form of the Greco-Egyptian word was first narrowed and then generalized in two different ways. In English the 'netting' has displaced the 'couch' element of the original meaning, and the term persists in the sense of 'covering.' In the modern languages of continental Europe, including Greek, the 'couch' component of the original meaning has survived.

cant

Latin *cantāre* 'to sing' was formed from the past participle, *cantus* 'sung,' or 'a thing sung,' of the verb *canere* 'to sing,' which is cognate with the English word *hen* (originally the "singing" male of the species). Unlike most of the terms derived from *cantus* and *cantāre*, such as *cantata, canticle, cantilation*, and *chant, cant* has had a negative flavor ever since its introduction into English in the Middle Ages.

Three factors, all connected with the early Christian Church, are generally held responsible for the negative connotations of Modern English *cant*. First, some clerics who chanted the Mass were believed to perform their ecclesiastical duties mechanically, without giving much attention to the meaning of the words they were uttering. Second, since beggars were permitted to attend services for the dead at which these clerics officiated, often expressing spurious grief in order to be given alms, their "chanted" pleas for money affected the meaning of the term for the performance of the ceremony. Third, in the early 1700s a famous father-and-son team of Presbyterian preachers, Andrew and Alexander *Cant*, lent their Anglicized name to the already suspicious sing-song of hypocritical clerics and beggars.

Thus, by the middle of the 18th century, *cant* referred to the ho-hum delivery of the priesthood, the whining of beggars, and, by extension, to the jargon of the class of rogues from which beggars came. Nowadays, we think of *cant* as a form of cliché-ridden speech with little music in it.

canter

As an equestrian term, this verb derives from Canterbury, the See of the Archbishop in England. The name of the town and its famous cathedral, where Thomas à Becket was murdered in A.D. 1170, probably comes from the Celtic word for 'border,' *cant*, a term still in use in Modern Welsh. It is likely that the southeastern county of Kent got its name from the same source. When the West Germanic tribes under the legendary chieftains, Hengest and Horsa, came to the region in A.D. 449, they built a fortified town which acquired the name *Cant wara burig*, literally 'hill (or hill fort) of the men of the border.' *Wara*, or its variant *wera*, was the genitive plural of the West Germanic word for 'man' (still preserved in the *were-* of *werewolf*), and *burig*, a West Germanic form derived from the Proto-Indo-European stem meaning 'high.' The name of the Old Irish goddess *Brigit* descends from the same word, as does the Old Norse *berg* 'mountain,' now preserved in the Modern English *iceberg*. *Cant wara burig*, later shortened to *Canterbury*, and its meaning faded from the knowledge of all but the most linguistically sophisticated scholars.

Following the murder in the cathedral of Thomas à Becket, the place became a shrine for pilgrims, many of whom came on horseback, and the pace at which they rode, slower and smoother than a true gallop, came to be called the *Canterbury rate*, *Canterbury gallop*, or *Canterbury trot*, among other appellations. Repeated use caused the meaning of the various phrases to localize in the first element, and the following elements were dropped. In time *Canterbury*, too, was shortened to *canter*, and the connection of the term with the city or its cathedral was forgotten.

canvas, canvass

If the origin of the Greek *kánnabis* (whence Latin and, later, English *cannabis*) and its German cognate, *hemp*, is obscure, the history of the uses to which this plant has been put is clear enough. If today the plant is more often smoked than pounded and braided into rope or woven into fabric, it was as the name for a 'heavy-duty cloth made from hemp' that *cannabis* in its Norman French form *canevas* was borrowed into English in the 14th century. The meaning of *can(e)vas* soon became extended to 'heavy-duty cloth made from hemp or flax,' a sense still in use today, along with a number of extensions of this meaning, all having to do with the specific purpose to which the cloth is to be put. Thus an artist's *canvas* is a 'painting on canvas,' while a *canvas* can also be a 'tent' or a 'sail.'

The original sense of the verb *canvass* seems to have been 'to toss (a person) in a *canvas* sheet for pleasure or punishment,' a usage dating from the early 16th century. A metaphorical extension of this meaning, current in the latter half of the 16th century was 'buffet, thrash,' and, a little later, 'criticize, buffet verbally.' This meaning broadened to include 'discuss thoroughly,' where it is the subject under discussion that is being thrashed.

Another extension of the meaning, dating from the 16th century and still current, is 'solicit (votes, support, opinions, etc.).'

carpet

The Roman poet Horace wrote, *Carpe diem*, literally, 'pluck the day,' or, more freely, 'harvest life's fruits,' or 'live now!' *Harvest* is the English cognate of *carpe*, and the Greek cognate, *karpós* 'fruit,' entered English in such botanical terms as *carpology* 'the study of fruit,' *carpel*, *endocarp*, or *pericarp*.

One semantic specialization of the Latin *carpere* 'to pluck' was the sense 'to pull out, disentangle, unravel' as applied to the separation of the material of cloth. The Italian word *carpeta* (also *carpetta*), originally 'plucked' or 'unraveled,' derived from the past participle, was first applied to the threads that resulted from such an unraveling, and then to the coarse fabric woven of those threads.

When the word *carpet* reached English in the 14th century, probably via French, it applied to such a fabric, then used to cover beds or tables. *Carphology* refers to 'the practice of plucking at bed-clothes,' as is sometimes seen in aged persons. In the 15th century, pieces of this material were spread on the floor for people to kneel or sit on, and by the following century those who could afford it began to leave the material permanently on floors and stairs, hence the present meaning. Modern *carpets*, of course, are frequently woven of virgin fibers rather than from the unraveled remnants of previously used cloth.

catsup, ketchup

According to a recently reported legal decision, the Food and Drug Administration prevented a manufacturer from calling a product *catsup* or *ketchup* because it used honey rather than refined sugar as a sweetening agent. The item failed to indicate whether a lexicographer had been consulted.

Although they disagree on minor details, most etymologists trace the word back through Malayan, and then perhaps Dutch, to a Chinese dialect (probably Amoy) where the first element, *köe*, meant 'shellfish' or 'seafood,' and the second, *tsiap* (related to the standard Mandarin *chih*[3]) meant 'brine' or 'sauce.' Clearly, the recipe has changed considerably since the early 18th century when the term first reached English, since tomato paste is now usually a principal ingredient, and it is unlikely that refined sugar was used in the early versions.

cave

This word was borrowed by English in the 13th century from Old French, which had inherited it from the Latin adjective *cavus* 'hollow,' which could also be used to mean 'a hollow place.' While English retains this meaning in the related *cavity*, *cave* seems to have been specialized since Old French times to mean 'hollow place in the earth.'

A matter of some debate among etymologists is the question of whether or not the Latin root underlying *cave* is also to be seen as the source of the English *cage* (and *jail/gaol*). Some argue that the original sense of Latin *cavea* 'cage (for birds or animals), beehive, fuller's frame' bears so little resemblance to that of *cavus* 'hollow' that any phonetic similarities between the two words must be accidental. The fact that *cavea* was used in Imperial Latin to mean 'cavern' and, by extension, 'theater auditorium' is said to be simply the result of the influence of the phonetically similar *cavus*.

Others maintain that the semantic connection between 'hollow' and 'enclosure' is not really farfetched, and that *cavus* and *cavea* should be seen as coming from the same root.

In any case, *cavea* did produce *cage* in Old French, and that form passed into English in the 13th century meaning 'a construction for confining birds and animals.' The diminutive, *caveola*, having become *gaiole* and *jaiole* in different dialects of Old French, was borrowed into English as *jail* 'cage for people' during the same period. *Cage* has subsequently become generalized to cover any barred enclosure, while *jail/gaol* has retained its original 13th-century sense to this day.

cemetery

The Proto-Indo-European root **kei* 'lie, sleep, lodge' has provided English with a variety of terms, all having some connection with these meanings. Through Germanic, *home* and *hamlet* are derived from this root, the one meaning 'a place where one lodges permanently,' the other, 'a collection of houses, a village'; and the Latin *cīvitās* 'community of people' (from which we get *city*) and *cūna* 'cradle' are also traceable to this source, each by extension of its original meaning. *Cemetery* comes to us through Latin, from the Greek form *keîsthai* 'to lie down.' A variant form of the root is derived from the verb *koimân* 'to put to sleep' or, in still another form, 'to lie down, to go to sleep.' From this comes the noun *koimētérion* 'dormitory,' which was taken over by the early Christians and applied euphemistically to designate 'a burial place,' that is, a place where people "sleep" until the Second Coming. It is in this sense that *cemetery* entered English in the 14th century.

censor

In ancient Rome, the agent responsible for assigning adult male land-owners into groups of 100 (*centum*) for military service, for voting (in those days balloting took place by companies of one hundred, in the *Comitia Centuriata* 'Assembly of Hundreds'), and, later, for tax purposes, was known as the *censor*, and the enumeration was known as the *census*. *Cent-*, the root from which all these words spring, is cognate with the *hund* of the English word *hundred*, plus *-t-*, the participial suffix.

When the cadres started falling short of their full numerical strength, the meanings of *census* and *censor*, as well as the related *centurion* 'officer in charge of a group of 100,' lost their numerical specificity, and the *census* became simply an enumeration of the citizenry and its wealth, usually for tax purposes.

The modern meaning of *censor* developed out of the specialization of that official's duties. At first, it was the *censor*'s task to assign the landowner to his appropriate group (*century*). As an outgrowth of this function, the *censor* became responsible for determining the composition of the senate by ruling on candidates' qualifications, including whether or not they were morally fit for the job.

When the term entered English in the early 16th century it still referred to the office of the Roman magistrate; but by the end of that century it had lost its technical meaning and was used to signify 'anyone who supervises or corrects conduct or morality,' the meaning generally accepted today.

center, centre

The Greek verb *kenteîn* means 'to prick, stick (with something sharp and pointed)' and the corresponding noun, *kéntron*, is 'a sharp, pointed thing; a spur, ox-goad, nail, thorn, stationary point of a compass,' and the like. From its particular use as 'the stationary point of a compass,' *kéntron* came to mean 'center of a circle.' It was borrowed into Latin (as *centrum*) in this sense, and the word then passed into Old French and thence into English in the 14th century.

From its introduction into English, *centre* (later *center*) seems to have been the radial point not only of a circle, but of any object or construction whose middle point could be fixed with precision. Since the 14th century the use of the term has been extended to designate any 'focal point,' as in the *center* of a town 'downtown focus of mercantile activity' or the *center* of the political spectrum.

The use of *center* in its political sense of 'between the radical and the conservative positions' derives from the seating arrangements of the French National Assembly in the late 18th century. The radicals were seated to the left of the president of the Assembly and the conservatives to the right in a semicircular auditorium. The *centrists* were legislators whose political views were neither consistently radical (leftist) nor conservative (rightist).

chagrin

In Turkish, a *shagri* is 'the rump of a horse' and, by extension, the 'leather' derived from the horse's hide. This leather in its untanned state is quite abrasive and was commonly used as one might today use a scouring pad. Sharkskin, which has similar properties, was also known by the same name at one time and put to the same use.

Subsequently, *shagri* (and *sharkskin*) came to be used, when properly prepared, as material for clothing. Commonly dyed green, *shagri*, the fabric, entered English through French as *shagreen* in the 17th century. In its untreated form, *shagri* gave rise to French *chagrin* 'anxiety, vexation' by transference of the sense 'abrasive cloth' to 'sensation produced by the application of an abrasive cloth to one's person,' usually figuratively. In this sense, *chagrin* entered English from French in the 17th century, and is used in this way today.

chap

This word, first abbreviated in the 16th century from *chapman* (which is still in use), probably goes back to some form of the Latin stem *caup-*, seen in *caupō* 'merchant, shopkeeper, innkeeper,' or *cauponārī* 'to engage in trade or business,' a form which entered the Germanic ancestor of English long before that tongue had separated from the parent stock. A variant of the same stem (minus the sound change caused by compounding with the Germanic-derived word *man*) appears in the word *cheap*, attested in English earlier than *chap*.

It is probable that the line of transmission starts with the Roman traders who followed the armies as they first engaged the Germanic tribes in warfare, and then administered the pacified territories. Early uses of *chapman* reflect the semantic range of the Latin source, which encompassed both sides of the commercial transaction, selling and buying, and made no distinction between the localized shopkeeper and the itinerant pedlar, although some lexicographers assume that many of the various meanings found in English usage—'seller,' 'customer,' 'shopkeeper,' 'business agent,' 'pedlar,' are specifically English developments.

All meanings of *chapman* eventually became obsolete or obsolescent except 'itinerant pedlar' or 'dealer at market booths.' The shortened form *chap*, however, developed through 'person who engages in any transaction' to simply 'person, fellow,' used as an informal term. Occasional dialectal uses of *chap* continue to display the meaning 'customer.' (See also **cheap.**)

chapel

St. Martin of Tours performed many miracles during his life, according to his disciple, Sulpicius Severus, but none is more famous than his act in sharing his cloak with a naked beggar at Amiens in the 4th century. After his death in A.D. 397, Frankish kings kept his *cappella* 'little cloak' as a holy relic in a shrine dedicated to his memory. Eventually the word for the garment became transferred to the building in which it was kept, later to any place that housed sacred objects, and then to places of worship. In accordance with the normal sound changes from Latin to Old French the word developed into *chapel*, in which form it entered English in the early 13th century, by which time the original meaning had long since faded.

Officials attached to *chapels* were called *cappelani*, now *chaplains*. The word *cape*, derived from the same source, still reflects the early meaning.

charm

The Latin stem *can-* 'sing' plus *-men* 'result of, act,' produced **canmen*, whence came *carmen* 'song,' following the regular shift of the first *n* to *r*. The English cognate of *can-* is *hen*, which at one time meant 'the singer,' referring to 'the bird that sang in the morning'; *Chauntecleer*, the common Medieval French name for the rooster, literally 'clear singer,' shows a similar semantic development. The *chaunte* was an extended variant of the same root, *can-*, as it evolved in the southern dialects of French (and, incidentally, entered English as *chant*). The Latin word *carmen* became the French *charme*, but extended its significance to 'magical incantation' or 'song possessing occult powers,' in which sense it reached English by the start of the 13th century. (See also **slogan.**)

This meaning became generalized to 'something possessing supernatural powers, often used to ward off evil or attract good fortune,' and was applied to an object, often an amulet. The song-related part of the meaning had been lost, although the magical connotation remained. The chief modern sense 'quality or trait that evokes admiration, interest, or fascination' appeared in the 16th century, possibly as an outgrowth of the idea of the fascination of things mysterious or unknown. (This development parallels the semantic evolution of *glamour*, which see.) It is likely that the shift to the later senses received some impetus from the existence of words like *incantation* and *enchant* (also derived from the same *can-* stem), which retain the transitional meaning bridging the gap from 'sing' or 'song' to a meaning that pertains to the supernatural. Modern linguistic theory holds that synonyms always differentiate in meaning, since true synonymy is redundant, and languages tend to evolve toward greater efficiency.

chauffeur

This word preserves the history of the automobile, which was originally driven by steam. The term is etymologically related to the first element of the phrase *chafing-dish*, and both derive from the Latin *calfacere* 'to make heat.' The French word *chauffeur*, first attested in the 17th century, originally meant 'one who makes heat,' that is, a stoker. When applied to stokers of steam-driven vehicles, the word acquired the connotation of 'driver,' a meaning that survived after the motive power of the automobile became self-regulating and no longer required someone to shovel coal or wood into the fire.

chauvinist

Nicolas Chauvin de Rochefort, a veteran soldier of the First French Republic and vocal supporter of Napoleon and his nationalistic policies, was so outspoken in his views that after the fall of the Empire his name became synonymous with extreme and even excessive patriotism. Ridiculed in a popular play, *La Cocarde tricolore* 'the Red,

White, and Blue Rosette,' the terms *chauviniste* and *chauvinisme* referred to 'an excessively patriotic person' and 'excessive patriotism,' respectively, and both were borrowed into English in these meanings.

During the past decade in the United States *chauvinist* has begun to take on the sense of 'male supremacist' by localization of the word in the phrase *male chauvinist*. Whether this sense of the term will take hold, supplanting the original sense, for which *jingoist* is a ready synonym, remains to be seen.

cheap

It is not clear whether the Latin *caupō, caupōnis* 'merchant' was borrowed by Germanic (giving the Modern German *kaufen* 'to buy' and *verkaufen* 'to sell') or if Latin-speakers borrowed the term for buying/selling from Germanic. Most etymologists favor the hypothesis that the Latin speakers were the original purveyors of the word among the Indo-Europeans, having perhaps acquired it from one of the non-Indo-European languages of the Mediterranean. Whatever its source, *cheap* appears as a noun, *cēap*, in Old English in the sense of 'barter.' It remained in use with that meaning until well into the 14th century, by which time it had become standard practice to modify the noun with an adjective describing the nature of the transaction. *Great cheap* was 'a great bargain,' and *dear cheap* was 'a costly bargain.' In Shakespeare's time, *cheapen* still meant 'to sell,' whether at a good price or a poor one.

In the 16th century, *good cheap*, *dear cheap*, and the like localized to *cheap* in something like its present sense of 'inexpensive,' from usage as 'a good, inexpensive bargain' from the buyer's point of view. Today the term has also acquired a pejorative sense, 'shoddy, skinflintish,' from that same connotation. (See also **chap**.)

cheat

The Latin *excidere* (later dialectal *excadere/excadēre*) meant 'to fall away' and, by extension, 'to become lost, forgotten.' By the Middle Ages, the past participle of this verb had come to have a specialized sense in its use as a noun, from 'that which has fallen away or been lost' to 'inheritance,' and specifically to 'lost inheritance, inheritance taken by the state, *escheat*' (Old French *eschete*).

It is not clear exactly what the range of meanings was when English borrowed the Old French *eschete* in the 14th century, but the word first appears in English documents as 'inheritance forfeited to the manorial lord or the state in the event of there being no legal heirs'; 'inheritance forfeited to the manorial lord or estate in the event of a person's dying intestate'; or 'inheritance forfeited to the manorial lord or the state in the event that the heirs were deemed unfit or criminal.' From the general sense of 'forfeited inheritance' a new word, *cheat*, and a new meaning, 'booty, stolen goods,' evolved between the 14th and 16th centuries as a cynical commentary on the legal system of the day.

From 'stolen goods' evolved the sense of 'someone who bilks another of his goods by fraud or underhanded dealing.' Such a person was known as a *cheater* as early as the 14th century, and as a plain *cheat* from the 17th, the verb *cheat*, meaning 'defraud, deceive,' having gained currency in the 1500s. Today one can be a *cheat* or *cheater* by *cheating* on an exam, on one's spouse, or on one's income tax return.

check, cheque, checker, chequer

As a chess term, this word entered English from Old French at some time before the 13th century. In Old French *échec* meant 'rout' (later, 'failure'), coming from the Late Latin *scaccum* 'chess piece,' which was itself derived from the Persian *shāh* 'king,' principal piece in the game of chess. *Checkmate* is similarly derived from the Persian *shāh māt* 'the king dies,' and a chess-player warns his opponent that his king is in danger by saying, "*Check.*" From this usage evolved the sense of *check* as 'warning, stoppage,' current in the 16th century.

Subsequently, *check* as a verb came to mean both 'stop' and 'stop to examine,' as in the Modern English "his spending went *unchecked*"; "I *checked* my answers before handing in the exam"; or "they *checked* into a motel" (which can mean either 'they stopped and examined a motel,' or 'they stopped and registered at a motel').

As a noun, *check*, while retaining its sense of 'a stopping to examine,' developed a specialized banking sense in the 18th century, when it came to mean 'a written request to a banker to pay out money from one's account,' presumably after stopping and examining the account; for this sense the spelling *cheque* is used in British English.

Other uses of *check* derive by what etymologists call "back formation" from *checker*, which comes from the Late Latin *scaccarium* 'chessboard,' the multi-squared rectilinear board on which chess pieces are maneuvered in play. Thus in the 13th century one could speak of a *checker*, denoting 'the board on which chess (and, later, *checkers*) might be played.' By the 14th century, the sense of the word had been expanded to refer to any pattern of squares like that of a chessboard. Indeed, *exchequer* is derived from such an extension, since early financiers transacted their business over a tablecloth patterned with squares. (See also **chess.**)

cheer

The Proto-Indo-European root **ker*, which seems originally to have meant 'horn,' in one of its Greek forms, *kára*, had the extended sense of 'face.' This word was borrowed into Late Latin with that meaning, and then passed into the Romance languages. (It is not clear whether *kára* formed the basis of the Romance adjective which appears in Modern Spanish and Italian as *caro/cara* and in Modern French as *cher/chère*, both meaning 'dear.') English borrowed *cheer*, in the sense of 'face,' from Old French during the Middle Ages.

Subsequently the word took on the extended sense of 'mood,' perhaps because the mood is generally reflected by the facial expression. This sense still lingers in the question, *What cheer?* and the admonition *Be of good cheer*. From the localization of the phrase *good cheer* comes the expression *to cheer a person (up)*, in use since the 14th century to mean 'to put a person in a good mood,' and *to cheer one's comrades (on)*, in use since the 15th century to mean 'to encourage one's comrades.' More recently, the verb *to cheer* is used without an object, in the sense of 'to applaud, shout for joy.'

The noun *cheer* has evolved from 'face' to '(happy) face' to 'good mood' to 'happiness' itself. When applied to food and drink, it is in the sense of their being the means for providing a feeling of happiness or pleasant satisfaction.

chess

The game of *chess* has been aptly called "the game of kings and the king of games," the latter because of the difficulty of mastering the rules and strategies of the game, which requires a high level of intellection. It was considered "the game of kings" because it was traditionally played by the nobility and because one of the playing pieces, the king, is the focus of play. Once the king is lost, the game is over. In most of the languages of Western Europe, *chess* is also etymologically the game of kings, since the name of the game comes from the Persian *shāh* 'king.' In Late Latin any chess piece was a *scaccum*, the borrowed form of Persian *shāh* with a Classical Latin neuter noun ending tacked on. This form passed into Old French, where it acquired the *e* seen in Modern French *échec* 'failure,' an extension of 'rout,' since the objective of the game of chess is to 'rout' the opponent's king. *Échec* in the singular gives us *check* (which see), while *échecs* in the plural gives us *chess*.

It is not clear whether the Latin word *scaccum* still retained its original kingly sense at the point when it worked its way into French, but when the Normans brought the game and its name to England, 'routing' was established as its essence on the winning side, with 'failure' on the side of the loser. All senses of 'kings,' 'routs,' and 'failures' have disappeared from the word, which now simply designates the game.

chignon, chain, catena

Both *chain*, which entered English in the 14th century, and *chignon*, which entered in the 18th, derive ultimately from the same Latin stem, via French. *Chain* comes from *catena* and *chignon* from *catenionem*, a derivative. The original word meant both 'a brace or bracket used to hold two beams together' and 'a chain.' The English descendants derive from the second sense, but in its transmission the French transferred the word *chignon* to the 'coil or knot of hair worn at the back of the head by women' because of a fancied resemblance of that adornment to the coils of a *chain*.

The Latin word *catena* also reached English in the 17th century as a direct borrowing, in the sense of 'a series of extracts from the writings of the church fathers,' a shortening of the semantic localization *catena patrum*, and, in the 19th century, with the original meaning of '*chain*.' This stem has entered into other English words, among them *catenation, concatenate,* and *catenary* (a mathematical usage signifying 'a curve formed by a flexible but uniform cable suspended between two points').

A direct Old English cognate of the stem, *heaðorian* 'to restrain,' which may refer to the earliest meaning, has become obsolete. The relationship of this form to *catena* is indicated by another Germanic word, the Old Norse *hadda*, which also meant '*chain*' (of rings or links).

chowder

The Latin *caldāria*, originally a place for warming something, became specialized to mean 'warm bath' and also 'pot for boiling.' In the latter sense, it became the French *chaudière*. Breton fishermen used to pool their resources to contribute bits of fish, other seafood, biscuits, and vegetables to a stew or soup boiled in a large *cauldron* (another variant from the neuter form of the same word). Eventually the term was transferred to the contents of the pot, and when the Bretons brought their dish to Newfoundland in the 18th century it entered the English of North America respelled as *chowder*.

The root *cal-* 'heat,' which served as the base for the Latin *caldāria*, also provides the word *calorie*.

circus, circle

The Greek *kirkos* 'circling hawk, circle, ring' and *krikos* 'circle, ring' come from the same Proto-Indo-European root **(s)ker*, which seems to have meant 'turn, bend.' This, in its Germanic form, gives the Modern English *ring* and Modern German *Ring* 'circle.' Latin not only had its own form of this root, which appears in *curvus* 'bent, crooked, curved,' whence comes the English *curve*, but seems to have borrowed the Greek *kirkos/krikos*, as well, to give *circus*. This word originally meant 'circle,' but soon took on the added meaning of 'circular arena for athletic contests.' The original meaning of 'circle' was then taken over by the form *circulus*, a combination of *circ(us)* and the diminutive suffix *-ulus*. It is from *circulus* that the English word *circle* is derived, having entered the language through French in the 14th century.

Circus is a direct borrowing from Latin. The word came into English in the 16th century with the sense of 'circular arena,' a meaning partially preserved today, although now it is restricted to a 'covered circular arena' in which a particular entertainment, generally featuring acrobats, clowns, and animal acts, takes place. *Circus* also refers to the entertainment rather than the arena and, by further extension, to any 'boisterous, disorderly gathering or event.'

A use of the term found in England but not in the United States is as a word for 'a circular intersection of roadways,' as Piccadilly *Circus*. This usage seems to have originated in England in the 18th century and never took hold in the United States, where the term for such a traffic pattern is *circle*.

cithara, guitar, zither

The ancient Greek word *kithára*, meaning 'a stringed musical instrument,' usually one having from seven to eleven strings, passed into Latin as *cithara* and descended to English by various routes as *cithara*, *cither*, *guitar*, *gittern*, *citole*, and *zither*. The different names reflect changes in the instrument itself. *Guitar*, for example, a form that went through Spanish and then perhaps French, is the word for an instrument of six strings that is normally held and plucked vertically, while *zither*, the variant which passed through Old High German as *zithera*, is the name for an instrument of thirty to forty strings played horizontally.

All the variants derive ultimately from the Greek form, but the origin of the *kithára* itself poses an intriguing puzzle. One possibility suggests itself. An identical stem appears in the word *kítharos*, which meant 'thorax' or 'breastplate' in the singular, and referred to the curved pieces of armor worn front and back by soldiers in ancient Greece. If one of these had had strings attached from side to side, it could have served as a sounding board, and it may be that a field soldier created the ancestor of the *guitar*, *zither*, and other more refined stringed musical instruments in this fashion.

cleric, clerk

Both *cleric* and *clerk* are derived from the Greek *klērikós* 'of or pertaining to an inheritance or (in New Testament Greek) to the Christian clergy.' Originally *klêros* meant 'lot' and came to mean 'inheritance' in the sense of 'a person's lot with regard to his parents' estate.' Subsequently, in the early days of the Christian church, it came to have the more general sense of 'share, portion.' From this usage developed the sense of 'one having a share in the Christian ministry,' which is reflected in the adjective *klērikós* in its later meaning 'of or pertaining to the Christian clergy.'

Clerk is attested as a noun from the 11th century with the meaning of 'ordained minister,' and by the 13th century its sense had broadened to any 'scholar, literate person,' probably because most literate Englishmen of the period were members of the clergy. By the 16th century the term had lost most of its ecclesiastical associations, although it is still used in Anglican circles to designate 'a lay minister who assists the parish priest.' Present usage developed from 'a lay officer of the church,' generally one with secretarial or other scribal duties, through 'a person in charge of correspondence, record-keeping, billing, and accounts,' to include, chiefly in American English, 'a salesperson,' who has no secretarial duties.

Cleric, the slightly more learned descendant of *klērikós*, retained its original adjectival sense until the 17th century, when it first came to be used as a noun to describe a member of the clergy, and was replaced as an adjective by *clerical*, in the sense of 'secretarial.'

club

Like its close relative *clump*, *club* seems to have come from a Proto-Germanic form of a Proto-Indo-European root meaning 'form a lump, lump together.' The oldest attested sense of *club* in English, and one in which it is found to this day, is that in use in the 13th century 'a heavy, tapered stick suitable as a weapon with which to bludgeon someone or something.' This may represent a specialization of the sense of 'lump' associated with the noun derived from the Proto-Germanic root verb, the 'lump' referring to the thicker end of the stick.

In the 15th century, *club* in the sense of 'tapered stick used for hitting' came to be used to designate 'a bat for striking a ball in sport,' and, in contemporary usage, a golf *club* is 'a wood- or metal-ended stick.' A further application of the term appeared in the 16th century, when it was used to denote one of the suits of playing-cards, that known in French as *trèfle* 'trefoil.' The corresponding Spanish playing-card symbol was the club-shaped *basto* 'stick, club' (now generally referred to in English as "wand"). The word *club*, translation of the Spanish name for the card suit, was applied in English to the quite different-looking suit in the French deck.

Starting in the late 16th and early 17th centuries, *club* as a verb came to have another sense, more closely related to its original Proto-Germanic meaning 'lump together,' when it came to mean 'collect, combine, assemble,' and, specifically, 'pool financial resources, share expenses.' It is not clear whether these related senses represent a throwback to the older meaning or are a "new" metaphorical use of the term, possibly influenced by *clump*.

Whatever the case, the verb *to club* in its sense of 'pool resources, gather together,' soon gave rise to the use of the noun to mean 'assembly of people [for example, at a tavern] among whom expenses would be shared.' From this sense arose the meaning '(secret) society, aggregation of people with shared interests,' and, from this, the use of *club* to designate 'a building in which a society or aggregation of people with shared interests may meet on a regular basis.' *Club* in all these meanings is still in use.

cobalt

The arsenic and sulfur that occur in the ores of the metallic element *cobalt* caused damage to the health of the workers who mined it and the metallurgists who refined it. At one time this damage was attributed to the ill will of the goblin or spirit known in German as a *Kobold*, who presided over the mines. It is from this notion that the mineral acquired its name. When the word traveled to England as *cobalt*, in the 17th century, the original significance was lost owing to English speakers' ignorance of German. (See also **nickel**.)

cockatrice

Many mythical beasts are physical hybrids. Dragons customarily have the body of a snake and the wings of a bird; griffins have the head and wings of an eagle grafted onto the body of a lion; the centaur is half man and half horse, and so on. The *cockatrice* is a semantic hybrid, with elements of the basilisk (which see), the weasel, the crocodile, and the rooster.

Originally, the word *cockatrice* comes from the Latin *calcātrix* or *cocātrix*, a loan translation of the Greek *ichneúmon* or 'tracker,' a weasel that 'tracks' crocodile eggs to eat. (*Ichneúmon* also designated a variety of wasp that 'tracks' spider eggs.) Apparently as a result of the garbling of myth, etymology, and phonetics, *cockatrice* in English took on two different meanings. On the one hand, it was held to be a crocodile, presumably because of a confusion between the weasel and its food—a sense that has disappeared in English. On the other hand, a *cockatrice* was 'a basilisklike monster,' a serpentine creature with a glance that could kill, that was hatched from a cock's egg (which may explain the rarity of the creature in the real world), and that was vulnerable only to weasels.

Ulisse Aldrovandi, the 17th-century naturalist, wrote that in order to kill a *cockatrice* a weasel first had to eat rue. Failing a rue-eating weasel, travelers were advised to carry a rooster, whose crowing was believed to be effective against the monster.

comet

The Greek noun *kómē* meant 'hair of the head,' but the corresponding adjective *kométes* came to signify 'wearing long hair,' since the Greeks often used the word to describe the Persians, who wore their hair longer than was the fashion in most of the Greek city states. Thus when the Greeks first observed a *comet* they called it *astèr kométes* 'a star with long hair,' referring to the tail of the *comet.*

Eventually the meaning of the phrase became localized in the adjective, which assumed the function of a noun when the superfluous noun was dropped. When the Romans borrowed the expression they sometimes added *stella* 'star' but generally did not, and the Latin *comēta* reached English in the 12th century without the *stella* and with no trace of the original etymological meaning of the stem, an instance of what etymologists call semantic "fading."

companion

The Vulgar Latin *compāniōnem* came into being and passed down into French on the model of the Gothic word *gahlaiba*, from *ga-* 'with' and *hlaifa* 'bread' (the cognate of the English *loaf*), which designated 'the associate with whom one broke bread.' The original significance of Latin *pānis* 'bread' came from the Proto-Indo-European stem **pā-* 'feed,' which ultimately underlies the English word *food.*

As Latin evolved into the Romance languages, *compāniōnem* pressed into French and was borrowed by English in the late 13th century, by which time the etymological core of the significance (*pan* 'bread') had faded, leaving only the sense of 'associate.' This meaning has extended even to inanimate units, as in one member of a pair of twin stars.

constable

Like *marshal* (which see), *constable* has its origins among horses, since *comes stabulī* was the Latin phrase for 'an attendant of the stable.' The Latin word *comes, comitis* originally meant simply 'one who goes with another,' from *cum* 'with' and *īre* 'to go,' but from this neutral sense evolved the specialized meaning of 'attendant'; presumably the people who 'went with' an important person were not his equals. This downgrading of the sense of derivatives of *comes* was not invariable, however, for the English *count,* which derives from the form of the noun in oblique cases, clearly rests on an upgraded sense of the word.

By the Middle Ages, *comes stabulī* had itself been upgraded, like its Germanic counterpart, *marshal,* to designate 'a high-ranking official in the service of the king or other member of the nobility.' In 13th-century England a *constable* was, in fact, the chief officer of a nobleman's household. By the following century, however, he had begun his fall from grace. No longer 'the manager of the royal household,' a *constable* had become an 'appointed officer of the peace,' operating at the parish or county level. This is a realm of authority which has steadily diminished as those administrative sectors have faded in importance in the English-speaking world.

In contemporary England, a *constable* is 'a police officer.' In America, the increasingly rare term designates 'a minor official at the county level of government.'

cop

This word has two oddly related senses in English slang. As a verb, *cop* means 'to grab, get,' as in *to cop a piece of goods, to cop a plea;* while as a noun, *cop* means 'police officer.' The first sense of the term

probably derives from Latin *caupō*, *caupōnīs* 'merchant,' a word of
obscure origin which appears in Modern German as the basis for the
verb *kaufen* 'to buy.' (See also **chap.**) In its Old Frisian form, the term
seems to have served as a euphemism for 'piratical stealing.' Thus, to
cop something, in Germanic, was to acquire it through accepted
mercantile channels, one of which—stealing—was outside the law.
This is the sense in which the English verb is used today.

Cop as a term for 'a police officer' may or may not have its origin
in buying, selling, and stealing. If it comes from the verb to *cop*, it is
possibly because the police officer seizes the criminal and hauls him
off to be punished. Another possibility, however, is that the noun *cop*
is an abbreviation for '*copper*,' and referred to a person whose uniform displays *copper* buttons. The characteristic buttons are taken to
stand for the uniform, and the word for the uniform is transferred to
its wearer.

In any case, the word carries a pejorative sense, since the verb
signifies an arbitrary and often illegal practice, while the noun is
generally considered a disrespectful term for an officer of the law.

copper, Cyprus

The ancient Romans imported most of their *copper* from Cyprus,
called *Kúpros* in Greek, and so it came to be called *cupreum aes* 'the
ore or metal from Cyprus.' The meaning of the phrase became localized in the single word *cupreum* or its variant *cuprum*, and it was in
that form that it reached the Germanic tribes, who understood it only
as the name of the metal. This borrowing, which became *copor* in Old
English, dates back to the period before English had separated from
its Germanic relatives.

Most, perhaps all place names once had some significance, and
one can speculate on their original meaning. Aphrodite, the Greek
goddess of love, was also called *Kúpris* or *Kupría*, a name often
attributed to the fact that one of the chief centers of her worship was
Cyprus. However, in antiquity Cyprus was famed both for its *copper*
deposits and for its fertility, and Aphrodite is also a fertility goddess.
What could be the same stem appears in the Latin name of her son
Cupid (*Cupīdo*), as well as in the verb *cupēre* 'to desire,' from which
English derives the word *cupidity*. Further, the Greek name for the
henna plant, *kúpros*, was identical with the name of the island, and

the Greek word *kuprismós* means 'bloom.' Thus it is possible that the island took its name from the goddess, rather than the other way round, or, more plausibly, perhaps, that both the goddess and the island received their names from the same underlying source.

coquette

In French, a *coquet* was, literally 'a little rooster,' from *coq* 'cock' plus the diminutive suffix *-et*. The term was applied to 'a male flirt,' that is, a male who struts like a cock to attract a female. The word entered English in the 17th century as *coquet* and was interpreted as an adjective, based on its use in an expression like *Il est coquet*, literally 'he is a flirt,' but understood as 'he is flirtatious.'

After its introduction into English the word seems to have applied to both men and women, but by the 18th century it had come to refer exclusively to women and was given the feminine French ending, becoming *coquette*. At about that time it also switched back to being a noun and was used in its present meaning 'a female flirt; a woman who plays fast and loose with a man's affections.'

corn

Corn, kernel, and *grain* all come from a Proto-Indo-European root, **grH*, which seems to have meant 'wear down, waste away.' A *grain* or *kernel* (the diminutive of *corn*) was thus 'a small or worn-down thing,' a sense still preserved in such phrases as *a grain of salt* or *a kernel of truth*. In English, *corn* and *kernel* soon became specialized to refer to 'the seeds of edible cereals,' and *corn* came to designate as well the adult plants grown from such seeds.

It was this latter sense that the English colonists brought to the New World, where they encountered the native American maize. This they quickly dubbed *Indian corn* or *corn*. In America, English-speakers tended to call the native plant *corn* with no qualifier, since it was the only variety of edible grain cultivated locally in New England; but English-speakers in England were careful to distinguish *Indian corn* from other varieties grown there.

Corn in America has subsequently taken on two other meanings. It may refer to 'whiskey,' that is, *'corn liquor'* an alcoholic beverage made from *corn* mash, reminiscent of the brew of John Barley*corn* in

England. (When asked how he was able to survive on a diet of bourbon, William Faulkner is reputed to have replied, "There's an awful lot of nourishment in an acre of *corn*.")

The other sense of *corn*, 'bumpkin humor,' comes from the association of *corn*-growing with American rustics.

cove

The Old English word *cofa* was originally used to designate 'a small room, a closet,' a sense which was occasionally extended in compounds, such as *gast-cofa*, literally 'soul-chamber,' 'breast,' '(hollow) enclosure.' The Middle English form *cove* not only retained the Old English sense of 'closet,' but took on the extended meaning of 'hollow area, cave, recess.' It was this last which formed the basis for the present meaning of the word. By 1600 *cove* had come to mean 'a recess in the coastline, an inlet,' and the earlier meanings were forgotten.

It is possible that this extension and specialization of the meaning was influenced by the phonetically similar, but apparently etymologically unrelated word *cave* (which see). (See also **alcove**.) The British slang *cove* 'chap, fellow' is not related.

cummerbund

This word, meaning 'a sash worn around the waist,' has literally come up in the world. It is an Urdu loan word from the Persian *kamarband*, where the second part has the same meaning as, and is cognate with the English *band*. The first part, however, means 'loin.' Thus the word has clearly been transferred from an item of clothing similar in appearance but different in function.

cynosure

When the beautiful Arcadian nymph Callisto, whose name means 'the fairest,' bore a son to Zeus, she was transformed into a bear and placed in the heavens as the constellation later dubbed *Ursa Major* 'Larger Bear' by the Romans. According to one version of the story this was accomplished by Hera, Zeus's jealous wife; according to another, Artemis was responsible, for she demanded that her attendants remain chaste; and according to a third, Zeus himself performed the transformation in order to protect his mistress from Hera's wrath.

In one of the versions, Callisto's hunting dog went with her, and the hound's tail, *kunós oura* in Greek, forms that part of the constellation that contains Polaris, the polestar. *Kuno* is a cognate of the English word *hound* and the Latin *canis*, whose stem appears in *canine*.

In any case, the phrase *kunós oura* passed into Latin as the word *cynosura*, reaching English, as *cynosure*, by way of French at the end of the 16th century, with a number of different meanings. One use of the term was as the name of the polestar itself or of the constellation in which it appears. Another, derived from a connotation attached to the first, is 'a beacon or point of reference that serves to give guidance or a sense of direction, a guiding star.' A third meaning is 'something which stands out from its surroundings by virtue of its brightness or beauty, and therefore serves as a center of interest or attraction.'

Another version of the myth, in which Callisto's son also became a bear, gave rise to the name more commonly used for the constellation containing the polestar, *Ursa Minor* literally 'Smaller Bear.'

D

dactyl

The word *dactyl* 'a metrical foot consisting of one long syllable followed by two short syllables,' derives from the Greek *dáktulos* 'finger'
when it refers to humans, 'toe' when it refers to animals. The Greeks
applied the word to the metrical foot because of a supposed resemblance to the single long and two short joints of the digit, as well as
because the word itself embodied the measure, since the first syllable
was long, according to the rules of Greek prosody, and the second and
third syllables were short. Unfortunately, in English *dactyl* is a
trochee.

The same word entered English as part of scientific nomenclature, and appears in its primary sense 'finger' in such compounds as
dactylitis 'inflammation of the finger,' *syndactylism* 'a condition in
which the fingers or toes are joined,' and so on.

In Greek itself *dáktulos* also had the meanings 'grape' and 'date,'
possibly arising from the similarity of clusters of grapes or dates to the
fingers of a hand. The word even entered English in the 14th century
in the sense of 'date,' but by the second half of the 17th century this
had become obsolete.

There is a distinct possibility that the *dak-* of *dáktulos* represents
the exact cognate of the English word *toe*, since by normal sound
changes known as Grimm's Law, Proto-Indo-European *d* became *t* in
the Germanic branch of the language, and *k* became *h*. The Old
English form of the word is *tāh*. If the occasional use of *dáktulos* in
the sense of 'toe of an animal' did not already suggest such a semantic
connection, the phonological analysis may demonstrate that even metrical feet may have toes.

decimate

The Late Latin verb *decimāre*, derived from the Classical Latin *decimus* 'tenth' by adding the first conjugation endings, meant 'to tithe,' or to exact a tenth of a person's produce or earnings as a tax. *Decimate*, made from the past participle of *decimāre*, first appeared in English with the Late Latin meaning in the 15th century and remained in use until the end of the 18th. In the early part of the 18th century it acquired the now obsolete sense of 'divide into tenths.'

Another meaning, however, is first attested in English in the 16th century. This is 'to put to death one in every ten individuals as punishment for their collective crimes.' This means of punishment, which involved choosing the victims by lot, was known in the Roman army and was occasionally used in the armies of other nations, including England, as a way of punishing mutineers or deserters without reducing the numbers of soldiers by too great an extent. The practice was not long employed in England, however, and by the 17th century *decimate* had begun to be used in a more general sense, as 'to slaughter, destroy a large part of, lay waste to,' the common meaning of the term today.

delirium, last

The Latin word *līra* meant 'a furrow, track, or rut' such as might be made by a plough. To depart from this straight line was *dēlīrāre*, from the prefix *de-* 'from' plus the stem *līra*. To the Romans, one who deviated in such a way was demented or irrational (at least metaphorically), and these connotations accrued to the term. The noun formed from this verb, *delirium*, acquired the meaning 'madness.' Physicians applied the term to the temporary derangement induced by illness, and thus the word assumed the medical significance it still carries. The Romans undoubtedly remained aware of the etymological origins of the term, since the stem continued to exist in its early meaning, but that sense had faded by the time the word reached English in the late 16th century.

English retains a cognate word derived from the same Proto-Indo-European form that produced the Latin *līra*, namely *last*, 'the block shaped like a human foot that is used in making shoes.' The modern meaning represents a specialization of the earlier Old English meaning 'footprint,' itself a development from the 'track' sense of the Indo-European word. Part of the phonological difference between the Latin *līra* and the English *last* arose from the regular Italic shift of *s* to *z* and then from the Roman shift of the *z* to *r* when it occurs between vowels.

The Latin *līra*, of course, bears no relationship to the Modern Italian name for a particular unit of currency. That *lira* derives from the Latin *libra*, the Roman pound, whose abbreviation, *lb.*, still signifies 'pound' (the unit of weight) in English.

derrick

Originally the surname of a famous 17th-century executioner in the employ of the Earl of Essex at Tyburn, *Derrick* was so well known in his lifetime that his name became synonymous, first, with 'hangman' and then, by extension, with 'gallows.' It retained the latter meaning long after the eponymous *Derrick* had died and been forgotten.

By the 18th century *derrick* had come to be used to designate 'a crane; device for hoisting' which bore a certain physical resemblance to the standard gallows. It is still in use in this sense, and has come as well to be used in the terminology of modern oil-drilling, where it means 'a framework surmounting a drill hole and used for hoisting pipe or supporting drilling apparatus.'

domino

The Latin *dominus* meant 'lord, master.' During the early Middle Ages, *dominus* (or *domino*, as it became in semi-learned Romance) was used to refer to, among others, 'a member of an ecclesiastical order.' By the time the term had entered English in the 16th century from French, it had acquired a new meaning from the characteristic hooded winter cloak worn by such ecclesiastics and referred to that 'cloak.' During the following century *domino* came to designate only 'the hood' that formed part of the winter cloak.

In the 18th century, when masked balls were popular among the rich, one costume frequently worn was a sleeved cloak with a black hood and half-mask, modeled on the clerical *domino* and referred to as such. By the mid-19th century the term had come to be applied solely to the costume's 'mask.'

Today the primary meaning of *domino* has come to be 'a playing piece in the game of *dominoes*,' where each piece is a black rectangular tile with white pips on one surface. The reason for the name is unclear, although it may be that the playing pieces were so called because of their resemblance to the black hood and mask of that name. Alternatively, the game and its pieces may have taken their name from the cry of *"Domino!"* ('Master!') originally uttered by the winner at the close of play.

dreary

The Old English noun *drēor* meant 'blood,' and the corresponding adjective, *drēorig*, 'gory' or 'bloody.' The adjective also, however, meant 'sad, full of sorrow,' a sense still preserved in the cognate German *traurig*. The sanguinary sense appears to represent a specialization from the general meaning 'drop' or 'fall' that survived in the related Old English verb *drēosan* 'to fall.' The phrase *dropena drēorung* 'falling of drops' referred to rain, not blood.

The transition from 'bloody' to 'sad, full of sorrow' (if that was, in fact, the chronological sequence) would appear to be an extension of the connotative meaning, since anyone dripping blood might be assumed to be full of sorrow. Subsequently the denotative core faded.

An alternative explanation could proceed from the 'falling' sense to 'raining,' whence comes the notion of 'dismal, gloomy,' an interpretation which would accord well with the meaning of the German cognate. If this derivation is the correct one, the 'bloody' sense would simply be a divergent development.

In any event, by the late 19th century the meaning of the term had weakened to mean simply 'unpleasantly gloomy, boring, or unattractive.'

dromedary

In the taxonomy of mammals, one subfamily, the *camelidae*, contains six species, two of them varieties of camel and the other four the llama, the guanaco, the alpaca, and the vicuna. These are camellike animals distantly related to the true camels but surviving only in South America, chiefly in Peru. The two camel species are the one-humped type, *Camelus dromedarius*, and the double-humped *Camelus bactrianus*. The latter gets its name from Bactria, one of the provinces of the ancient Persian Empire, in spite of the fact that in antiquity these animals were found also in parts of Central Asia and in the desert regions of China (where some may still exist, close to extinction, today). The *Camelus dromedarius* got its scientific name from the Latin phrase based on the Greek stem *dromad-* found in the word for 'runner' with the addition of the Latin adjective-forming suffix. The Romans used the term to signify 'a camel specially trained for riding,' and, more specifically 'for running.' Normally this was the one-humped variety, although the two-humped Bactrian could receive similar schooling and, if so, might properly also be identified by this description. Even in Roman times, the phrase was often shortened to *dromedarius*.

The word reached English as *dromedary* in the 14th century, probably via French transmission. In popular usage it is specialized as the term for the one-humped animal, a practice that conforms loosely to the scientific nomenclature but seems to restrict the name camel to the Bactrian variety. This is a sense at variance with internationally recognized biological taxonomy, since both species are properly camels.

dunce, Scotist

It is most ironic that *dunce* 'a stupid or ignorant person' comes to us from the name of John *Duns* Scotus, one of the great scholars of the Middle Ages. His surname, *Duns*, may bear some relationship to the name of the village in Berwickshire, Scotland, where he was born around the year 1265. Either the family took its name from the village, a common practice at the time, or the village may have derived its name from a family ancestor. The *Scotus*, often mistakenly believed to be part of the philosopher's name, is actually a Latin epithet used by those outside the British Isles to identify him as the man from Scotland.

In the early Middle Ages, Europe derived much of its philosophical and theological learning either directly from Scripture or indirectly from the writings of the church fathers, particularly from those of St. Augustine. In the first half of the 13th century, the translation into Latin of many of the works of Aristotle and of many Greek and Arabian commentaries on these works initiated a great controversy among Christian scholars as they sought to determine the extent to which pagan philosophy might be valid for Christians. Some of the finest intellects of the time grappled with the real or apparent contradictions between pagan ideas and biblical revelation.

One of these was John *Duns Scotus*, a Franciscan theologian, dubbed "Doctor Subtilis" from the acuteness of his philosophical reasoning. He undertook the task of mastering the teachings of Aristotle so as to use Aristotelian precepts and reasoning to clear away discrepancies and correct what he felt were shortcomings in that philosopher's conclusions. The synthesis at which he arrived did much to shape Western thought of his time, and consequences of his thought persist to the present day. That the name of this great scholar and philosopher developed into a word meaning 'a fool' is indeed ironic.

At first, however, his followers came to be called *Duns men*, a phrase with a wholly favorable connotation of reasoning both clever and sophisticated. Unfortunately, however, the students were not the equal of the master, and by gradual stages such phrases as *Duns men*, *Duns prelate*, *Duns learning* acquired new connotations signifying 'petty sophistry' and 'caviling purely for the sake of arguing.' Eventually this degenerated into meaning 'acting like a fool.' Occasional uses of the terms in the earlier sense of 'following the teaching of the Subtle Doctor, or reasoning like him' survived into the 16th century, but eventually only the pejorative connotation prevailed, and the original denotation with its connection to *Duns* Scotus faded.

The epithet *Scotus* 'of Scotland' also became applied, strangely enough, to followers of *Duns Scotus*, and they were referred to as *Scotists*. The terms *Scotist* and *Scotism* are still in use among modern philosophers in the technical sense of 'essentialist' and 'essentialism' by way of contrast with the terms *Thomist* and *Thomism*, referring to the metaphysics of St. Thomas Aquinas, with whose thinking the reasoning of *Duns Scotus* is often compared and contrasted.

A further lexical and semantic connection with *Duns Scotus* is through William of Occam (or Ockham), a *Duns man* most remembered today by the phrase *Occam's* (or *Ockham's*) *razor*. This phrase is used to express the principle that all unnecessary assumptions must be cut away in logical reasoning. Although he was a

Scotist, Occam came to disagree with certain points of the teachings of *Duns Scotus,* and his philosophy, which laid the groundwork for the beginnings of modern science, came to be called Occamism.

E

electric, electron

The Greek word *élektron*, related both to *ēlektris*, an epithet applied to the moon, and *ēléktor* 'the shining sun,' probably originally meant 'shining' or 'gleaming.' By the beginning of recorded history, however, it had specialized to mean both 'amber' and 'an alloy of gold and silver.' The semantic line leading from *élektron* to the modern word *electric* begins with the meaning 'amber.' *Elektron* passed into Latin as *ēlectrum*, and reached English by the 14th century. Early in the 17th century scientific experimenters had coined the term *electric* to refer to the electromagnetic phenomenon produced by rubbing amber, which evoked an electrostatic force. Under appropriate conditions this caused a flow of current by induction. Eventually the meaning of the term lost its connection to rubbing amber and focused on the current, however produced.

Ēlectrum has not been used in the sense of 'amber' since the end of the 18th century, but it still signifies the gold and silver alloy. Occasionally, metallurgists have applied it to other alloys which have a similar appearance, such as copper, nickel, and zinc.

Although the etymological source of *electric* is *élektron*, the modern word *electron* 'the fundamental negative particle of an atom' represents a new coinage based on the *électr-* stem plus a later addition of the word element *-on*. Since a flow of *electrons* is what we call an *electric* current, we have the paradox that physically *élektron* 'amber' originally produced the charge, but etymologically *electric* is the source of *electron*.

eleven, twelve

In many cultures, counting started on the digits of the hands and feet. Those peoples of antiquity who, like the ancient Sumerians, lived in a warm climate and either went barefoot or wore open sandals, counted on the combined number of fingers and toes, and used twenty as the basis of their counting system. This was reflected in their languages. Indo-Europeans, on the other hand, living in a region that was covered with ice and snow for part of every year, wore footgear that concealed their toes, and they counted on their ten fingers alone. When they needed to count beyond ten, different groups of Indo-Europeans resorted to different expedients.

Ancestors of the Greeks and Romans used the word for 'one' followed by the word for 'ten.' This became *héndeka* in Greek, a form that entered English in such compounds as *hendecachord* 'a scale of eleven notes' and *hendecasyllable* 'a line of poetry containing eleven syllables.' Greek *dōdeka*, from 'two' plus 'ten' reached English in such compounds as *dodecahedron* 'a twelve-sided figure.'

Ancestors of the Germanic and Lithuanian tribes also started with the word for 'one' but then added the word for 'left,' that is, 'left after the count of ten.' This compound stem became *eleven* in English, the *e-* a reduced form of *one* and the *-lev-* a variant of the word *leave*. For the next number they substituted the number 'two' for 'one', giving *twelve* 'two left' in English.

In time, the phonological changes obscured the relationship of the parts of the words to their fuller forms, and the original senses were forgotten.

equip

The Proto-Germanic root **skip-* meant 'ship' and is the ultimate source, through Old English, of Modern English *ship*; through Old French, through Lombardic, we have *skiff*; through Dutch *schipper*, the *skip-* of *skipper*. This root also provides the basis for the verb *equip* which, when it entered English in the 16th century, meant 'to outfit a ship.' Only later did it come to mean 'outfit, supply with necessities' in a general sense.

There is some question as to the precise route taken by the word *equip* on its way from Proto-Germanic to English. It is commonly held that *equip* is a borrowing of the Old French *esquiper* 'to sail.' This Old French verb is a descendant of the Late Latin *(e)skippare* 'to outfit or man a ship; to send by ship; to sail,' a verb created from the borrowed Germanic word for 'ship.'

The difficulty with this chronology is that the English meaning assigned to the verb *equip* is different from that of the French form from which it is supposedly derived. This may be owing to some filtering in the transmission from French to English; or English may have independently assigned a new meaning to the French verb, since by the time *equip* entered English the language already had a verb expressing 'to sail.' Still another possibility is that the meaning may have been influenced by other existing forms of similar shape and sense, whether Latin, Latinate, or Germanic; and finally, the word may not have come from French at all, but may have entered English directly from Late Latin.

ether

Like many other ancient peoples, the Greeks conceived of the universe in layers. The earth was the bottom layer, the atmosphere or "lower air" was the second, and the "upper air" was the third and topmost layer. The atmospheric layer was termed the *aér* (whence comes the Modern English *air*), from the Proto-Indo-European root **weH* 'wind,' the source of Modern English *wind, weather, ventilate*, and so on. The "upper air," which was believed to be bright and pure, was called the *aithér*, from the verb *aithein* 'to kindle, light up, shine' plus the agent suffix *-er*.

The *aithér* was believed to be the rarefied stuff breathed by the gods on Olympus, and 'a fifth essence or basic element; *quintessence*,' being composed neither of fire, water, earth, nor (atmospheric) air, but present in latent form in all things. It was in the sense of 'upper air, quintessential element' that *ether* entered English from French or Latin, which had borrowed the term from Greek, in the late Middle Ages.

As the theory of the four (or five) essences fell into disfavor, the term *ether* was used in other senses. In the 18th century, it designated the volatile anesthetic liquid now known as ethyl ether or $(C_2H_5)_2O$, possibly because of the compound's high flammability, its purity, its euphoric effects, or some combination of all three. The term also had an application in physics somewhat closer to its original sense of 'upper air.' Until the experiments of Michelson and Morley in the early 20th century definitively disproved its existence, the *ether* was thought to be an infinitely elastic, massless medium in which light and electromagnetic waves might be freely propagated.

All senses of the term are suggested by T. S. Eliot in the opening lines of "The Love Song of J. Alfred Prufrock:"

Let us go then, you and I,
Where the evening is spread out against the sky
Like a patient etherized upon a table...

F

fanatic

The Proto-Indo-European root *b^heH, meaning 'to speak,' entered English in a variety of ways via Latin, Greek, and Germanic transmission, having undergone the appropriate sound changes in each branch of the family. These involved b^h becoming f in Latin, p^h in Greek, and b in Germanic, producing the Latin *fa-ta* 'things decreed,' which gave *fate*, and *fa-ma* 'result of the speech, reputation,' which gave *fame*, and the Greek *-phēm-*, seen in *euphemism* and in the native English *ban* 'thing said against something' or *banns* 'marriage announcements.' One specialization led to the Latin *fānum* 'a place dedicated to a deity (originally consecrated by the uttering of prayers), a temple, or a sanctuary.'

An extension of this stem produced the Latin adjective *fānāticus* 'pertaining to a temple,' which later specialized its meaning to 'inspired by a god,' from the actions of those impelled by religious fervor while at the temple. This sense became extended to 'enthusiastic,' 'frantic,' and even 'mad,' but always with a religious or superstitious overtone.

It was with this significance, now generally obsolete or obsolescent, that *fanatic* first entered English in the 16th century. It then became generalized, passing from 'excessively enthusiastic by reason of religious or supernatural inspiration' to simply 'excessively or overly enthusiastic.'

(For another development of Latin *fānum* see **profanity**.)

fare

There is some doubt as to the original range of meaning of the Proto-Indo-European root *$*per$. Such forms of the root as the Modern German *führen* 'to lead,' whence comes *Führer* 'leader,' Latin *portāre* 'to carry,' and Modern English *'ferry'* together suggest an original meaning of 'carry, lead.' *Port, ford,* and *fare,* on the other hand, imply an original sense of 'pass, go.' (Cf. Modern German *fahren* 'to go, travel.') It is possible that **per* simply expressed 'forward motion' and that this meaning became specialized, possibly in Proto-Indo-European times, to 'lead, carry (forward),' and 'pass, go (forward).'

The Old English forms of this root include the noun *fær* 'journey' and the verb *faran* 'to go on a journey,' both of which appear as the Modern English *fare.* As a verb, *fare* has all but disappeared from current use, appearing in the word *welfare* and in the frozen expression *farewell* (literally 'go well'), reflecting a shift in sense attested from the 13th century, *How did you fare?/I fared well,* 'How did it go for you?/It went well for me.'

As a noun, *fare* is still in current use, albeit with a number of new meanings. By the 13th century, it could mean not only 'a journey' but also 'food, supplies (for a journey)'; this sense is still found, slightly modified, in the modern use of *fare* to mean 'food and drink; a meal.' By the 15th century, it had acquired another meaning, that of 'passage money; money to pay for a trip.' This too is a meaning of the word found today. Further, by the 16th century *fare* had come to mean 'passenger,' presumably 'one who pays a *fare.*' Taxicab passengers are to this day referred to as *fares.*

feint, faint

The Proto-Indo-European root **dheigh,* from which the English word *dough* is derived, seems to have meant 'knead.' The Latin form of this root, *fingere,* meant 'to touch, fashion, form,' and, by extension, 'to conceive of, devise, invent,' that is, to form in thought or speech. It was in this last sense that the word passed into Old French, where it acquired the connotation 'to invent in a self-serving way; pretend.' French *feindre,* with its past participle, variously spelled *feint* and *faint,* entered English in the late 13th century, giving *feign, feint,* and *faint.*

The original English sense of *feign,* preserved to this day, was that of the Old French verb. *Faint,* as the past participle of that verb, meant 'pretended, simulated.' By the 14th century, however, the word had taken on the meaning of 'lazy, cowardly,' and this sense was soon extended to 'weak, feeble, inclined to swoon.' The connotation of 'pretense, simulation' began to fade, and by the 16th century not only could a person be *faint* in the sense of '(genuinely) weak, feeble, inclined to swoon,' but the term could be applied to such things as a *faint* sound 'a weak sound.'

In the 17th century, after the sense and spelling of *faint* had become fairly well established in English, *feint* was reborrowed from French, this time with the meaning of 'simulated attack.' This sense, now largely associated with such sports as fencing and boxing, has been maintained to the present day.

felon

Two etymologies have been proposed for this term of ultimately obscure origin, each implying a different kind of semantic change. One hypothesis is that *felon* is derived from the Latin *fēlāre/fellāre* 'to suck; perform fellatio.' From the latter meaning the sense became generalized to 'a wicked person; person who has committed a serious (capital) offense,' meanings presumably borrowed with the term from French and attested in 13th-century English.

The other hypothesis takes the word from Celtic, the Bretonese *fall* and Irish Gaelic *feal*, meaning 'evil.' In this case the assumption is that the general sense of 'evil' became narrowed to 'evil (person); person who has committed a serious (capital) offense.'

Whatever its origins, *felon* seems from its earliest days in English to have denoted 'a very bad person,' one whose crimes might, in fact, be punishable by death. From this sense has evolved the modern meaning of 'person convicted of a serious crime.' The term, less its final *n*, also survives in the legal expression *felo-de-se* 'suicide,' in which *de se* is Latin for 'by, of himself,' and the *felony* committed is no less a crime than murder.

forlorn hope

The Proto-Germanic verb *ferliusan*, from which comes the Old English *ferlēosan* and the Modern German *verlieren*, with past participle *verloren*, meant 'to lose, forfeit.' Modern English *lose* comes, in fact, from this verb without its prefix, while *forlorn* is the modern outcome of the past participle of the Old and Middle English form with the prefix. In the 12th century *forlorn* had the sense of 'lost, forsaken,' and by the 16th century it had acquired the extended meaning of 'sad, pitiful, wretched,' a remnant of which we have in the archaic *lovelorn*.

It was in the 16th century that the English encountered the Dutch expression *verloren hoop*, literally, 'lost heap,' a military term that designated specifically 'an advance group of troops sent to the front lines,' the implication being that they did not have much chance of returning alive. The English readily and rightly recognized *verloren* as cognate with *forlorn*, although the meanings of the two words were no longer quite the same. *Hoop* was just as readily, but incorrectly, perceived as cognate with *hope*, a word whose pronunciation was similar to that of the Dutch *hoop* but which had quite a different etymology and meaning. Dutch *hoop* is actually cognate with English *heap*, while *hope* is of obscure origin.

Thus, what had originally been 'a lost troop' became thought of as 'a sad or desperate wish; a hopeless enterprise.' Today, both the original sense of the Dutch expression, 'advance troops sent on a dangerous mission,' and the English misinterpretation of the phrase, 'hopeless undertaking,' are current.

fornication, furnace

Variants of the Proto-Indo-European root $*g^{hw}er$ 'warm,' extended by various suffixes, entered into a great many words, which reached English by diverse routes, with different meanings and often with strikingly divergent forms. Augmented by the suffix -*m*-, the root gave the Greek *thermós* 'hot' preserved in the English *thermometer* and *thermonuclear*, and the English *warm*. In Latin, where the Proto-Indo-European $*g^{hw}$- developed to *f*-, an extension with -*w*- gave the word that eventually entered English as *fervent*. An extension with -*n*- gave *fornācem* (*fornax* in the nominative), which is the direct ancestor of the English word *furnace*, via French.

A different Latin word, *fornix* (*fornicis* in the genitive), meaning 'vault' or 'arch' probably evolved on the basis of the stem of *fornax* from the shape of some of the ovens or kilns used by the Romans. This process represents what semanticists call a connotative extension with fading of the core denotation. The term *fornix* later became

attached to the underground vaults in Rome often cheaply rented to
the poor and to prostitutes, and thus acquired the connotation, which
later became the denotation of 'brothel.'

The same stem with a feminine agent suffix became *fornatrix*
'prostitute.' With the masculine agent suffix, it was *fornicator*; and the
activity became *fornicationem* (accusative case), the direct ancestor of
fornication, a term which appears in English by the end of the 13th
century.

Strangely enough, *fornication* again entered English as a respectable term of architecture in the earlier sense of 'vaulting' or 'arching'
in the 18th century, and has occurred sporadically with that significance since.

frank

The *Franks* were a Germanic tribe from the upper Rhine who subjugated all of modern-day *France* and much of modern-day Germany,
Italy, and the Balkans in the latter half of the first millennium of the
Christian era. They seem to have taken their name from a Germanic
word meaning 'javelin' (cf. Old English *franca* 'javelin'), a weapon
associated with the tribe. It is interesting to note that the Saxons, too,
are thought to have taken their name from a weapon, in their case
from a Germanic word meaning 'knife, sword,' which appears in
Modern English as *saw*, *scythe*, *sickle*, and *section*. (See also **javelin**,
at **gable**.)

By the 13th century, two uses of the word *Frank* or *frank* were
current in English. The first was as the tribe name, and the second
was as an adjective meaning 'free.' This latter meaning apparently
arose from the notion that in the Frankish Empire only those who
belonged to the tribe or were under protection were free.

From the sense of *frank* as 'free' arose two extended uses of the
term. The first, which appeared in the 16th century, was as an adjective meaning 'candid, open.' A person who spoke *frankly* ('freely') or
was *frank* ('free') was one who spoke 'candidly' or was 'candid.' This
sense of *frank* persists to the present day. The second use of the term,
which appeared in the 18th century, was as a verb meaning 'to affix
an official signature on a written message to allow its free delivery,'
later, 'to affix a stamp on a piece of mail (to show that its delivery was

prepaid and is free to the recipient).' From this usage, *frank* came to be employed as a noun, meaning 'signature or mark on a piece of mail to allow its free delivery.'

furlong

The actual measure of the *furlong* has varied at different times according to the standard to which it was pegged, but the form of the word betrays its agricultural origin. The Old English *furhlang* consisted of *furh* 'furrow' and *lang* 'long.' This early standard was the length of the furrow plowed in the common village field, generally a square area containing about ten acres. In the 9th century, the measure approximated the length of a Roman *stadium*, one eighth of a mile, and this became the standard length, varying with the measure of the mile. The *furlong* is now officially 220 yards. (See also **mile**.)

furtive

The stem *fūr*, on which the Latin *furtīvus*, ancestor of the English *furtive*, rests, meant 'thief,' as does the cognate Greek *phŏr*. If, as is generally assumed, it is a phonological variant of *fer-*, meaning and cognate with the verb 'bear,' it represents what linguists call a specialization of sense: 'one who bears something off,' with the connotative extension, 'illicitly.' The adjective *furtīvus*, then, meant 'stolen' or 'taken illegally,' by implication 'in a clandestine manner.' Even during the Classical Latin period the latter part of the meaning sometimes came to be the central core of the significance, although the potential meaning 'stolen' coexisted with the derivative sense 'stealthily or secretly' as long as the word remained in Latin. Once it passed into English at the end of the 15th century in the adverbial form, as *furtively*, and then in the 17th century, as an adjective, the derivative sense became predominant. The meaning 'obtained by theft' does occur, but it is likely that this is a *re*specialization of the 'stealthy' sense.

G

gable, javelin, cephalic

The Proto-Indo-European stem $*g^heb^hl$-, or its variant $*g^hob^hl$-, meaning 'vertex' or 'point of intersection,' reached English through three different major lines of transmission, each exhibiting different senses. One version descended through Germanic, Old Norse, and Old French—when the Norsemen conquered Normandy under the leadership of their chieftain, Rollo. From French, the word reached English in the late 14th Century as *gable*, in the specialized sense of 'triangular vertex extending to the peak or summit of a roof,' or 'any similar-appearing vertical canopy over a doorway or window.'

Some Germanic forms, such as the Modern High German *Gabel* or its Yiddish cognate, preserve a slightly different specialization, 'fork' (the eating utensil). The Celtic, through which it was transmitted, however, includes 'fork of a tree,' or 'branch that forks off from the main stem.' An expanded variant of this transmission, possibly based on the Old Irish *gabul*, passed into Old French as *javelot* 'javelin, spear,' or *javelin*. The semantic line leading to these two forms, which entered English at the end of the 15th century or beginning of the 16th, passed from 'fork used as a spear,' from the multi-pronged spear used by the Celtic tribes, to, simply, 'spear.' It is possible that the 'spear' significance arose from the simple 'branch' sense ('branch of a tree used as a spear'), but the other line seems more likely. The Old Irish word *trethan* 'spear' is the exact cognate of *Triton*, the sea god of ancient Greece traditionally depicted with a forked spear, whose name itself probably derives from an ancient word for 'spear.' (See also **frank**.)

The third major descendant of Proto-Indo-European $*g^heb^hl$- to reach English is the one that passed through Greek, becoming *kephalè* 'head,' which entered English in the 16th century in words like *cephalic* 'of or pertaining to the head,' and *cephalalgia* 'headache.' An extension of the same stem, with the added prefix *en-*, meaning 'in,' gave the Greek word that entered English in the form *encephalo-*, which appears in such compounds as *encephalogram*, and means 'brain,' since that organ is located 'in the head.'

galosh

The word *galosh* (plural *galoshes*) entered English from the French *galoche* in the 14th century with the meaning of a type of 'clog' or 'wooden-soled shoe.' It may have evolved to the later sense of 'over-shoe (often made of a rubberized material)' when it served to protect more fragile shoes or boots from mud or snow. The precise date at which the transition occurred is unclear, since most of the early citations are ambiguous.

The history of the French *galoche* itself is a matter of dispute among etymologists. One theory traces the term back to Late Latin *gallicula*, the diminutive of *gallica*, from the phrase *solea gallica* 'Gaulish sandal.' This would trace the form back to a word meaning 'pertaining to Gaul,' which, as beginning students in Latin used to learn, was an area that once included what are now France, Belgium, parts of the Netherlands, Switzerland, Germany, and northern Italy.

According to a different theory the word can be traced back to the late Latin term *calopia*, a variant of *calopodes* or *calopedia*, which go back to the Greek *kalopódion/kalopódia*, based on the stems *kâlon* 'wood' and *pod*, 'foot.' If this theory is correct, it would involve a transfer of the word from its use to denote 'a shoemaker's last,' the Greek sense, to one signifying the 'shoe' itself, the Latin sense.

During the 17th century there were abortive attempts to expand the final *-sh*, making the word "*galoshoes*."

gamut

The notes of the medieval hexachord musical scale were illustrated by the singing of certain initial syllables taken from the words of a Latin hymn for St. John the Baptist's Day, which began, "*Ut* queant laxis *re*sonare fibris *Mi*ra gestorum *fa*muli tuorum, *Sol*ve polluti *la*bii rec-tum Sancte Iohannes," and the first, or lowest, note was the G, called *gamma* from the Greek letter, and *ut*, giving *gamut* for short. When the word first entered English in the 16th century it applied only to the first note of the scale, but in time it came to signify the entire

musical range. This was probably what etymologists call a semantic
localization and shortening of *gamut scale*. A later generalization
dropped the musical element of the sense, permitting the word to
signify the entire range of anything, and allowing Dorothy Parker to
jest that a certain actress ran the whole *gamut* of her emotions from A
to B.

The Greek letter got its name by adding a Greek ending, *-a*, to a
reduced form of the corresponding Phoenician letter *gimel*. This name
originally meant 'camel,' from a resemblance of the written form of
the letter to a simplified picture of a camel. The Latin *ut* was an
adverb compounded of a relative pronoun, cognate with such English
words beginning with *th* as *the, this, then,* and *there*. In Latin, the
combination acquired a variety of meanings such as 'in accordance
with, thus, or as.'

garble

The Arabic *gharbala* 'select or sift,' related to *ghirbāl* 'sieve,' first
entered Italian and then passed into English in the late 15th century,
probably by way of the spice trade. It referred to the straining of the
foodstuff through perforated barriers in order to separate the spices
from extraneous material. From the early 16th century to the 19th,
the term *garbel* in one of its uses applied to the residue separated
from the mixture, a meaning now obsolete.

For a time in the 16th century the word also applied to any
mixed materials that contained unwanted elements. One possible specialization of this semantic line may be the technical use of *garbel* in
the sense of 'alloy consisting of precious and base metals,' first
attested in the 19th century.

The semantic branch leading to the main modern meaning, however, generalized the sense away from the physical act of straining
and focused on the process of selection. Sometimes the emphasis was
on getting the best elements of the mixture or set of objects; one
vestige of this semantic sequence appears in the technical phrase
garble the coinage, that is, 'pick out the physically unblemished or
unworn bullion.' Sometimes the emphasis was on the negative aspect
of weeding out undesirable units or members. In this sense, found

from the mid 17th century down to the early 19th, but now obsolete, one could *garble* the army, the House of Commons, a corporation, or a college.

Toward the end of the 17th century the term took on a pejorative connotation, and to *garble* an utterance, a quotation, or an idea was to select elements of it so as to misrepresent or distort it. Part of this connotation carried the idea of malicious distortion, although in recent years this aspect has begun to fade. Now one often hears the term used in a way that suggests confusion because of mental incapacity, rather than deliberate intent, as in "You've got that story all *garbled*."

Ironically, some linguists believe that the Arabic source of this etymology itself goes back to the Late Latin *cribellum* 'sieve,' which rests on the same root seen in *discern*, meaning 'to separate the ideas accurately.'

gargoyle

Originally, the grotesque sculptured figures to be seen near the roofs of certain buildings were primarily functional, rather than ornamental: they served the purpose of draining rainwater from the roof gutters by spewing it out of their mouths. The term *gargoyle* comes from the Old French word *gargouille* 'throat,' derived from the Latin *gurguliō* 'windpipe, gullet, throat.' This term, in turn, is derived from the Proto-Indo-European root *g^werH 'to swallow,' which also gives us *craw*, by way of Germanic, as well as *gurgle*, *gargle*, *gullet*, *gorge*, *regurgitate*, and *gulf*, by way of Latin and the Romance languages.

Later the form of the *gargoyle*, rather than its original function, came to be primary, and these grotesque pieces of decorative masonry or metalwork were incorporated into building designs simply as sculptural adornments. By extension, a particularly unattractive person may be referred to as a *gargoyle*.

gasket

Etymologists generally agree that *gasket* 'seal' is a 19th-century specialization of the 17th-century nautical *gasket* 'rope used to bind a furled sail to a boom'; both uses of the term are still current. There is further agreement that the nautical *gasket* was a corruption of the French word *garcette* 'braided rope, cat-o'-nine-tails.' Braided rope was used to secure the sails on a ship, and (braided) rope (or, later, rubber and other materials) might be used to pack or seal machine parts so that they would stay in their proper places and not allow any interstitial leakage.

The disagreement is over the source of *garcette*. Some suggest that *garcette* in the meaning 'braided rope, cat-o'-nine-tails' is derived from *garcette* 'girl' (to be compared with *garçon* 'boy'), since *garcette*, *garçon*, and *garce* 'bitchy woman' are all of ultimately obscure origin. Just what is the connection between 'girl' and 'braided rope' is not clear, although a number of more or less far-fetched suggestions have been offered. One holds that girls are rope-slender or that they can be manipulated as sailors handle rope; another, that their effect on men is the same as that of the cat-o'-nine-tails; none is particularly convincing.

A more likely possibility is that the *garcette* in question was 'a hairstyle featuring side-locks' (made popular by Anne of Austria in the early 17th century). This term came into French in the early part of the century as a borrowing from the Spanish *garceta*, the name for the hairstyle worn by Spanish-born Anne.

giddy

The *gyd-* of the Old English *gydig*, the direct ancestor of *giddy*, is a variant of the word *god*, with the original root vowel (once *u*) shifted to a *y* (later to become *i* by assimilation to the *i* of the second syllable). The Old English word meant 'possessed by a god or spirit,' hence 'insane, not in control of one's mind, frantic,' or, sometimes, 'foolish or stupid.' It acquired part of its contemporary meaning through compounding with *turn* (*turngiddy*, *turngiddiness*) in the late 15th century, a development which probably arose from the notion of becoming mad or frantic through turning or whirling about—the rotary motion resulting in a sensation of vertigo or dizziness. The compound word, with its meaning of 'dizzy,' appeared regularly down to the end of the 16th century, but by the last few decades of that period the word *giddy* had begun to occur in that sense by itself, and in mid century was already being used to mean 'inconstant of mind, incapable of weighty or serious thought.'

It is difficult to determine precisely when the word lost the meaning of its original Old English stem, tying the form to the independent word *god*, but one guess might suggest that this development coincided with the sound changes that took place in Middle English. (For the pre-Old English meaning of the base, see **God**.)

glamour, grammar

The ancient Greek stem *graph-* 'to write' probably originally meant 'to cut or carve,' since much of the earliest writing was incised on wood, stone, or bone. With the addition of appropriate suffixes the specialization **graph-ma*, later *grámma* 'a written character or letter,' which in the plural *grámmata* meant 'letters' or 'literature,' appeared. Variants of the word passed into Latin, and thence into French. Since most medieval studies centered on literature in Latin, one specialization of the Old French derivative *gramaire* shifted the meaning to 'Latin grammar.' A later generalization, 'grammar' itself, was the signification with which the word entered English in the 14th century.

By the same phonological shift of *r* to *l* that caused the Latin word *peregrīnus* 'wanderer' to become *pelegrīnus*, the ancestor of the English *pilgrim*, an early form of 'grammar' became *glamour*. The early sense of the word survived in the old Cambridge University title *Master of Glomery* 'Master of Grammar,' but by the beginning of the 17th century the term had specialized to the meaning of 'enchantment, aura of wonder,' probably because such an aura surrounded the study of subjects as arcane and mysterious as grammar in the mind of the average unlearned individual.

God

English preserves no more spectacular example of what etymologists call "amelioration" than the etymological development of this word, which goes back to an ancient Proto-Indo-European phrase meaning 'enjoyer or consumer of that which has been poured forth' (presumably wine or blood, as a sacrifice). The full phrase survives in Sanskrit as *huta-bhug*, where it was one of the epithets of Agni, the god of fire, whose name is cognate with the Latin stem from which English gets the word *ignite*. The Sanskrit *huta* 'that which has been poured forth, the sacrifice' is the exact cognate of the English word *God*, following localization in which the full meaning of the phrase centered in its first element, which occurred in the Early Germanic ancestor of English. The Slavic branch of Indo-European reversed this choice, localizing the meaning in the second element of the phrase, and leaving the Slavic *bog* 'God' as the survivor.

With what linguists call "connotative extension," the meaning became 'Deity who enjoys the sacrifice,' but as sacrificial offerings vanished from religious practice, that part of the meaning which had once been primary faded, leaving only the sense in use today, 'Deity.'

goodbye

This word, not found until the latter part of the 16th century, is a contraction of *God be with you*. Its sound changes appear in various forms side by side in the works of such authors as Shakespeare, who has the clown Costard say, "God be wi' you!" in *Love's Labour's Lost* (1588), whereas Joan of Arc, in the first of the King Henry VI plays (1591), says, "God buy, my lord!" When the changes by which *be with you* evolved to *bye* had run their course, the earlier, denotative meaning of the phrase had disappeared through a process that linguists call "fading," and a connotative meaning, a vague or often perfunctory expression of good will to conclude a social exchange, was all that remained. Subsequently the first element of the phrase, *God*, was reshaped by analogy with such phrases as *Good day* and *Good night*, which serve a similar function in social intercourse.

gorilla

This term first appeared in an early Greek translation of the Punic account of the voyage of the Carthaginian explorer, Hanno, to the northwestern shores of Africa in the 5th or 6th century B.C. On one of their stops, Hanno and his party reported that they encountered a group of "wild people with hair all over their bodies." Capturing a few of the females, whom they later killed and skinned, the Carthaginians asked their native guides what these "people" were called. The Greek rendition of the answer given is *"Gorillas."* Whether the Carthaginians actually considered or referred to the creatures as "people" or not is unclear, since we have only the Greek rendering of the original Punic account, but the Greek translation is unequivocal in its choice of words. The *gorillas* are consistently referred to by words appropriate to people and not to lower animals.

Thus, for centuries, *gorillas* were 'the hirsute African people discovered by Hanno.' In 1847, however, an American missionary to West Africa, T. S. Savage, employed the term to refer to the native great ape which we now know as *Troglodytes gorilla*, popularly, simply *gorilla*.

gossamer

This term was originally a compound of the English words *goose* and *summer*, *goose-summer* having been the phrase used in England from Middle English times to designate the "Indian summer" which occurs during the month of November. As to why this phrase should have been used to refer to those warm days of autumn, the best conjecture seems to be that it was at that time of the year that geese were traditionally plucked and eaten.

More mysterious is the 14th-century transference of the meaning of *goose-summer/gossamer* from 'Indian summer' to 'cobwebs.' One possibility is that the reference was to the fact that it is in autumn that spiders produce the fine webs that hang from the bushes and are blown through the air. Another possibility is that these webs were seen to be similar to the *goose* down associated with the season. Whatever the reason, *goose-summer* came to be associated with cobwebs, as did the dialectal variant *summer-goose*, restructured by folk etymology to *summer-gauze*. Later, *gossamer* took on the more general sense 'anything light, delicate, wispy, insubstantial.'

gossip

Originally, the term was a compound of the English words *God* and *sib*, and formed a part of the Middle English kinship terminology relating to baptism. A *godsib* was 'a sponsor at a baptism,' that is, godfather or godmother to the baptized child and god-relative to the child's parents and to each other. *God* seems to have been prefixed to the standard kinship terms *father, mother, daughter, son, child*, and *sib* to betoken the spiritual nature of the relationship. By the 14th century, however, *godsib* had become generalized to mean any 'friend or acquaintance,' not necessarily a sponsor at a baptism.

During the following two centuries, the term underwent a further change of meaning, to 'idle prattler, tale-teller.' This was its basic sense until the 19th century, when *gossip* took on the additional meaning of 'idle prattle, tale-telling.' Presumably the change from 'familiar friend or acquaintance' to 'person engaging in trifling talk or rumor-mongering' came about because of the nature of the talk in which the *godsibs/gossips* engaged at the baptism. Does such an explanation help to explain why *gossips* are more often thought of as being female than male?

grog, groggy

Both evolved, ultimately, from the French phrase, *étoffe à gros grain*, literally 'material of a coarse grain,' later shortened simply to *gros grain*. Originally a description of a stiff fabric woven of wool, silk, and mohair, the phrase later evolved into the name of the fabric itself. It became reduced to the single word *grogran* or *grogoran* and was finally borrowed into 16th-century English as *grogram*.

At the beginning of the 18th century, the British navy regularly issued the sailors a daily ration of rum; but in 1740 Admiral Edward Vernon (1684–1757), the hero of the battle of Porto Bello, recognizing that too much rum was conducive neither to discipline nor efficiency, ordered his men to dilute their drinks with water. The Admiral, affectionately nicknamed "Old Grogram Cloak" or "Old Grog," after his habit of wearing a cloak of *grogram* while at sea, has achieved immortality by giving his name to just that mixture of rum and water known to this day as *grog* (from the phrases *Grog's ration* or *Grog's mixture*).

The adjective *groggy*, in its original meaning 'under the influence of grog' or 'inebriated by grog' eventually came to signify intoxication by any alcoholic beverage. In contemporary usage it has come to mean any mental befuddlement, whether caused by alcohol or any other agency.

groom

The Middle English *grom*, a word of uncertain origin, meant 'boy, male child,' and appears in that sense in the 13th century. By the following century, the meaning had been generalized to 'man, male person, especially a male servant.' It was presumably this general sense of *groom* that caused the Middle English word *bridegome* 'man about to be married or just married,' in which the -*gome*, cognate with Latin *homo*, meant 'man,' to be remade into *bridegroom* in the 16th century.

During the 15th and 16th centuries, *groom* as an extension of its sense of 'male servant,' was used to designate 'an officer in a royal or noble household,' as in the titles *Groom of the Stole*, *Groom of the Privy Chamber*. By the 17th century, however, the only such *groom* was the *Groom of the Stable* 'male servant in charge of the horses,' the basic sense of the noun today.

From this last usage evolved the verb *to groom* 'brush and curry a horse' in the 19th century. Today the verb has taken on the more general sense of 'to attend to the personal appearance,' as in the phrase *well groomed* or such usages as *to groom one's hair*, or the figurative *to groom someone for office*.

grotesque

The Greek term *krýptein* meant 'to hide,' and a *kryptế* was 'a vault, place where something might be hidden,' from which we get the Modern English *crypt*. The noun *kryptế* was borrowed into Latin as *crypta*, and, in Late Latin, became *crupta* and *grupta*. From this last we derive *grotto* 'cave, cavern.' The adjective *grotesque*, formerly also spelled *crotesque*, is a combination of *grotto* and *crotto* and the suffix -*esque*, from the Romance -*iscus* 'resembling, having the characteristics of.' The term was originally narrowly applied to a form of fantastic wall paintings found in ruins excavated by the Romans and imitated in the 16th century by Italian painters.

The 16th century *pittura grottesca* 'grottolike painting' typically combined monstrous human and animal forms with elaborate floral patterns, and so gave rise, in the 17th century, to the generalized use of *grotesque* to mean 'bizarre, incongruous, absurd,' the generalized sense of the term today, with the added connotations of 'unpleasant' and 'ugly.'

H

hackney, hack

Two etymologies have been proposed for *hackney* and its abbreviated form, *hack*. The first traces the two words to the Middle English *Hakenei*, a borough of London now known as *Hackney*, where a particular breed of horse was raised. The other derivation holds that the name of the *hackney* horse comes from the verb to *hack*, presumably because the animal's gait approximated the regular chopping of an axe. In either case, the fact that the *Hackney* or *hackney* horse was typically available for hire to draw passengers in a coach and was steady and stolid in its task gave rise to a number of senses of the terms.

By the 16th century, *hackney* had come to designate not only the horse, but any 'common drudge, prostitute,' a sense which has since been extended, in the abbreviated form, *hack*, to include specifically fee-for-service writers and low-level political time-servers. The *hackneyed phrase*, originally 'words for hire,' now 'an overused, trite expression' is said to be the stock in trade of both the literary and the political *hack*.

Another line of development, involving the localization of *hackney coach* rather than *hackney horse*, has resulted in the use of *hackney* and, later, *hack*, to designate 'a coach for hire.' With the advent of the automobile, *hack* has come to mean 'taxicab,' and even 'taxicab driver.'

hag, haggard

Both *hag* and *haggard* come from a Proto-Indo-European root **kagh*, which seems to have meant 'seize, catch,' and, by extension, 'fence (in).' *Hag* appears in English in the 13th century in the sense of 'female evil spirit,' probably as a result of shortening the Old English *haegtesse* 'witch, fury.' This may be an extension of 'seize' to '(female) person who seizes her victims,' but the reasoning that underlies the semantic change is not at all clear.

A similar shift in meaning from 'seize' to 'creature that seizes its prey' has been suggested for the Old French *hagard* 'wild hawk.' From its phonetic shape, however, one would judge this Old French term a borrowing from Germanic, so its sense may reflect some filtering in the transmission. Other explanations of the term involve the hypothesis that a 'wild hawk' was 'something to be seized by humans' so they might train it to hunt; or that the hawk was somehow associated with a *hedge* 'a fence made of bushes, to fence in property.' The semantic connection between *hagard* 'wild hawk' and *hedge* is obscure, to say the least.

However *hagard* came into Old French, *haggard* was borrowed into English in the 16th century, with the meaning 'an adult hawk that can be trained to hunt,' a meaning it still carries. Soon it became current as an adjective, probably as the result of a misinterpretation of the word's grammatical status in the expression *haggard hawk*. As an adjective it first had the sense of 'wild,' which, by the 17th century, had been generalized to 'wild-looking, gaunt,' from which comes its later and current meaning, 'old-looking, worn-out-looking.'

Between the 17th and 18th centuries, *haggard* could also be used as a noun with the same sense as *hag*, since the suffix *-ard* had by then become well established as a pejorative noun ending in such words as *bastard, drunkard, sluggard,* and the like. This use of the noun has since disappeared from the language, although the extended use of the adjective in the sense of 'an old-looking, worn-out-looking person of either sex' persists.

handkerchief

The French word *curchief*, later to be spelled as *kerchief*, had entered English by the beginning of the 14th century. It represented a reduced form of *couvre* ('cover,' the same element appears in *curfew*) and *chief* ('head,' a word element actually cognate with the English word). Then, as now, the compound referred to a cloth, but at that time it was a cloth specifically intended as a head covering. Although the word denoted a single function, the cloth could obviously be used for other purposes, and since many English speakers did not understand French, the meaning of *kerchief* soon changed to the more general meaning of 'a cloth of the particular size and shape generally used as a head covering.' By the early 16th century the fashion arose of carrying a *kerchief* in the hand, and thus the compound form *handkerchief* came into being. A further specialization occurs in the phrase *pocket handkerchief*: 'a covering worn on the head, held in the hand, and put in the pocket.'

harlequin

While its ultimate origin is uncertain, *harlequin* seems to have come from the Old English *Herla Cyning* 'Herla the King' associated by legend with the Norse god Woden (Wotan, Odin). Herla was said to have been the leader of a band of itinerant demons who terrified people by night. As such, *Herla Cyning* passed into Old French as *Herlequin* and then into Italian. There he appears as the buffoonish stock character *Arlecchino*, in the 16th century commedia dell'arte, typically costumed in a suit of varicolored patches and a flared mask. It is from this costume, which entered England with the theatrical character, that the adjectival use of *harlequin* is derived. This is applied, variously, to a variety of duck with colorful plumage, to a kind of ice cream with mixed colors and flavors, and to a style of eyeglasses whose frames flare in the manner of *Harlequin's* mask.

Since the original sense of 'demon king' had been lost by the time *Herlequin* entered Italian from Old French, a number of folk etymologies were proposed for the name of the theatrical character. One derived the name from Hachille du Harlay, a member of Parliament and patron of one of the members of a commedia dell'arte troupe. Another derived the name from Charles V, Carlos Quinto, King of Spain and Holy Roman Emperor during the first half of the 16th century. It has also been suggested that the name is a diminutive of Old French *herle* or *harle* 'a colorful water bird,' or *hierle, herle* 'tumult.'

harlot

The Late Latin term *arlotus/erlotus* was a word used to designate 'a (male) glutton.' Somehow, it came to be associated exclusively with 'gluttons' of the lower classes, and when the word entered Old French it was with the meaning of 'vagabond, knave, beggar, lowlife.' It was in this sense that the word was introduced into English in the 13th century by the Normans. It is unclear whether the Old French sense represents what etymologists call "filtering," or if it is an instance of local extension of meaning.

In any case, from the 13th to the 15th century, *harlots* were 'young male rogues of slovenly habits.' By the end of the 14th century, however, *harlotry* came to be applied to the slovenly behavior of both sexes, *hordome and harlotry* being a common boxed set of vices said to have been practiced by 'vagabond' women of the day. During the 16th century the sense of *harlot* as 'a slovenly, obscene woman' was well on its way toward displacing the original meaning, although men could still be *harlots* for another hundred years.

By the middle of the 16th century the association of the term with women was sufficiently strong for a folk etymology to have emerged. This derived the term from the name of William the Conqueror's mother, *Arlette*, since the King had been known as William the Bastard before his accession to the throne.

Today *harlots* are exclusively women, specifically 'women of ill repute, prostitutes,' a "refinement" in usage resulting from two narrowings of the 16th-century meaning. First, the 'slovenly, obscene behavior' associated with those to whom the term was applied came to refer specifically to 'obscene sexual behavior'; second, the term came to designate 'a female practitioner of obscene sexual behavior.'

harridan

Like *jade¹*, (which see) *harridan* seems originally to have meant 'broken-down horse, nag' in its Old French form, *haridelle*, a word of uncertain origin. The term came to be used in the sense of 'old, broken-down woman, old whore' in Old French, and it was with this meaning that it entered English at the end of the 17th century.

Today, a *harridan* may be 'an old, worn-out woman' (not necessarily a whore); 'a vituperative scold'; or 'a lewd woman' of indeterminate age, all of which are clear extensions of the metaphorical use of the Old French term borrowed into English. While she may still be a nag, in the colloquial sense of the term, a *harridan* is no longer thought of as a horse.

hassock

In Old English *hassuc*, the ancestor of Modern *hassock*, referred to 'tall grass' or to 'clumps or tufts of grass,' usually the *Aira caespitosa*, either alone or mingled with the sedges *Carex caespitosa* or *Carex paniculata*. Some etymologists have suggested that the Old English word is a variant of the Welsh word *hesg*, which means 'sedge,' in which case the clumps would be clumps of sedge mingled with grass.

In any event, the custom arose of taking these clumps into the house or into church to rest the feet on or to kneel upon during devotions. Since crude bundles often disintegrated in use, they were tied or shaped and stuffed into fabric bags, thus evolving into 'cushions' or, with further elaboration, 'upholstered stools,' a development that had taken place by the beginning of the 16th century.

In the 18th century, the word was further applied, by a process etymologists call "transference," to 'a shock or clump of hair,' probably from its visual resemblance to tufts of grasses.

heathen

The Old English word *hæþ*, ancestor of Modern *heath*, meant 'waste, desert, or uncultivated land.' An extended form of the term, *hæðen*, originally meant 'one who inhabits the *hæþ*.' Some etymologists hold that a shift in the meaning took place following the introduction of Christianity into England by Bishop—later Saint—Augustine in 597. Starting in the Kentish region, missionaries concentrated their efforts on centers of population, chiefly towns and cities, while people in rural outlying areas remained untouched by the new teachings. Thus the connotation 'unbeliever, non-Christian' accrued to the word that was to become the Modern *heathen*. The connection between *heath* and *heathen* was forgotten, and the term became generalized, so that any pagan or unbeliever was a *heathen* no matter where he lived.

Other scholars hold that the shift in meaning took place far earlier, in the 4th century, when Gothic speakers received the message of Christianity from Bishop Ulfilas. This would pinpoint the term first in the East Germanic language, which subsequently influenced the West Germanic cognates as a loan translation.

Since the shift took place before the time of the earliest written records, the point remains moot.

heir

This English word descends, via French transmission, from *herem*, a Late Latin variant of the Classical Latin accusative form *heredem*. To understand the early Latin sense of *heres*, however, it is necessary to understand the legal and economic structure of the family system of ancient Rome.

The *pater familias* 'father of the family' in ancient Rome was the oldest male in the direct genetic line, and he exercised absolute control over all the family's possessions and, in the earliest period, over all family members. With a few exceptions, most of them devised later, no member could dispose of any property or spend any money—even if he himself had earned it—without the permission of the *pater familias*. So extensive was his control that the *pater familias* could (in the earliest period and subject to certain restraints) impose the death penalty on those in his power. He could also sell them into slavery, and if a son so enslaved were to be freed by his master, the *pater familias* could resell him for a second or even a third time. Few Romans chose to exercise this right except under the most extreme conditions, but it was a vested privilege under the old law. As long as the 'father of the family' lived, none of his offspring was *sui juris*, that is, 'under his own legal jurisdiction,' but each remained *in potestate* 'in the power,' under his father's total economic and legal control. Even if one were to rise to become consul, the highest administrative officer in the government, he remained entirely subordinate to the *pater familias*, without the ability to pay a single private bill except at the father's pleasure.

Technically, although the *pater familias* controlled all the family possessions, he was not the sole owner. Ownership was vested in the entire family, all genetically descended or adoptive members *in potestate* of the father. A daughter who married passed out of her father's power and into that of her husband. Economically, this family structure resembled that of a modern corporation, with the *pater familias* as chief executive and family members as shareholders. If the administration of the *pater familias* became too capricious or irresponsible and seemed likely to dissipate family assets, family members could petition to have him removed from control of the purse strings. There were formidable obstacles to such action, but it was legally possible.

In nontechnical usage, the modern English word *heir* refers to 'one who acquires possessions or transmissible rights on the death of the current owner.' Under ancient Roman law, no one could be an *heres* 'heir' of a living person; and when the *pater familias* died, no one 'inherited' his property in the modern sense. Since each family member was already an "owner" prior to the death of the *pater familias*, all that changed was the administrative control.

What, then, was the meaning or significance of the word *heres*? The *heir* was the one who entered into 'the rights and place of the deceased.' In a sense, he "became" the living embodiment of the deceased. If the deceased owed money, the *heir* had to pay; if the deceased owed services, the *heir* had to fulfill them. Certain exceptions were permitted through Roman concepts of equity, among them obligations that originated in wrongdoing—although the *heir* was required to return any material gains accruing from such acts. Since, under the old tradition, the *pater familias* was the family priest, the *heir* assumed the duty of presiding over the religious rites, sacrificing to the family gods, and so on. He could now spend the family money and dispose of property, having obtained administrative control over what had already been his own—at least to the extent of his own original share. His percentage of the total depended on the number of others who stood in the same degree of legal relationship to the *pater familias* as he did.

In later law, the Romans developed various refinements of the concept of *heres*, but in the early period the most important characteristic was that the *heir* could not refuse his obligations. This could prove highly embarrassing if, for example, the inheritance was insolvent—especially in view of the fact that the *heir* himself could be sold into slavery for nonpayment of debt. Under later praetorian law, those *heirs* who came to be called *heredes sui et necessarii* 'personal and obligatory heirs,' who included sons, daughters, the widow, and any grandchildren whose fathers were not under the paternal power, acquired the right to refuse an inheritance.

Such was the legal significance of the word in early Roman times; but etymological evidence suggests a yet more ancient significance. A Greek cognate, the adjective *kheros* meant 'bereft.' Used as a noun, with appropriate endings to denote masculinity or femininity, the same Greek stem meant 'widow' or 'widower.' This suggests a relationship to the notion that no one could be *heres* of a living person. A possible cognate in Old English, the verb *grætan*, meant 'to mourn,' and this was one function—possibly the primary function—of the *heres*, although it is possible, too, that the meaning of the Old English word represents a semantic specialization by connotative extension.

The word *heir* reached English in the 13th century in the sense 'person entitled to acquire property or rank of another on the latter's demise,' and popular usage preserves this meaning. Technical usage, however, retains the limitation that reflects the ancient restriction that the word *heir* does not apply until after the demise.

hen

This word comes from the Proto-Germanic offspring of the Proto-Indo-European root **kan* 'sing,' which also gave us, via the Romance languages, such words as *cant*, *chant*, *incantation*, and *accent*. Apparently the original *hen* was 'a male domestic fowl noted for his "singing."' Just how the name for the male came to be transferred to the female is not clear, although the most likely possibility is that *hen* was generalized from 'male fowl' to 'any fowl' and later became specialized to 'female fowl' on the introduction of a new term for the male.

Whatever the process, by the 11th century *hen* was firmly established in the sense of 'female domestic fowl,' whence came its extended meaning, attested from the 14th century, of 'any female bird,' and even the contemporary '(fussy or maternal) human female.' (See also **charm**.)

henchman

According to Bede's *Ecclesiastical History of the English People*, completed in 731, one of the West Germanic chieftains summoned in 449 by the Celtic king Vortigern to help drive away the invading Picts and Scots bore the name *Hengest*, which at that time meant 'stallion.' Since *Hengest*'s men went on to drive away the Celts as well as the invaders, and then remained to found the English nation, the name is coeval with the country. In Old English, theoretically dated as in the 5th century although it has no written evidence until the 7th, the word *hengest* also signified 'horse, steed, gelding.' This range of meanings is found in cognates in other Germanic languages. In Old High German *hengist* is 'gelding,' but in Modern German *Hengst* is 'horse'; in Old Frisian *hengst* is 'horse,' while in Dutch it is 'stallion,' and so forth.

Except in dialectal usage, the English word survived only in proper names, where it became *Hinks*, spelled in various ways but usually showing the normal phonetic shift of *e* to *i* before a nasal plus another consonant, or in the compound *hengestmann*, now *henchman*. This originally meant 'a groom, one who takes care of horses,' as it does today in the Modern German *Hengstmann*. Since, in the Middle Ages, such a person in a nobleman's household was often his squire or page, the compound took on that sense, first as a connotative addition and later as the chief meaning of the term.

In Scotland the word specialized to mean 'the major attendant to a Highland chief,' a sense popularized when Sir Walter Scott used the word in *Waverley*, the first of his historical novels. Eventually generalization occurred with the dropping of the 'Highland chief' reference, leaving simply 'supporter' or 'follower' as the central meaning.

hint

Both as noun and verb, *hint* seems to have originated in the Old English *hentan* 'to seize, grasp,' a word of Proto-Germanic parentage. Already archaic, it appeared in English at the beginning of the 11th century with that meaning. From this verb is derived the now-archaic noun *hent* 'the act of seizing, grasping,' which dates from the 16th century. *Hint*, as a noun with the meaning 'opportunity,' is first attested in the early days of the 17th century and is probably derived from that source, an opportunity being 'a thing to be seized (and used to advantage).' It is from this sense of the term that its modern meaning 'suggestion, clue (to be used to advantage)' is derived.

The verb *hint* appeared in English toward the middle of the 17th century in its modern sense, 'to offer a suggestion, a clue,' and may be presumed to have been derived from the noun *hint*. Thus the shift in meaning from *hent* 'seize, grasp' to *hint* 'offer a thing to be seized, grasped, understood' seems to have come largely as a result of interference from the derived noun *hent/hint*.

hippopotamus

When the Greeks first encountered this aquatic mammal not indigenous to their own country, they called it a 'river horse,' from *hippo-* 'horse,' cognate with the Latin *equus*, seen in the English *equine* and *equestrian*, and *potamos* 'river,' which appears also in the name of the geographical region *Mesopotamia* 'between the two rivers,' that is, the Tigris and the Euphrates. *Hippo-* appears in many other words that have entered English, among them *hippodrome*, originally 'a running place for horses,' and in such proper names as *Hippocrates*, from which we get the *Hippocratic oath* sworn by contemporary physicians. The Old English cognate of *hippo-* was *eoh*, but this word has not survived.

Although Pliny the Elder, who first employed the Greek word *hippopotamos* in Latin, probably knew its meaning, other Romans did not, and the fading of its original significance started with the transmission of the term through Latin.

hobby, hobbyhorse

Robin, Robby, Dobbin, Dobby, Hob(b)in, and *Hobby* were all at one time common diminutives of the name *Robert*, and most have acquired other applications over the years. A *robin* is a bird, the American *Turdus migratorius* and the British *Erithacus rubecula*; a *dobby* is variously a 'silly old man' and a 'poltergeist, brownie,' and a *dobbin* is 'a common draft horse.' All of these extended uses came about as the result of the friendly application of the human nickname to other creatures.

Hobby and the earlier *Hob(b)in* in the sense of 'small horse' represented a similar use of the nickname as a name and then a generic term for an animal. As such, it dates from the 14th century. Somewhat redundantly, in the 16th century *hobbyhorse* came to be used, first to designate 'a small horse,' as *hobby* had earlier, and, shortly thereafter, to refer specifically to 'the mock horse used by morris dancers.'

From the latter sense soon evolved the *hobbyhorse* of today 'a child's toy consisting of a fabricated horse's head fixed to a stick or pole.' In the 17th century, *hobbyhorse* took on a more general meaning, that of 'idle pastime, interest, or activity.' This occurred through a combination of what etymologists call "generalization," from 'child's toy horse' to 'plaything in general,' followed by transference from 'plaything' to 'activity involving plaything, play.' In the 19th century the term *hobbyhorse* in this sense localized to *hobby*, thus regaining its original form, if not its original meaning.

hulk, sulcate

The Greek word *holkás*, based on a stem meaning 'to tow or drag,' originally referred to 'a barge or ship that was towed,' but later came to mean 'a trading vessel or merchantman.' In this sense it reached many of the languages of the Mediterranean area whose peoples engaged in maritime trade. When it first entered English, it designated 'a light ship,' probably still reflecting the notion that a towable ship was a small one in the days before the advent of steam. In time, however, trading vessels became increasingly large and unwieldy, and the connotation 'clumsy' became attached to *hulk*. By the late 16th century the term could be applied not only to a 'clumsy ship' but also to 'a big or clumsy person,' a sense still prevalent today.

In the 17th century, when some of the clumsy trading vessels no longer deemed seaworthy were beached and pressed into service for temporary housing or for storage, *hulk* came to be applied to such dismantled ships, and still later to structures resembling them but built expressly for these purposes. By the 19th century the term had become generalized to apply to anything large and unwieldy, and the original meaning of 'drag or tow' had disappeared.

A Latin cognate *sulcus*—the initial *h* of the Greek having developed from the Proto-Indo-European *s*—referred to 'a furrow made by a plow.' It is suggested that this came about because the plow is dragged or towed by oxen. The Latin stem survives in specialized senses such as the anatomical use referring to 'a fissure or groove in an organ or tissue' or, in the engraving industry, to 'a groove made with a pointed tool.' It occurs as well in various other loan forms, like *sulcate* 'marked with furrows,' *sulciform*, and *sulculus*.

hussy

Like many other gender-specific words in English that designate members of the female sex, *hussy* started out as a term with essentially positive connotations that have gradually been replaced by negative ones. It comes from the Middle English *hūsewīf*, from which the Modern English *housewife* is derived; this is a compound of the words for 'house, household' and 'adult woman' and was at one time a term of unqualified respect. A *housewife* was 'the mistress of a household, (female) manager of a household,' as a *husband* was 'a freeholding peasant who owned and inhabited his own house and worked the land belonging to it,' the *-band* suffix coming from a verb meaning 'to dwell.'

By the 16th century *hussy*, the result of a localization of meaning in the first part of the compound plus the diminutive suffix *-y*, had come to mean not only 'the little woman' in a rather demeaning, if not pejorative sense, but 'a rude woman, a harlot.'

In the course of time, both *husbands* and *housewives* came to be thought of as married people, each with a particular set of responsibilities in running a household, although originally both could be single. It is not clear whether the original sense of *hussy* implied anything about the marital status of such a woman, but today it does not.

hypocrite

Greek drama is generally held to have originated in the festivals held each spring to honor the god Dionysios. A major feature of these ceremonial productions was the recounting of the god's exploits by a chorus and its leader. It is said to have been Thespis, the legendary actor-playwright, who added a solo actor, known as the *hypokritḗs*, to answer or enter into dialogue with the leader of the chorus. The appellation is derived from the verb *hypokrinesthai* 'to answer,' later, 'to discuss,' and, still later, 'to play a part.' As the drama was further elaborated by Aeschylus and Sophocles and more solo actors were added, *hypokritḗs* came to be used to designate any '(solo) actor.'

In the early days of the Christian Church, however, *hypokritḗs* came to be used in the sense of 'a person who claims to have religious beliefs which he does not in fact have,' that is, a person who plays the part of being a Christian. It was in this specialized sense that *ypocrite* entered English in the 13th century, either through Old French or directly from ecclesiastical Latin. Its initial *h* was restored in the 16th century.

Soon the sense of *(h)ypocrite* was extended in English, as it had been in Classical Greek, to mean 'any dissembler, person who pretends to believe that which he does not believe, or who pretends to be a person other than he is.' This general sense is the common one today.

hysterics

The Greek word *hýsteros* meant 'latter, lower.' In its feminine form, *hystéra*, it came to be applied specifically to 'the lower part of a woman's anatomy, the womb,' a sense revealed in the modern surgical term *hysterectomy* 'excision of the uterus.' Physicians attuned to the traditions of Classical Greek medicine—which is to say, most European physicians up to relatively recent times—ascribed fits of uncontrolled laughter or weeping in women to a dysfunction in the womb and, accordingly, used the Greek adjective *hysterikós* 'of or pertaining to the womb' to characterize both the malady and the behavior associated with it.

Thus, in the 17th century, one could refer in English to *hysteric passion* (also known as the *vapors*, since the condition was believed to be caused by "exhalation" of the womb) and, in the 18th century, to *hysterics*, with reference to these symptoms.

By the 19th century both men and women could suffer from *hysterics* or from its newly coined synonym *hysteria*.

I

inaugurate

The early significance of *inaugurāre*, the Latin verb from which this word derives, referred to divination by observing the flight of birds (the *au-*, meaning 'bird,' being the same stem preserved in the *av-* in such words as *aviary* and *aviation*). Since the ancient Romans formally consulted the will of the gods by divination before embarking on any important public enterprise, the word came to refer to the ceremonials that preceded such enterprises, particularly those concerned with the installation of high-ranking officials. After the actual consultation of the oracle of the birds was no longer considered essential as a guide to the success or failure of a course of action, the ceremony of *inauguration* remained to dignify and consecrate important investitures. Thus the original specialized significance has disappeared, by a process known as "fading," while the word *inaugurate* continues to describe the installation of public officials.

indri, lemur

Indri, the name for a lemurlike primate of Madagascar first observed by the French naturalist Pierre Sonnerat in 1780, entered scientific nomenclature and reached English in the first half of the 19th century as the result of a misunderstanding. When the natives pointed out the animal to Sonnerat, crying "Indry!" he thought they were giving him its name, when, instead, they were saying, "Look!" The actual native name for the creature was *babakoto*, a term which entered English as *babacoote*. The animals were regarded by the Betanimena tribe of Madagascar as "the embodiment of the spirits of their ancestors," as the *lemurs* themselves derived their name from the Latin word for 'ghosts' or 'shadows of the departed.'

97

insect, entomology

The Greek phrase *éntoma zôa* meant, literally 'cut in, or notched, animals,' a description based on physicial appearance. The *-tom-* of the adjective is the same as that preserved in the Modern English *atom*, derived from the Greek, and meaning 'not (capable of being) cut or split,' and in the suffix *-tomy*, as in *lobotomy*, *tonsillectomy*, etc. Eventually the meaning of the phrase became localized in its first element, and the second element was dropped. Similarly, the Latin phrase *insectum animale*, a direct translation from the Greek, dropped its second element and reached English by the start of the 17th century as *insect*.

In its earlier English use, as well as in present nonscientific use, the term applies to numerous invertebrates such as spiders, mites, and various small crustaceans, as well as to the hexapods. In technical scientific nomenclature the word specialized to include only segmented arthropods ('joint-footed animals') which have six legs in at least some stage of their adult development—a specialization that excludes the arachnoids, mites, and crustaceans, but includes approximately one million named species and, when current classification studies are completed, may number about three million. In nonscientific use, the word has been extended to include any creature of little or no significance or importance, a shift from the sense of 'physically small' to the sense 'of small value.'

The *entomo-* stem of *entomology* 'the study of insects' represents an 18th-century borrowing by scholars from the original Greek.

iodine, violet

When she recalled how her friend Atthis had adorned her "hanging locks with *violets* and little roses," the word used for *violets* by the Greek poet Sappho was *íon*. In some of the contemporary dialects of the 6th century B.C., the word still had an initial *w*. The cognate Latin term *viola*, also meaning 'violet,' reached English and appears in the works of the 15th-century poet John Lydgate: "Swettest *viola*, that neuer shal fade." The word *violet* represents a diminutive of the French descendant of the Latin word.

Iode, from the Greek *iódēs*, a combination of *íon* 'violet' and *eidēs* 'resembling,' was the name given to the powder which produced a violet-colored gas and which was identified as an element by the

French chemist Gay-Lussac after it was isolated in 1811 by a French manufacturer of saltpeter. Sir Humphry Davy added the suffix -*ine*, a word element coming into use (*bromine, chlorine*) to identify chemical substances, thus giving *iodine*.

The term is still used to refer to the pure chemical (atomic number 53), but after C. J. Davaine discovered the bactericidal property of a *tincture of iodine*, that liquid came into widespread use as an antiseptic, and is generally referred to, simply, as *iodine*. While the gas and many solutions of *iodine* are *violet*, solutions in alcohol or water are brown, so the etymological sense of the term has faded.

J

jade¹

Judging from the most likely cognate forms in the Scandinavian languages, one might conclude that a *jade* was originally a 'mare,' although since its earliest appearance in English the term seems to have applied to 'a horse' of either sex, and, specifically, to 'a broken-down horse, a nag.' Thus, before Chaucer's time, when *jade* is used in the sense of 'broken-down horse,' the word had already undergone two changes in meaning, although it is not clear whether 'mare' became 'broken-down mare' and then 'broken-down horse,' or 'horse' and then 'broken-down horse.'

By Shakespeare's time, the term had undergone two further transformations. It had come to be used as a verb meaning 'to wear out,' both transitively and intransitively; as a noun, it had come to mean 'a worthless person' of either sex. Subsequently, the noun *jade* came to mean, first, a 'worthless woman' and then 'a disreputable woman,' the sense in which it is used today. The past participle *jaded* 'worn out, sated' is now the form in which the verb is most frequently found.

jade²

When the Spaniards encountered native American *jade* (probably *nephrite* rather than *jadeite*) in the early days of the 16th century, they called it *piedra de ijada*, literally 'flank stone,' because it was believed to have the quality of curing or preventing renal colic. The Spanish word *ijada* means 'flank, small ribs,' and is derived from the Late Latin *iliata*, a form based on the Latin *ilium* 'flank, loin.' As the term passed into French, it became localized and slightly modified phonetically, becoming *éjade*. Subsquently, *l'éjade*, where the *l'* represented the definite article, was remade to *le jade*, by a misanalysis, and it was as *jade* that it entered English in the 18th century.

101

A full century before the term entered the language, *jade* and its curative properties had been described in English by Sir Walter Raleigh, who spoke of the stones "which the Spaniards call *Piedras Hijadas*, and we use for Spleene stones." This was a reference to the fact that while the Spanish located colic near the short ribs, the English attributed it to the spleen, and both sought to cure it with *jade*. Interestingly enough, the Greeks believed that colic originated in the kidneys, and it is from *nephrós* 'kidney' that *nephrite* is derived.

As it became evident that "Spleene stones" by any name did not have any curative properties, *jade* came to be used in carving jewelry and objets d'art.

jingo, jingoism

The earliest attested English use of this word appears around 1670 as part of a magician's incantation which ends, "high *jingo*, come again." The exact sense is not clear, nor is it certain that the word is not simply a bit of stage gibberish coined to produce an effect of wonder. The meaning 'god (God), deity,' however, would not be inconsistent with the context, and, in fact, a late 17th-century translation of Rabelais renders the French *par Dieu* 'by God' with 'by *jingo*,' Some etymologists have considered the possibility that the term derives from *Jinko*, the Basque term for 'God,' perhaps transmitted by way of Basque sailors. If this conjecture is correct, it would be one of the very few English borrowings, and conceivably even the only one, from that language, which is of uncertain but probably non-Indo-European affinities. It was once spoken in part of the area that is now Spain, and has influenced certain Spanish dialects now also called Basque because of that influence.

In any event, the word came into use initially as a magical call for an object to be conjured out of the air, then as a simple accompaniment, almost an expression of surprise, at such prestidigitation. By the end of the 17th century, the phrase, *by jingo*, sometimes intensified to *by the loving jingo*, was appearing as a simple asseveration, not unlike *by gosh*, or *by golly*, where the noun occurs as a substitute for the forbidden use of the divine name.

In 1878, when Disraeli was Prime Minister of Britain, his party adopted a belligerent policy, sending a fleet into Turkish waters to deter Russia from its threatened acquisition of Constantinople, a martial song supporting this stance became popular in England. It went,

We don't want to fight,

But, by *jingo*, if we do,

We've got the ships, we've got the men,

We've got the money too.

Thereafter, those who sang this *jingo* song and supported such get-tough foreign policy came to be known as *Jingoes*, and their point of view became *jingoism*.

jovial

Latin *joviālis* meant 'of or pertaining to *Jovis* or Jupiter,' the Roman version of the Greek god *Zeus*. In fact, *Jovis* and *Zeus* are cognate forms of the Proto-Indo-European **dyēus* 'heaven, daytime sky,' from which comes the Latin *diēs* 'day,' the source of English *diurnal, diet,* and many other words having to do with days. *Jupiter* is the Latin form of **dyēus-pHter* 'heaven-father,' or 'Father *Jove*,' since that Graeco-Roman god had originally been associated with the majesty of the sky.

There is some question as to the immediate source of *jovial* in English. Its earliest sense, attested in the late 16th century, agrees with that of the narrow French use of the term at the time 'born under the sign of Jupiter,' although the word is found in English less than a century later in the more general Latin meaning of 'of or pertaining to *Jove* or Jupiter.' There already existed in English an adjective *jovy* 'jolly, happy,' which had been derived from Latin *Jovius* 'of or pertaining to *Jove*' in the 15th century and which had been completely replaced, by the 18th century, by *jovial*, in an extension of its narrow French sense. It may well be, then, that *jovial* was in fact borrowed from the French, but its meaning was influenced by an awareness of its Latin origin and a certain familiarity with the sense of the underlying Latin term.

Both *jovy* and *jovial* seem to have evolved their sense of 'jolly, happy' from the notion that the planet Jupiter was the source of joy and happiness.

jubilee

The Hebrew *yovel* originally meant 'lead ram,' but came to designate only 'a ram's horn' rather than the whole animal, and soon became specialized in the sense of 'trumpet,' although not necessarily one made from a ram's horn. By a process etymologists call "transference," the term came to mean 'the blast of a trumpet,' and from that, any 'loud noise of announcement; a cry, especially a cry of joy.'

It is from this last sense that *jubilee* in its biblical meaning (Leviticus 25: 8–17) is derived. Every fifty years, blasts of the trumpet announced the beginning of a year of general rest and recuperation, during which slaves were freed, lands returned to their original owners, and creditors temporarily kept at bay. The *jubilee* year was originally one that came at the end of the seventh of seven sets of sabbatical years, and the association of the number fifty with the notion of *jubilee* is still strong in English, which acquired the term in the 14th century. Today, however, a *jubilee* may be any special anniversary on or during which a general celebration is appropriate. This loosening of the numerical constraints on the periodicity of the *jubilee* with its attendant celebration was largely the result of experimentation on the part of the medieval Christian church fathers in setting the interval between the years of general dispensation for the sinners in their flock. Christian years of general reprieve and celebration first came at 100-year intervals, then at 50-, 33-, and finally, 25-year intervals.

These days it may come well before the passage of 50 or even 25 years, last for considerably less than a year, absolve nobody of debt or sin, and be ushered in by no blast of ram's horn or trumpet. But a *jubilee* still calls for a celebration.

juggernaut

In Sanskrit, *jagannātha* 'world-protector' is a common epithet of Krishna, the eighth avatar of the god Vishnu. The Hindi form of this word has been used for centuries to designate both Krishna himself and the immense idol of the god which is pulled through the streets of Orissa on an over-sized cart during the festival of Pūrī every year. The earliest European accounts of this festival, which date from the first half of the 14th century, report that it was the practice of at least some of the devotees of Krishna to throw themselves under the wheels of the great cart that hauled the *Jagannāth*.

Whether this was actually the practice or merely a misinterpretation of the deaths of those caught in the crush of people pulling the cart, the British associated willful self-destruction with the *Jagannāth* cart. This gave rise in the 19th century to the use of *juggernaut*, the English rendering of the Hindi term, to mean 'a thing or idea that arouses blind, self-sacrificing devotion in people.' That sense is still prevalent today along with the more generalized sense of 'destructive force.'

jumbo

This word, with its meaning 'gigantic, oversized' seems to have originated in the name of *Jumbo* the Elephant, one of P. T. Barnum's star attractions in his famous traveling circus. Anything elephantine, or simply larger than ordinary, came to be called by the name of the famous elephant, this hyperbole being no more than circus-goers and the general public had long since grown accustomed to in English.

Barnum seems to have come up with the name for his elephant by abbreviating the 18th-century term *mumbo-jumbo*, a word with an appropriately exotic flavor and a vague meaning. Possibly originating in the West African Mandingo *māmá-gyombō* 'shaman who causes the troubled spirits of the ancestors to go away,' *mumbo-jumbo* has been used in English to mean, variously, 'African idol, shaman, meaningless object of worship, meaningless incantation, and gibberish,' all more or less simultaneously.

jungle

This word was borrowed into English from one of the native Indo-European languages of northern India, probably Hindustani or Marathi, during the heyday of the British Empire. In Sanskrit, *jangala*, a term of obscure, probably non-Indo-European origin, meant 'arid, desert land.' In the modern languages descended from Sanskrit, the term was first used for any patch of uncultivated or uncultivable land, and was then specialized to refer to the lush forests described by Kipling and other British sojourners in India. Thus the term for a land which could support little or no vegetable life came to be used for land superabundant in vegetable life. The apparent paradox is explained by the uncultivability of both regions, the one because it is too dry and the other because it is too wet.

junk

In Latin, *juncus* meant 'reed, rush.' This form is the basis for English *junk* 'trash,' *junket* 'a sweet confection,' and, by extension, 'a pleasure trip masquerading as business,' and *jonquil* 'a rushlike plant with yellow flowers.' Until the 20th century, *junk* 'trash' was a sailor's term referring to bits of rope too small to save, the original sense presumably having been 'reeds,' then 'rope made from reeds (or hemp),' and then, 'pieces of rope too worn or torn to be of any use.' From this is derived the modern, more general meaning of the term, 'something unusable, worn out.'

The current slang use of the word as a synonym for heroin is an ironic extension of its meaning of 'trash,' just as the heroin addict's *rush* is a perversion of the noun meaning 'a charge (to repel someone or something)' from the Late Latin verb *recausāre*.

A *junket* was originally a sweet dessert served on a plate of rushes, another example of a word whose meaning has been transferred from the mode of presentation of something to the thing itself.

There is no etymological connection between either *junk* as trash or *junket* as pleasure trip and the Chinese boat known as a *junk*, which is derived from the Malay *jong* 'seafaring vessel.'

L

labyrinth

The *lábrus*, or 'two-headed axe,' whose name goes back to ancient Lydian or Carian, served as one of the predominant religious symbols in Minoan Crete. The *labúrinthos* or 'place of the *lábrus*' was, according to Greek legend, an intricate mazelike building designed by Daedalus, the great artificer of antiquity, to house the Minotaur, a half-bull, half-human monster to whom the Cretans sacrificed Athenian youth. The myth relates how Theseus slew the monster and then found his way out by following a thread provided by Princess Ariadne, who had fallen in love with him.

In his *Natural History* Pliny the Elder claims that Daedalus modeled his creation on a vastly larger Egyptian edifice with "passageways that wind, advance, and retreat in a bewilderingly intricate fashion" (Book XXXVI).

The word *labyrinth* reached English by the 14th century in the sense of 'any building with complicated or convoluted passageways.' Physicians of the 17th century applied the term to part of the inner ear, and metallurgists of the 19th century to a device with winding channels used to sort out particles of ore of varying sizes.

lace

The Latin word *laqueus* 'noose, snare' might have been derived from the verb *lacere* 'to seduce, entrap,' or it might have been a borrowing in its original sense from Etruscan or another non-Indo-European language. If the former, *lacere* might have been used in the specialized sense 'to snare with a rope or noose,' and the derived noun *laqueus* thus came to mean 'rope, noose.' In any case, it passed into English via Old French in the general sense of 'string, cord.' (Modern

107

English *lasso*, a much later addition to the language from the Spanish form of *laqueus*, *lazo* 'rope, snare,' preserves much more of the original meaning.)

The word *lace* came to be used in two increasingly different senses in English. On the one hand, the noun was 'a piece of string for tying shoes or stays,' and on the other, 'a decorative braid for adorning clothing or a uniform.' The Major in the Gilbert and Sullivan operetta *Patience* sings of it in this sense: "Gold *lace* has a charm for the fair/ And I've plenty of that, and to spare." In its decorative function, braided cord, linked metal, or cloth gave *lace* the sense in which it is now understood when it appears as a noun without the qualification *shoe*, *boot*, or *corset*.

As a verb, *lace* has three current senses. First, it means 'to tie up with string,' as to *lace* a shoe. Second is 'to adorn with *lace*,' and the third use is an extension of the second: to *lace* a drink, whether with alcohol or arsenic, is to embellish it.

laconic, Spartan

The *Spartans* were called many things by the Athenians, their arch foes. Among the more polite epithets applied to them were *Spartiâtai* 'Spartans,' *Lákōnoi* 'Laconians,' and *Lakedaimónioi* 'Lacedaemonians,' each derived from a place name of ultimately uncertain origin. From the adjectives formed of two of these, we have inherited *Spartan* and *laconic*.

In its more general sense today, *Spartan* is used to mean 'austere, self-disciplined,' like a citizen of Sparta. *Laconic* 'terse,' spelled with a small *l*, has largely lost its original geographical association, although when the term entered English in the 16th century it could still be used to describe a 'Spartan/Laconian/Lacedaemonian,' as well as 'a person of succinct speech habits.'

Terse speech was characteristic of the *Spartans*. It is recorded that when, at the fall of Thebes, the victorious *Spartan* general sent the message, "Thebes is taken," the home command replied, " 'Taken' would have been sufficient." Again, in response to a challenge to the ephors in which a besieger said, "If I take Sparta, I will raze it," the *Spartans* are said to have replied, simply, "If."

left

The Old English word *lyft* 'weak,' which appears in the compound *lyft-adl* 'palsy or paralysis,' literally, 'weakness disease,' is cognate with the East Frisian *luf* 'weak.' The word had a variant, *left*, in the Kentish dialect of southeastern England, and it was this nonstandard, local form that evolved into the Modern English antonym of *right*. The semantic evolution derives from the fact that for most people the *left* hand is the weak one. The impetus to shift from a sense dealing with strength to one relating to relative location may have come from the introduction into English of the French-derived word *feeble* at the end of the 12th century. Citations showing the use of *left* in its directional sense start to appear almost immediately thereafter, demonstrating what etymologists call a "fading" of the then-synonymous denotation in favor of what had originally started as a connotative extension.

lethargic, latent

To the Greeks of antiquity, a *lethargic* person was one who died and sipped the waters of forgetfulness, the river *Lēthē*. By the time the term entered English in the 14th century it had already taken on the extended sense of 'sleepy, apathetic, torpid, or morbid,' meanings which have remained associated with it to this day.

The Proto-Indo-European root from which *Lēthē* and *lethargic* are derived, **ladh*, seems originally to have meant 'to lie (hidden).' It is the source of *latent*, as in a *latent* volcano, a *latent* tumor, or a *latent* hostility.

lewd

Two etymologies have been suggested for this word, first attested in English in the sense of 'lay person, noncleric' in the early Middle Ages. The first derives the word from Latin *laicus* 'lay, nonclerical,' which is itself derived from the Greek *laikós* 'of or belonging to the people,' the adjective formed to *laós* 'people; common people.'

The second explanation of the form, which accounts for its otherwise mysterious final *d*, derives *lewd* from the past participle of Middle English *lǽwan* 'to weaken,' on the assumption that 'weakened' might have been extended to mean 'ignorant, illiterate,' characteristics of the early lay brothers of the Church.

Perhaps a more likely possibility is something of a compromise between these two: the Latin *laicus* formed the basis of the borrowed term and, perhaps through the influence of the Middle English *læwan*, the past participial ending *-(e)d* was added.

No matter how it acquired its form, in the early Middle Ages *lewd* meant 'lay, nonclerical,' and, by the 13th century, had taken on the more general sense of 'ignorant, unlettered.' By the following century, it had come to mean 'rude, lascivious,' by extension of its sense of 'illiterate' and the association of illiteracy with the lower classes.

John Taylor's palindrome, "*Lewd* did I live and evil I did dwel,' believed to be the first in the language, seems to show that by the end of the 16th century the term had acquired both connotations. Today it would be reasonably accurate to say that we think of *lewd* and *lascivious behavior* as being one and the same.

licorice

This English word, also spelled *liquorice*, represents the modern development, via Latin and French, of the Greek *glukús* 'sweet' plus *rhiza* 'root.' Variants of *glukús* reached English without the loss of the g, in such words as *glycose* and *glucose*, while *rhiza* is the cognate of both the Germanic-derived *root* and the Latin-derived *radish* (from *rādix*). Today *licorice* refers to the candy made from the boiled juice of the root as well as the *rhizome* itself.

lilac

In Sanskrit, the stem *nil* meant 'to appear dark' and *nila* 'very dark' and covered a range from black to dark blue or sapphire. In Persian, a language closely related to Sanskrit, since it represents the Iranian branch of the subfamily from which Sanskrit is descended in the Indic branch, *nilak* meant 'bluish.' Before starting its wanderings en route to English, the Persian form of the word underwent an assimilatory sound change by which the n shifted to l by way of anticipating the following consonant. In this form the term entered Arabic, then Spanish, then French, and finally, in the 17th century, English. On the way it had been applied to a flowering shrub, *Syringa vulgaris,* perhaps originally as part of a descriptive phrase. By the time it reached the end of its journey only the *lilac* part of the phrase remained, and it signified the plant itself and not the color.

Today, the *Syringa* has many varieties, ranging in hue from white to violet, but by the end of the 19th century that variety which was a shade of pinkish violet had become so well known to English speakers that *lilac* again became the name of a color, albeit not the same color it had been originally.

lumber

As a verb, *lumber* is first attested in English in the 14th century with its modern meaning of 'move clumsily, heavily'; it is probably to be derived from a dialectal Swedish verb *lomra* 'to resound' beside which appears *loma* 'to move heavily.' Because of the paucity of cognate forms for *lomra* and *loma* and the uncertainty as to which of these verbs reflected the primary sense of the word from which both were derived, there is some disagreement among linguists as to the Proto-Indo-European or Proto-Germanic root to be posited for their source. One school of thought has it that *loma* reflects the original sense and is to be derived from a root meaning 'to break to bits, cripple' (also seen in Modern English *lame*). The other maintains that *lomra* reflects the primary sense and is to be derived from the root that gives Modern English *loud* and which seems to have originally meant 'sound, noise.'

The derivation of the noun is no less troublesome. Appearing in the 16th century with the sense of 'useless odds and ends,' the word seems to have been derived from the verb *lumber*. In that case the connection might have been either that the 'odds and ends' were large and bulky, that they were an encumbrance, or both. It has also been suggested that the sense of the term may have been influenced by the phonetically similar but etymologically unrelated *lump* and by the word *Lombard*. The *Lombards* had made a name for themselves in the late Middle Ages and early Renaissance as bankers and pawn-brokers, and in the 17th century a *Lombard-house* was 'a bank or pawnshop,' thus a place where a variety of odds and ends might be stored. In England today, a room used to store unused household goods is called a *lumber room* and the goods are called *lumber*.

The 17th century saw a further change in the meaning of *lumber* as the term came to designate 'rough-cut timber,' the sense of the term in America today, this possibly representing an extension of the earlier sense of 'bulky item.'

lunatic

The Latin word *lūna* 'moon,' from earlier **louksnam*, rests on the same Proto-Indo-European stem that yielded *lūmen*, from **louksmen*, and *luminōsis*, eventually *luminous*, as well as, via Germanic, the English word *light*. The corresponding Latin adjective, *lūnāticus*, from which *lunatic* comes, meant 'that which pertains to the moon,' later, 'moonstruck,' and then 'acting peculiarly because of the moon,' that is, 'mad, insane.'

M

macabre

During the Middle Ages, as the plague raged throughout Europe, many artists produced *Danses macabrées* depicting corpses from all walks of life in a dance led by Death itself, sometimes accompanied by short verses on the transitoriness of life. One of the earliest of these is credited to Jean de Fèvre, whose *Danse macabrée* appeared in the middle of the 14th century. The first *Daunce of Machabree* in England appeared in the 15th century. The sense associated with the term *macabré(e)* in French, as in English, seems to have been 'gruesome, funereal, ghastly' at that time, although the original meaning was quite different.

Two derivations have been suggested for *macabré(e)*, which eventually lost its final-syllable stress, giving both French and English *macabre*. The first posits a painter named *Macaber* or *Macabré* after whom the dance was named—although no such painter is known to have existed. The second derives the phrase from the Late Latin *Chorea Maccabaeorum* 'dance of the Maccabees,' a feature of certain morality plays of the period which dramatized the slaughter of the *Maccabees*. The troublesome feature of this derivation is that although *Maccabee* seems to underlie the Modern French slang term *macchabé* 'corpse,' the origin of the *r* of *macabré(e)* poses a problem for which no solution has been suggested.

machine

The Doric Greek term *mākhaná* meant simply a 'contrivance,' or a 'means of accomplishing something.' One specialized use of the word referred to a crane, or machine for lifting weights. The playwrights of ancient Greece used a *mākhaná* (*mēkanē* in the literary dialect of Attica and Ionia) to hoist actors portraying gods through the air. When the word was borrowed into Latin, this practice produced the

113

phrase *deus ex machinā*, literally, 'god from a machine or contrivance.' The Latin form passed through French and entered English in the 16th century in the sense of 'a structure of any sort.' During the following century it was applied to various vehicles, such as carriages or coaches, and even to sea vessels, a sense which had become obsolete by the beginning of the 19th century.

Occasional uses in the 17th century reverted to one of the specialized meanings the word had acquired in Greek and Latin, an 'engine of war,' but by the latter part of that century it began to take on its principal modern meaning, 'device or means for applying force or power.' In the 19th century the term began to be used in American political parlance to mean 'a controlling organization for acquiring or applying governmental power.'

The Old English cognate of *machine* was *magan*, the ancestor of the modern word *may*, which meant 'to be able, to be strong,' a sense that survives in the past *might*.

mackinaw

The Ojibway Indian name for the island which lies between Lake Michigan and Lake Huron is *mitchimakinak*, which means 'big turtle.' This name was shortened and adopted by the French Canadian trappers as *Mackinac*, and it now applies not only to the island but to the strait and the nearby state park in Michigan. As so often happens with place names, and particularly with those in a foreign language, the original meaning was soon forgotten. In linguistic terms, it "faded."

Mackinaw blankets acquired their name from a variant of the name of the region, when the U. S. Government distributed blankets woven in bright woolen plaids to the local Indians. The same heavy blanket material was made into short, double-breasted jackets that became known as *Mackinaw coats* or, later, simply *mackinaws*. A *Mackinaw boat* is a particular flat-bottomed sailboat widely used on the Great Lakes, and *Mackinaw trout* are a variety of fish (*namaycush*) indigenous to the area.

Although the original meaning, 'big turtle,' has long since faded, the multiple specializations, illustrating a process linguists call "radiation," might lead one to agree with Ogden Nash's couplet:

How very clever of the turtle
In such a fix to be so fertile.

madrigal

Although this term, applied both to a 'pastoral form of verse' and a 'musical setting of a secular poetic text,' is, by all accounts, Latinate in origin, the precise Latin word from which it is derived is a matter of some debate. Debatable also are the secondary forms which may have influenced the development of *madrigal*, which entered English via French from Italian in the 16th century.

The most popular etymology derives the word from the Late Latin *(carmen) matricālis* '(song) of the womb, of infancy.' The adjective *matricālis* means 'of or pertaining to a mother' in the most literal sense; four explanations, all with some degree of semantic difficulty, have been proposed for the extended use of the adjective to describe this poetic/musical form. One holds that *madrigals* are so called because they were written in the 'mother tongue,' that is, the vernacular, rather than in the language of the Church. A second, that since they were liturgical in origin, they belonged to the 'Mother Church.' A third suggests that the subject matter of the *madrigal* was pastoral and often amatory, or affectionate 'as a mother might be toward her children.' And fourth, it has been suggested that *madrigals* were so simply constructed that they could be performed by one 'fresh out of the womb.' Regardless of which explanation is the true one, on the basis of the phonetic evidence *matricālis* seems the most likely underlying form of the word.

This has not prevented etymologists from suggesting other possibilities. One of these is that since *madrigal* is the name for a secular piece, it derives from *materiāles* 'secular.' Or, it may have originally been a *(carmen) mandriālis*, since *mandriālis* is an adjective formed from the noun *mandra* 'flock,' a Latin borrowing from the Greek *mándra* 'sheepfold.' This suggestion is based on the pastoral nature of *madrigal* texts.

Perhaps the best guess is that some elements of all these suggested derivations played a part in determining the final form of the word, whatever its actual source.

magazine

This is one of the few notable exceptions to the rule of thumb that when nouns are borrowed into English from Arabic, they begin with the Arabic definite article *al*. The Arabic word *mahsan* is a 'storehouse; a place where things are stored.' In French, a *magasin* is a 'department store,' while in Spanish, where the term kept the Arabic article, an *almacén* is a 'warehouse; department or grocery store; literary or photographic periodical.'

English has taken over two of the senses of the Spanish word. *Magazine* in the meaning of a 'storehouse for explosives' entered English in the 16th century, probably by way of the wars between the British, French, and Spanish nations at that time. By the 17th century, the term had come to be used in the sense of a 'storehouse of (published or publishable) information'; the booklike *magazines* of the period were publications of miscellaneous knowledge on a given topic. When, in the 18th century, literary periodicals of the kind we have today began to appear, the old meaning of *magazine* became extended to refer to them.

mail[1]

This word, in its meaning of 'flexible armor,' is derived from the Latin *macula* 'spot, mark, or stain,' which entered English directly from Latin and acquired a variety of specialized senses. These include a 'spot on the sun,' as a technical term in astronomy; a 'mark of a contrasting color in a mineral, caused by the presence of a different element,' as a technical term in mineralogy; and a 'stain or spot, especially a permanent mark, on the skin,' as a technical term in medicine and entomology. The same stem in a slightly different form reached English as *maculate* 'spotted.' The negative version, *immaculate*, preserves a meaning acquired during the Latin period, from the application of the term to a moral quality, 'unblemished, without stigma or disgrace,' as in *immaculate conception*.

Also during the Latin period, the word took on a figurative use as 'the mesh of a net.' In the transmission through Old French, one specialized use applied it to any of the small metal rings that interlocked to form the flexible body armor used in the Middle Ages, perhaps because of their resemblance to little marks or spots. By this time, following normal sound changes, the French had become *maille*, whence the form *mail*. It was in this sense that the word first reached English by the early part of the 14th century. Within decades the meaning had been extended to include the entire network composed of such links. The transition from a 'single link' to 'the unit made up of such links' probably involved one or more of the many phrases like *coat of mail* 'garment composed of metal links' which after a time localized the meaning of the entire phrase in the single word and then dropped the other phrasal elements. (See also **mail²** and **blackmail**.)

mail²

This word, in its meaning of 'correspondence, postal matter, or the organization or means for delivering such matter,' probably derives from the Old High German word *malha* 'bag or pouch.' This was cognate with the Greek *molgós* 'oxhide sack; wineskin' and had a variant sense of 'something made from a hide or skin,' which suggests that an earlier Proto-Indo-European form with this meaning was ancestral to both terms. The Germanic word passed through Old French, becoming *male* en route, and then reached Middle English by the beginning of the 13th century in various spellings, among them *mail*, *mayl*, and *malle*. The word is still used, chiefly in Scotland, in the meaning of 'sack, pouch, traveling bag.'

The major semantic shift to the contemporary meaning began in the 17th century when the word occurred in the phrase *mail of letters* 'a pouch containing correspondence.' As often happens, the meaning became localized in a single element of the phrase, and *mail* came to signify not only the container, but also the contents. In time the original core of the meaning 'bag' faded, leading to a strange result, the formation of a new compound, *mail bag*—an etymological redundance. (See also **mail¹** and **blackmail**.)

man

The ultimate etymology of *man* remains a matter of dispute, but both possibilities start with words that are neutral with regard to sex. One traces the word back to the Proto-Indo-European **mon* 'one,' attested in the Greek *mono-*, which has reached English in such words as *monocle*, originally 'one eye,' *monomania* 'person with a single obsession,' *mononuclear* 'having one nucleus,' and so on. Another hypothesis holds that *man* represents a variant of the same stem seen in the Latin *mēns* 'mind, intellect,' or in *mental*, cognate with the English word *mind*.

Knowing these possibilities, many professional etymologists regard with derision the efforts of feminists to avoid the use of the word in compounds such as *chairman*. The German cognate *Mensch* still preserves the general sense 'human being, person,' while the Yiddish *mensch* has taken on a decidedly favorable connotation, signifying 'a person of distinguished character.' In this sense it sometimes appears in the usage of English speakers; "a real *mensch*" is an expression of great approval.

manure

The earliest use of *manure* in English, in the sense of 'tilling the land,' already shows a specialization from the French sense 'work by hand,' a meaning still visible in the phonological variant *maneuvre*. England in the late 14th century had an agricultural economy, and tilling the land was the most common work.

Contemporary with this use was another one, also now obsolete, that represents what etymologists call "generalization." This was the meaning to 'manage or administer,' and usually referred to land, but was not limited to the management of land. A number of other divergent semantic lines arose, including to 'improve or train a person,' but these fell into disuse when the term specialized to mean the single operation of working the land to which it refers today, namely, to 'spread fertilizer.' The noun refers to the fertilizing material itself.

map, napkin, apron

All three of these words have a common origin, the Latin *mappa*, which, according to the Roman rhetorician Quintilian, was a loan word from Phoenician. The Latin form meant 'tablecloth, napkin, towel, cloth waved as a starting signal for racers in the circus.' Quintilian's surmise is probably correct, and Hebrew, the language most closely related to the ancient Phoenician, still has a word *mapa* meaning 'flag,' which is undoubtedly a cognate form.

In medieval times cartographers often drew their charts on cloths (tablecloths or napkins, in other uses) since they were relatively durable, and thus the word for 'cloth' became specialized to mean 'drawing of a geographical projection,' which entered English, via French transmission, in the 16th century.

A phonological variant, with an *m* to *n* change, gave *nape* 'tablecloth,' which preserves one of the Latin meanings. An expansion of this, *napery*, came to mean 'linen used for any purpose, but usually for table use.' Since the Latin failed to distinguish between the large cloth used to cover the table and the small cloth used to protect the clothing or wipe the fingers, a diminutive suffix *-kin* produced the specialization *napkin*. It is surmised that this expansion first took place in a Middle Dutch or Flemish environment, although no manuscript source supports this conclusion. In any event, the form entered English in the early 15th century.

A second diminutive expansion, with *-eron*, took place in Old French, producing *naperon*, later *napron*. This had appeared in English by the 14th century with the specialization 'fabric garment worn to protect the clothes.' The initial *n* appears in all the earliest English citations. When combined with the indefinite article *an*, however, the phrase *an napron* produced two *n*'s, a combination that sound changes at the end of the Middle English period, around 1500, were simplifying to a single *n*. Both *a napron* and *an apron* occurred, but the latter eventually prevailed, giving us the contemporary *apron*, whose close relationship to *napkin* and more distant one to *map* became obscure.

A similar change took place in *orange*, which was originally *nāranja* in Sanskrit. Only after the word was borrowed by English speakers as *a naranj* was the *n* dissimilated, creating (with a change in spelling) modern *an orange*. Other English words underwent a reverse process in which the *n* of the indefinite article assimilated to the word it preceded; thus *an ewt* (seen in *eft*) became *a newt*.

marshal

In Old High German, a *marahscalh* was, literally, a 'horse servant,' that is, a person in charge of the horses, from *marah* 'horse,' from which we get the English *mare*, and *scalh* 'servant.' This compound was borrowed into Latin in its original meaning, survived into Old

French, and then passed into Middle English. In both French and English, the term took on a more general sense as the farriers to kings and noblemen were given broader duties, with concomitant amelioration of their social status. *Marshals* became responsible not only for the care and feeding of horses but for the acquisition and maintenance of other military ordnance as well. Soon there were *marshals* in charge of managing a variety of generally, but not exclusively, military aspects of the royal or noble household.

Today, a *marshal* is a person charged with maintaining order in a variety of realms. *Field marshals* are top-ranking military officers; *parade marshals* oversee the orderly comings and goings of their charges; the *provost marshal* in the army or navy is the one who sees to it that the prisons run smoothly. As a verb, *marshal* has taken on an even more general sense, though clearly related to the noun from which it is derived. One may *marshal* an army, or *marshal* evidence, 'collect and organize evidence toward a particular end.'

marshmallow

Originally a *marshmallow* was 'a variety of plant which grows in the marshes.' *Marsh* comes from the Proto-Indo-European root **mori*, which seems to have meant 'body of water, lake, sea,' and which, in its Germanic form, gives us *mermaid*, *meerschaum* (which see) as well as *marsh*, and, through Latin, *maritime*, *marine*, and many other sea terms. *Mallow* is probably of non-Indo-European origin, appearing in Greek as *malákhē* and in Latin as *malva*. From these we derive not only the name of the pink-flowered plant, but the color term *mauve* and the name of the mineral *malachite*, although it is neither rose nor mauve, but dark green or black.

The discovery that the *marsh mallow* has a root which, when pressed, yields a sticky, gummy substance that can be used as an unguent or as an ingredient in a candy paste seems to have been made relatively recently, but the sense of *marshmallow* as a confection is the more common one now. Indeed, nowadays *marshmallows* are commercially made from a substance synthesized in the chemical laboratory, rather than from the root of the plant that has given them its name.

martyr

The ancient Aeolic Greek word *mártur*, which is the ancestor of *martyr*, meant 'witness, one who testifies,' and *martúrion* originally meant 'testimony.' The semantic development of the term arose from the treatment of early Christians in the first century. Since legal theory of the time regarded the testimony of slaves as unreliable, it was common practice to interrogate them under torture, and since many early Christians were slaves, many were tortured. Gradually the Greek word, as well as the Latin form *martyr*, took on the connotative extension a 'witness who suffers or even dies for his religion.'

By the time the word entered English at the end of the 8th or beginning of the 9th century, the 'witness' part of the meaning had begun to fade, and the focus centered on the suffering on behalf of religious belief. In the time of the 14th-century religious reformer John Wycliffe, the term was applied to those who suffered for a cause regarded as misguided or evil, a sense obsolete, or at least obsolescent, today. By Shakespeare's time, *martyr* could be used to describe 'someone who suffered or endured for any cause.'

Current use has generalized the meaning to include anyone who suffers, even without belief in a cause or principle.

mathematic, mathematics

In Classical Greek, the adjective *mathēmatikós*, from the verb *manthánein* (aorist *matheîn*) 'to learn,' could refer either to a person ready and able to absorb the learning or science of the day or to that body of knowledge itself. In the plural, *tá mathēmatiká* referred to the sum of human knowledge and the principles by which it might be acquired and manipulated. Over the years, with the multiplication of discrete, and discretely named, fields of academic endeavor, the sense of the original Greek term has narrowed. Today, *mathematics* specifically names the science of numbers and numerical manipulation, while the adjective *mathematic* or *mathematical*, in its technical sense, refers to the science of *mathematics* and, in a more general way, may be used as a synonym for 'rigorous, precise.'

The original form of both the adjective and the noun which entered English from French or learned Latin in the 14th century was *mathematic*. Later, in the 16th century, the noun form acquired the English plural -*s*, although the word continued to be treated, as it had been in Greek, as a collective noun taking a singular verb. The adjective is now in the process of acquiring a technically redundant adjectival -al ending, to clarify its grammatical status. Thus, the process which linguists call "radiation" has been very nearly completed.

maudlin

Mary *Magdalen*, 'Mary of Magdala,' was the prostitute redeemed by Christ, according to the New Testament. The city of her birth, as incorporated into her name, gives us both the proper name *Madeleine* as well as the adjective *maudlin*. The pastry called a *madeleine*, made famous by Marcel Proust in *A la recherche de temps perdu*, is named after a particular *Madeleine*, the 19th-century pastry chef *Madeleine* Paulmier.

Maudeleyn or *Maudelen*, as it was first spelled in English, was borrowed from the French in the 14th century. The French form represented a borrowing from the Latin *Magdalena*. *Maudlin* seems to have been an English creation of the 16th century, derived from the specialized use of the name as it applied to St. Mary *Magdalen*, frequently depicted in early Christian iconography as a weeping penitent. Soon anyone given to weeping could be called a *Maudeleyn* or *Maudlin* (person), and in time *maudlin* as an epithet of a weeping person came to be spelled with a small *m* and lost its original association with Mary *Magdalen*. By the 17th century, *maudlin* had come to mean 'weepily sentimental.'

meat

While there is some disagreement among Indo-European specialists as to the ultimate source of the English word *meat*, most derive the word from the root **med* 'measure,' attested in such terms as *mete*, *mediate*, *modicum*, and *mantra*. If *meat* does come from 'measure,' it is as the result of the specialization of the sense of 'portion' to 'portion of something to eat.'

Whatever its ultimate origin, *meat* appears in Old and Middle English, as *mete*, in the sense of 'food.' A related form, *gemæte* 'companion, person with whom food is shared,' has subsequently yielded our word *mate*. Indeed, the general sense of *meat* as 'food' is still visible in such relics as *sweetmeat* and *mincemeat*, and in the use of the term to designate the 'edible portion of a nut or other fruit.'

More common, however, is the specialized use of *meat* to mean '(edible) flesh,' which arose as the result of the workings of three separate processes in the language.

One of these was simply the increasing use of the term *food*, from a root meaning 'protect, feed,' to express the general term. Another was the localization of the compound *flesh-meat*, which had been coined, along with *bake-meat*, *milk-meat*, *sweet-meat*, *mince-meat*, and the like, to differentiate among the varieties of *meats* 'foods.' Thus the *meat* of *flesh-meat* 'edible flesh' came to stand for the whole. Finally, such contrastive expressions as *meat and bone* and *meat and hide*, which were originally meant to set the edible (*meat*) portion off from the inedible (bone, hide) portion of a food, came to be seen as opposing, specifically, '(edible) flesh' to '(inedible) concomitants of (edible) flesh.'

meerschaum

The Germans translated the Persian phrase *kef-i-daryā*, which described the frothy white clay known technically as *sepiolite*, a type of hydrous silicate of magnesium, as 'sea foam' *meerschaum*. The first element, *meer*, is the exact cognate of the English word *mere*, which once meant 'sea,' a sense now preserved only dialectally or in archaic or poetic usage, but which now has come to signify either a smaller body of water, a 'lake or a pool,' or a 'marsh or fen.' The *mer-* of *mermaid* reflects the same English root, and the Latin *mare* 'sea,' found in such English words as *marine* or *maritime*, descends from the same ancestral source. The German *Schaum* 'foam, froth,' a High West German word, is cognate with the 13th-century loan word *scum*, which entered English from Middle Dutch, a Low West German dialect.

Meerschaum is first attested in English toward the end of the 18th century in the purely mineralogical sense 'sepiolite.' The poetic and descriptive significance had faded in the passage to English, whose speakers usually did not understand German. Pipes made with *meerschaum* bowls became so well known that the phrase *meerschaum pipe* became common enough for the entire meaning to localize in the first element of the phrase, causing the second word to drop.

Curiously enough, the first element of the word *sepiolite* derives from the Greek *sēpion*, which meant either 'the bone of the cuttlefish' or 'pounce,' a fine powder made from cuttlefish bone. The noun *pounce* is cognate with the English word *foam*.

melancholy

In ancient times, medical theory held that the state of an individual's health was determined by the mixture of the so-called humors of the body, the yellow bile, the black bile, the phlegm (which see under **phlegmatic**), and the blood. The Greek word for 'black bile condition' was *melancholía*, from *melan-* 'black,' *chol-* 'bile,' and *-ia* 'condition.' The term actually illustrates a strange etymological contradiction, since *chol-* 'bile' preserves a specialization of the Proto-Indo-European root for 'yellow.' Indeed, since the Greek k^h (respelled in English as *ch-* after passing through Latin) descended from an earlier g^h, this g^h became g in Germanic and later passed to *y-* in certain positions. Thus, a variant of the same stem, $*g^hel$-, gave the *yel-* of English *yellow*. The stem $*g^hol$- itself also gave the English *gall* 'bile,' without the *g-* to *y-* change. Thus, *melan-* plus *chol-* could have meant 'black yellow,' except for the earlier specialization 'yellow' to 'yellow fluid' to 'gall.' Since an excess of 'black bile' was believed to cause mental depression or unhappiness, the word took on that sense. It passed through Latin and entered English in the 14th century, still with the early Greek medical significance. As changing medical concepts swept away the theory of the humors, the once technical term generalized to become simply the popular word for the mental state.

meretricious

The Proto-Indo-European stem *smer-*, often shortened to *mer-*, meant 'portion, part, share,' as attested in the Greek *méros*, which eventually became a productive suffix in such English chemical terms as *polymer* and *isomer*. The same stem in the cognate Latin *merērī* meant 'to deserve (a portion or share); to earn or acquire (a share).' The corresponding Latin adjective *meritum*, from which English *merit* is derived, came to mean 'that which one deserves.' One specialization of *merē-* as a verb, extended by an agent noun suffix *-tr-* plus a feminizing diminutive *-ic-*, gave *meretrix*, which probably once meant 'a female who works for hire.' However, since the number of gainful trades open to women in ancient Rome, where the law decreed that they could neither own property nor money as long as there was a single extant male relative, was limited, *meretrix* came to mean 'prostitute.' The Latin adjective based on this stem was *meretricius* 'that which pertains to harlots or prostitutes.'

Spelled *meretricious*, the word entered English in this sense in the early 17th century, as a direct loan from Latin. It soon acquired an additional significance derived from one connotative extension, 'presenting a false or superficial appearance of beauty or attractiveness,' as a harlot might. This sense is occasionally extended to art criticism. Both meanings represent pejorative developments of the original nonjudgmental sense.

migraine, megrim

As popularly used today, the word *migraine* refers to a severe recurrent headache accompanied by nausea, although specialists in the area still use it in its etymological sense, a headache restricted to half of the head. The word represents a reduction, via Latin and then French transmission, of the Greek term *hēmikrānia*, literally 'half the skull.' Greek *hēmi-* is the cognate of Latin *semi-*; the *krāni-* stem entered English as *cranium*. A phonological doublet of the same word, one more common in British usage, is *megrim*, which first reached English in the 15th century with its original significance. By the following century it had acquired the additional specialized sense of 'vertigo,' since that symptom frequently accompanies the ailment and, by further connotative addition, the sense of 'whim,' apparently because headache is sometimes used as a pretext for avoiding unwanted obligations.

By the 17th century *megrim*, or its plural, *megrims*, had become extended to signify 'despondency' or 'low spirits,' presumably because these accompany headache, possibly also by attraction to *grim*.

mile

The ancient Romans measured long geographical distances by thousands of steps, *milia passuum* in Latin. The phrase was often shortened to *milia*, with the meaning localized in that word. The actual distance, then about 1618 yards, varied according to the time and place as the term passed from Latin, whose speakers still associated the word with the specific numerical measure, to the early Germanic ancestor of English, whose speakers understood no Latin. Thus the original sense faded, becoming a measure of 1760 yards in much of the English-speaking world.

money, mint

The Greek goddess Mnemosyne, a name which means 'remembrance' or 'memory,' was the mother of the Muses. The Romans translated this as *Moneta*, a word based on a cognate Latin stem that retained a semantic similarity to the Greek word; but in the course of time the verb *monere* 'to call to mind' came to mean 'to call to mind with the intent of instruction or admonition.' *Moneta* then seemed more appropriate as a function of Juno, and the Romans added the epithet to Juno as a surname.

Since the Romans coined their money in the temple of *Juno Moneta*, the term came to refer, by transference, to the place where the coins were stamped out and to the money itself. As the word passed down through Late Latin and then through Old French, the *t* disappeared owing to a normal sound change, and the word was borrowed into English in the late 13th century as *money*.

An earlier version of *Moneta*, however, had passed from Latin into the primitive Germanic languages, including the West Germanic ancestor of English. From this, with the phonological development characteristic of that language family, came Old English *mynet* 'coin' and *mynetian* 'to coin money.' It was the etymological doublet *money*, which had descended via Old French, that displaced this variant; but the variant survived to produce modern *mint*. It is uncertain whether the survival was through direct Old English transmission by way of still another variation in a related Germanic dialect, but in any case a loan translation of the same name split in both form and meaning to produce two totally different words.

muscle

The Latin *musculus*, from which *muscle* derives, meant 'little mouse,' so called from the fancied resemblance of some *muscles* rippling under the skin to the movement of such a little animal. For the

Modern English speaker the original visual signification has disappeared completely, although *mus*, the Old English word for 'mouse,' and the Latin *mus* 'mouse' were once identical.

mustard

This word actually descends from an extension of the stem of the Latin word *mustum*, which referred to the 'new or fresh wine' that was mixed with ground *mustard seed* to produce the paste we know as *mustard*. In time vinegar 'sharp wine' replaced *must* as the more common moistening and flavoring agent, but the name remained.

The Latin word for the *mustard* itself was *sināpsis*, ultimately of Egyptian origin, via Greek. This reached Old English as *senep*, but this form did not survive beyond the early Middle Ages. It was replaced in the 13th century by *mustard*, the word used by the French-speaking nobility.

N

nausea

The same stem, *naut-*, which produced *naútēs*, the ancient Greek word for 'seaman' or 'sailor,' also produced *nautia* 'sailor's condition,' or 'seasickness.' This meaning eventually became generalized to mean 'any illness with symptoms resembling seasickness.' In the East Greek dialects the *t* became *s*, a regular change before the *i* which came from an earlier palatal laryngeal sound. Borrowed by Latin as *nausia*, later *nausea*, in both senses, the word entered English in the 16th century with only the generalized meaning. It is interesting to note that while the ancient Greeks considered these symptoms so characteristic of sailors that they named them the 'sailor's condition,' today those who become nauseated from the motion of a ship consider themselves to be not very good sailors.

An additional generalization has shifted the meaning from a physical to a mental sensation, 'disgust,' a sense that coexists with the medical signification. Although this change, recent in English, is not inherited from the Latin transmission, it is attested in the early Greek.

The same Proto-Indo-European root *nau-* without the *-t-* extension descended directly to Latin and produced the words later borrowed by English as *navy* and *naval*.

nemesis

The Proto-Indo-European root **nem/*nom* seems to have meant something on the order of 'apportion, divide,' the primary attested sense of the Greek verb *némein*. The noun associated with this verb, *nómos* 'something apportioned or divided,' and hence, a 'custom or law,' forms the basis for the *-nome* of *metronome*, the *-nomy* of *economy*, and possibly even the *num-* of *numismatics*, all revealing extended senses of the word. The verb root, which appears also in the Modern German verb *nehmen* 'to take,' gave rise to the noun *Nemesis*

129

'goddess of divine retribution,' whence *nemesis* with a small *n*. In the 16th century this meant 'divine justice' and now means 'avenger, insurmountable foe or rival.'

The logic underlying the development of *Nemesis* and *nemesis* from *némein* would seem to have been that to divide or apportion was to do so according to local custom and accepted notions of justice, and that one form of fair apportionment was that involved in the meting out of divine retribution against those who have done evil.

The general noun *nemesis*, which originally had the meaning 'distribution, apportionment,' produced the specialized noun *Nemesis* the 'personification of divine retribution; dispenser of divine retribution.' From this last sense evolved two different meanings for *nemesis*: 'divine retribution,' by what etymologists call "transference," and 'foe with quasi-supernatural powers' by what is called "general extension." The first sense has disappeared, but the second remains current.

nest, nidus

Both of these terms, one Germanic and the other Latin-derived, come ultimately from the Proto-Indo-European **nisdos*, based on **ni*, a root meaning 'down' (the preposition), **sd* (from earlier **sHd*), a reduced form of the word meaning 'to sit,' and *-os*, the case form marking subjects. Thus the word referred to a place used 'to sit down.' *Nidus* is now a technical term in zoology, meaning 'a place where small animals place their eggs,' and in botany, meaning 'the site in which the seeds develop.' The same *ni* appears as the *ne-* of *nether*, as in *nether regions*, and the *-nea-* of *beneath*. The word *sit* itself comes from the other element, and the word *sedentary* rests on the Latin extension of the stem.

Both *nest* and the Latin *nidus* underwent the regular sound changes normal to their respective branches of Indo-European. In the development from **nisdos* to *nest* the *i* became influenced by the following *o* of *-os*, which dropped off after the change, and the *d* became *t*. In the development from **nisdos* to *nidus* the first *s* disappeared because of the following consonant, lengthening the preceding vowel. These changes helped to obscure the individual constituents of the compound, and thus the original denotation "faded."

nice

Since its introduction into English from Old French in the 13th century, *nice* has undergone a series of changes in sense rivaled by few other words in the language. The original source of the term is the Latin *nescius* 'ignorant, stupid,' from the verb *nescire* 'not to know, to be in ignorance,' which passed into Old French and then into English in its original sense.

By the 14th century, *nice* had come to mean 'silly' and, by extension, 'wanton,' a silly woman being assumed to be a wanton one, a person whose favors might be easily obtained. From this meaning evolved the sense, in the 15th century, of 'coy, shy,' possibly because a 'wanton' woman might be 'coy,' while another woman, whose behavior the 'wanton' woman aped or caricatured, might be 'shy.'

By the 16th century, in an extension of the positive 'shy' sense, *nice* had come to mean 'fastidious, subtle,' a sense that remains today in the phrase *a nice distinction*. In the 18th century a *nice* person was an 'agreeable, good' person, whether male or female, the sense of the term today.

A further change, however, is beginning to be visible. *Nice*, like *bad*, is now increasingly used cynically to mean its opposite. A *nice bit of flim-flam* is not necessarily 'nice,' just as a *bad dude* can be a 'good man.'

nickel

Like *cobalt*, this metal owes its name to a German origin. Originally called *Kupfernickel* 'copper-nickel,' the word is a compound whose first part is derived from the island of Cyprus, where copper was once mined. The second part is a German word meaning 'dwarf' or 'scamp' (compare *Old Nick* 'the devil'), referring to the same sort of malicious goblin held to inhabit the mines, and this 'imp,' or *nickel*, is all that remained when the term for the mineral entered English. (See also **cobalt**.)

nicotine

Jean Nicot, French ambassador to Lisbon in the middle of the 16th century, is credited with reporting the discovery of *tobacco* in the New World to France; the French named the plant *herba nicotiana* in his honor.

According to Bartolomeo de las Casas, the term *tobacco* comes from the Carib word for the plant or, possibly, from the word for the pipe in which the leaves were smoked. Although *nicotine* was retained as the name of the plant in the French- and English-speaking world until well into the 17th century, the term *tobacco* was also used, and in the 19th century *nicotine* became specialized to denote 'the active ingredient of *tobacco*,' the sense the word has maintained to the present.

noggin

The ultimate origin of English *noggin* is uncertain, although the best guess has it that the word comes from the Gaelic *noigean* 'wooden cup,' a term of obscure derivation. The word entered English in the 17th century in the sense of 'cup, mug,' and soon became specialized to mean 'cup or mug of liquor.' From this sense, *eggnog* (or plain *nog*) evolved, with the meaning 'alcoholic beverage made with whiskey (and eggs).'

Modern American use of *noggin* to mean 'head,' much as Modern German *Kopf* 'head' was derived from the word for 'cup' and Modern French *tête* 'head' from the Latin *testa* 'earthenware pot,' is probably derived from the early sense of 'cup, mug.' While the French and German words may have acquired their meanings because of the fragility of the original vessel, the American use may come from the sense of 'a container (of spirits).'

noon

The Romans divided the hours of daylight, from sunrise to sunset, into twelve divisions which, of course, were longer in the summer and shorter in winter. Thus, figuring dawn at what we today would call six o'clock, the Roman ninth hour, *nona hora*, would be about three o'clock by today's reckoning. In the early Catholic Church, certain services normally took place at that time, and the phrase shortened to *nona* and then, in Old English, *non*, applied to that time for the prayers. At a later date the Church rescheduled the same observances somewhat earlier, but the use of the term, now *noon*, remained, despite the change in the actual hour. This settled at what would later be called twelve o'clock.

In Middle English a *none shemch* 'noon cup or drink' (*shemch* from Old English *scenc* 'draught, cup') became a *nuncheon* 'beverage,' later 'a refreshing snack' which might include food, taken at around midday. This was later shortened to *nunch.* This word undoubtedly influenced the pronunciation and possibly the meaning of another term whose precise etymology remains speculative, *lunch* (and *luncheon*). Some scholars derive it from *lump* 'mass, piece,' and others from an old variation of the Spanish *lonja* 'slice of ham.'

The more remote meaning of the Latin *nona* 'ninth,' the antecedent of *noon,* is also a matter of uncertainty. It undoubtedly represents an extension of the root seen in *novem,* cognate with the English *nine* and the Greek *énnea;* the month *November,* an extension of this stem, was the ninth month in the Roman republican calendar (later shifted to the eleventh in the Julian calendar). The *nov-* root may be identical with that seen in Latin *novus* 'new,' cognate with English *new* or Greek *néos,* and the meaning may provide a clue to the mode of counting in very early times. Dialectal variants of the word for *eight* have led some analysts to suggest that the Proto-Indo-Europeans originally counted by fours, the number of fingers on one hand not counting the thumb. Thus, the word meaning 'nine' would represent the 'new' unit in the sequence after both hands of four fingers had been counted.

nun

Nana, nanny, and *nun* all come from a Proto-Indo-European children's word for 'an adult woman' other than the mother. In Greek, *nénna* meant 'aunt,' and the corresponding masculine form, *nénnos,* meant 'uncle.' A related form, *nánnos,* meant 'dwarf,' possibly as a generalization of the 'little, (old)' aspect of the meanings associated with 'aunt' and 'uncle.' Latin used *nonna* and *nonnus* as informal terms for 'aunt, adult woman,' and 'uncle, adult man.'

Like the more standard kinship terms designating members of the immediate family, *nonna* and *nonnus* were used by the early Christians in a quasi-familial sense. *Nonna* (whence *nun*) designated 'a female member of a religious community who has not received the sacrament of ordination,' and *nonnus* designated a man in the same condition. Today we would more commonly refer to the unordained members of a religious order as 'sisters' and 'brothers.'

Later, *nonnus* was upgraded to refer to 'a senior member of the religious order,' and could even be applied to the Pope; but eventually the term disappeared from use in the religious community. It continues in use in Modern Italian with the meaning 'grandfather.' *Nonna*, on the other hand, remained current, passing into English as *nunne* in the Middle Ages with the sense of 'a woman who has taken religious vows,' the essential meaning of *nun* today.

O

orang-utan, orang-utang, orang-outang

The Malay *ōrang-ūtan* literally means 'man of the forest,' from *ōrang* 'man' and *(h)ūtan* 'forest, jungle.' The specific reference was to 'a wild man, a forest-dwelling human.' The term is first recorded in Dutch by one Bontius, a physician stationed in the Dutch East Indies in the first half of the 17th century. He applied the term to the nonhuman jungle-dweller to which we now apply it, and the word passed into English and the other languages of Europe shortly thereafter.

Whether Bontius had misunderstood or misapplied the term himself, or was simply aping the Javanese, who apparently used the word to designate the animal, is not clear, although he did gloss the word 'man of the forest' in his account of life in the East Indies which appeared, in Latin, in 1631. Whatever he intended, his description was sufficiently ambiguous for Tyson to class the *orang-utan* more nearly with humans than with apes or monkeys in his work, *Orang-Outang, sive Homo Sylvestris, or the Anatomy of a Pygmie, Compared with that of a Monkey, an Ape, and a Man*, which appeared in 1699.

ostracism

In ancient Athens, any citizen could be banished for a period of five or ten years by a vote of his fellow-citizens. These votes were recorded on fragments of earthen vessels, or shells, *óstrakon* in Greek. According to Plutarch, himself a Greek, this practice, *ostrakismós*, was intended as a nonviolent means for dissipating envy or hostility toward those who had become too powerful or too popular. It fell into disuse when it began to be used against individuals of no public stature or importance.

When the word first entered English toward the later part of the 16th century, it referred to the Greek practice, but before the end of the century it had become generalized, first to 'banishment,' regardless of how the decision was arrived at, and subsequently to 'exclusion from approval,' without physical removal of the *ostracized* individual.

P

pagan, peasant

The Latin word *pāgus* seems originally to have designated a 'boundary,' that is, 'staked out, marked by stakes.' Later it came to be used in the generalized sense of 'district, province,' and, still later, 'countryside.' A *pāgānus* was, then, a 'countryman,' both in the sense of a 'person under Roman jurisdiction' and a 'person who lives in the countryside; a rustic.' *Pagan* and *peasant*, both from *pāgānus*, reflect different extensions of these two meanings.

Pagan entered English in the 14th century as a learned borrowing from Latin, where the term had acquired the specialized sense of 'non-Christian, heathen,' as a result of the early Christian use of *pāgānus* to mean 'citizen, person under Roman jurisdiction' as opposed to 'Soldier of Christ, person under the jurisdiction of Christ.' This usage may be compared to the use of *gentile* (from Latin *gens* 'clan, i.e., Roman clan') by the Jews to designate a 'nonbeliever.'

Peasant, on the other hand, entered English from Old French with the sense of 'person who lives in the countryside, person who works the land.'

Neither word has changed much in its sense from the time of its borrowing into English. A *pagan* is still a 'nonbeliever,' though no longer specifically a 'non-Christian,' and a *peasant* is still a 'person who works the land for a living.'

pain

The Proto-Indo-European stem *$k^{w}oin$*- 'cost, price, that which is given as recompense,' the ultimate ancestor of the English word *pain*, took three major lines of semantic development in the languages to and through which it descended. These may be considered a neutral continuation of the original sense, exemplified by the Old Church Slavic *cĕna* 'price,' and two major lines of specialization from that meaning. One, a positive sense, led to such meanings as 'reward,' or even 'honor' (that which is given for something which is appreciated); another, negative, sense led to such meanings as 'fine, penalty,' or even 'vengeance,' as in the Avestan *kaênâ*.

The path leading to the English derivatives starts with the Greek, in which the sound k^w- became p when followed by an o. The word *poinḗ* in Greek demonstrated all three semantic lines, positive, negative, and neutral, but as a legal term it signified 'blood money' or 'were-gild,' the fine paid as compensation by a slayer to the kinsmen of the victim. Sometimes it shaded off to the simple sense 'penalty.' Personified, the word became the name of the goddess of vengeance.

The Romans borrowed the Greek word as *poena*, but only in the negative senses, including the name of the goddess. Since penalties commonly took physical forms, the Latin word acquired an additional meaning, 'torment, suffering, pain.' This probably came about first through the connotation, and only later did that sense become the primary focus of the meaning.

Descending through Old French, the word entered English at the end of the 12th century in what is now a nearly obsolete meaning, 'penalty or fine levied for commission of a crime.' This sense is still preserved in the legal phrase "*pains* and penalties."

By the 14th century the signification of suffering appeared in English, first with reference to the pangs experienced in hell, and later in the general sense of physical or mental anguish experienced anywhere. The start of the same century also showed an occasional weakening to the sense of 'trouble' or 'effort,' as in the phrase "to take *pains*."

Such words as *punish* and *punishment* also derive from the early Latin *poen-* stem. The normal development of *oe* was to *u* in Latin, except for a small group of words, including *poena*, that were used in legal and religious formulas. Since the Romans laid great stress on precise adherence to early rituals and traditions, these words retained what later was to become an archaic pronunciation. It is this aberrant sound development that led to the modern English word *pain*.

A variant of the same Proto-Indo-European root, $*k^wi$- (an unaccented variant of $*k^woi$-), extended by a different suffix, also entered English, but was so transformed by the regular Greek sound change as well as by a divergent semantic development that the relationship usually passes unnoticed. Although k^w- became p- in Greek when followed by a back vowel like o, it became t- when followed by a front vowel like i. Thus the Greek word *tīmē*, meaning both 'honor' and 'value,' comes from the same source. Plato wrote of *tīmokratia* 'rule by those who value honor.' Aristotle used the same word, but chose the 'value' sense for the first element, using the term to mean 'rule by those with a certain amount of wealth,' that is, those who have sufficient property to qualify for the right to vote or govern. This word entered English as *timocracy*, with the Aristotelian sense, at the end of the 16th century. It entered again, with the Platonic sense, about seventy years later, but only philosophers take the *pains* necessary to differentiate the uses.

pajamas, pyjamas

English travelers in India at the end of the 18th or beginning of the 19th century became familiar with a type of loose trousers made of a light material, usually cotton or silk, well adapted to the climate, and fastened with a string. They brought this garment home as a useful and comfortable item of nightwear, adding a jacket in the colder temperatures of England, but keeping the name *pajama*. This became pluralized to *pajamas* on the model of such words as *breeches* or *trousers*.

The practice of wearing only *pajama* tops is etymologically paradoxical, since the Hindi word is borrowed from a Persian form compounded from *pai* 'foot' (a word element exactly cognate with the English 'foot') and *jamah* 'garment, clothing.'

palace

According to legend, Romulus founded the ancient city of Rome on the seven hills that rise above the Tiber around 753 B.C. The most readily defensible hill, and the first, therefore, to be fortified, was that known as *Palātium*, or *Mōns Palātīnus*. An oblique case form of *mōns* 'hill' is the source of the English word *mount*, and the English *palace* is descended, via French, from *Palātium*. Lexicographers disagree on the etymology of the term, some scholars deriving it from an extension of the stem seen in the Latin *pālus* 'stake' or 'pole.' According to this line of reasoning, the poles driven into the ground to form a defensive *palisade* around the original settlement provided the basis for the name. Other scholars derive *Palātium* from *Pales*, the name of the ancient Roman deity sacred to shepherds and cattle.

In time, the hill itself became the home of many of the more important Roman families; Caius Octavius, in particular, later to become Augustus, the first Roman emperor, in 27 B.C., had his residence there. He reportedly boasted that he "had found Rome brick and left it marble." The imperial domicile eventually expanded to cover most of the hill, and became the official residence of the later emperors. The name of the hill became transferred to the edifices resting on it, and came to signify the 'residence of a ruler.' Still later, it became extended to cover royal dwelling places other than the one set on the Roman mount.

Connotative extension specialized the meaning to 'mansion or building of great splendor inhabited by a ruler,' but later generalization allowed the 'ruler' aspect of the meaning to fall away, so that today any well-appointed dwelling may be referred to as a *palace*.

pandemonium

In Milton's *Paradise Lost*, *Pandaemonium* is the 'capital of Hell.' The word, apparently coined by the poet, is a compound of Greek *pân* 'all, whole,' *daimōn*, originally 'god' but in New Testament Greek 'evil spirit, devil,' and the Latin suffix *-ium*, which generally designates an 'area, place' in which that which is specified by the rest of the word is gathered together. Thus, *Pandaemonium* was 'the place in which all evil spirits are gathered together,' or 'Hell.'

By the 18th century, less than a hundred years after *Paradise Lost* first appeared in print, *pandemonium* had come to be used to designate any 'place in which evildoers are gathered' and, more specifically, any 'place characterized by lawless violence or uproar.' Since then, the term has lost its associations with hell and lawlessness, although the sense of 'uncontrolled uproar' is still present. Today, it may refer either to a 'place characterized by uncontrolled uproarious behavior' or, by extension, to 'uncontrolled uproarious behavior; general noise and confusion.'

pander

Pandarus, Pandare, or *Pandaro* was the name of the go-between in the ill-starred romance of Troilus and Cressida made famous by Boccaccio, Chaucer, and Shakespeare. In the Chaucerian version of the tale, *Pandare* was Creseyde's cousin and a friend of Troilus, who worked successfully to get the two lovers together. Later, when Troilus and Creseyde are separated in an exchange of prisoners during the Trojan War, *Pandare* acts as go-between for the lonely Creseyde and her new love, Diomede. As a result of the popularity of Chaucer's poem, a *pandar* or *pander* came to be used to mean a 'go-between in affairs of the heart.'

With the appearance of Shakespeare's *Troilus and Cressida* in the early part of the 17th century, however, the meaning of the word began to take on rather more sinister connotations. In Shakespeare's version, *Pandarus* is Cressida's uncle, and a not very sympathetic character. As a consequence, *pander* came to designate a 'person who caters to another's baser, usually sexual, lusts,' or a 'pimp, procurer.'

In the course of the 17th century *pandar* became *pander*, partly on phonetic grounds and partly by the influence of the agent suffix *-er*. Another change that took place at that time was the use of *pander* as a verb, with the sense of to 'cater to the baser lusts.' This use then gave rise to a new noun form, *panderer*, which is now displacing the older *pander*.

pane

In Latin, *pannus* was a 'piece of cloth; a rag,' and it was in this sense that the word entered English from Old French in the 13th century, appearing as such as a constituent of Modern English *counterpane*. In isolation, however, *pane* soon came to have two distinct senses, both still in current use.

In the 14th century, the term was generalized to mean any '(flat) section or side of something,' as the *pane of a quadrangle,* the *pane of a stone* or *timber,* or the *pane of a nut* or *bolt.* By the 15th century, *pane* also came to designate a 'section of window glass.' This specialization probably came about through the practice of covering windows with pieces of cloth in the days before glaziers were able to produce pieces of glass large enough to fill a window. On the other hand, it may have simply been a specialization of the general sense, a '(flat) section or side of something.' (See also **panel**.)

panel

This word came into English in the 13th century from Old French, which had inherited it from the Latin *panellus*, a diminutive of *pannus* 'piece of cloth, rag' (see also **pane**), and meant a 'little piece of cloth.' In Old French, as in 13th-century English, the term was applied specifically to the 'piece of cloth placed under a horse's saddle, a horse blanket.' By the following century, *panel* had also come to mean 'saddle (made of a rough pad of cloth).'

At about the same time, the term acquired another meaning 'piece of paper or parchment attached to a legal writ and containing the names of prospective jurors.' This may have been because the slip of paper with the names on it was considered to stand in the same relation to the writ to which it was attached as the horse blanket did to the saddle that was placed over it. It is from this metaphorical use of *panel* that the modern sense of the word as a 'collection of (appointed or selected) people' is derived. The meaning has been transferred from 'list of names' to 'people (named on a list).' Thus, from the 16th century onward, a *panel* might be a 'group of jurors' or some other such group, as the members of a *panel discussion*.

In the 17th century, *panel* took on still another meaning, influenced, in part, by the already existing *pane* '(flat) section or side of something.' The new sense was a 'thin board within a frame,' as the *panel of a door* or a *paneled wall*. This architectural usage gave rise to a succession of artistic associations. In the 18th century, a *panel* could be a 'thin board on which a picture or part of a picture was painted'; in the 19th century, a 'large photographic print'; and in the 20th century, a 'frame of a cartoon.' Further, generalizing from the 'thin board' meaning, *panel* has also come to be used to designate a 'switchboard containing the control switches for an electrical or electronic device.' Virtually the only one of the many historic meanings not in current use is that of 'horse blanket.'

panic

The Greek god *Pan*, part man and part goat, was a rural deity who frolicked in the woods with nymphs and played on the syrinx, or pan-pipes. He had another side, however, and both Plutarch and Polyaenus document his propensity for terrifying night-travelers. The fear he inspired, a sudden terror without visible or reasonable cause, was called in Greek *deîma pānikón* 'Panish fear.' Thus, *panic* was originally an adjective meaning 'of or pertaining to Pan,' and it was in this sense that it was borrowed from French into English in the 17th century. In the course of the 18th century the term became localized in such expressions as *panic terrors* and *panic fears*, and came to be used as a noun in the sense of 'fear, terror; especially, sudden fear or alarm,' the meanings it carries today.

pants

In the improvised street dramas of the 16th century known as the commedia dell'arte, *Pantalone* was a stock character, the silly, avari-cious old man ever in danger of being cheated or cuckolded, and, like the other stock characters of the commedia dell'arte, he was always associated with a particular costume. This included a mask with a hooked nose, a black cape, a dagger and purse (strongly suggestive of the genitalia), and a pair of tight trousers. It is from these trousers that the noun *pants* is derived.

Toward the end of the 16th century, *Pantalone*, or *Pantaloon*, entered English, and by the next century had given his name to the tight trousers then in fashion. Subsequently, *pantaloons* became short-ened to *pants*, although this term was largely displaced in England by *trousers*, a word derived from Gaelic *triubhas* 'riding chaps.' In the United States, however, *pants* remained the common term for 'trou-sers.' The term was later slightly modified, to *panties*, to designate female 'underpants.' In the clothing trade, one encounters *pant*, a back formation from *pants*, used to denote a single pair of trousers.

parasite

The ancient Greek word *parásitos*, from which the English *parasite* derives, once signified merely 'one who sits near the food,' from *para-* 'near' or 'beside' and *sit-* 'food' or 'grain.' The original sense of the form still survives in various scientific terms in English, such as *sitol-*

ogy the 'study of food or nutrition,' *sitomania* 'passion for food,' and *sitosterol* a 'type of alcohol derived from grain.' In its early Greek use *parásitos* had favorable, rather than negative connotations, for it frequently designated those fed at public expense, usually priests, government officials, heroes who had rendered exceptional service, and the children of soldiers who had perished in battle. It was also applied to citizens whom the priests invited to share in the feasting after religious sacrifices, a signal honor.

By the 4th century B.C., however, abuses of the custom caused the word to start acquiring the pejorative sense it still has. It shifted from 'one who feeds at another's expense' to the further specialization of 'toady, one who justifies his dependent consumption by (often insincere) flattery or some other means of ingratiating himself.'

The Romans borrowed the word both in its neutral sense, roughly equivalent to 'table companion,' and in the negative meaning. By the time *parasite* reached English in the 16th century via French, it was in the negative meaning, one of the two main significations it retains today. Classical scholars of the 17th to 19th centuries occasionally reverted to the honorific use of the term, but that sense never received general acceptance in English.

In the 18th century the process linguists call "generalization" allowed the word to apply to a nonhuman organism that has a dependent relationship with another organism.

pariah

The Tamil word *parai* refers to a type of large drum used in India, and the *Paraiyar*, literally 'drummers,' are members of the Dravidian group who played the drums at certain festivals. Of non-Indo-European origin, these people had customs and traditions that violated the Hindu precepts of purity that determine, to a great extent, placement in the caste system of India. Many, for example, worked as domestics for Europeans, and thus handled forbidden foods or laundry and performed other duties regarded as polluting. Some worked as shoemakers and in other forbidden occupations. Thus they ranked very low in the caste hierarchy, which determined a whole range of marital, social, and economic opportunities and obligations. They were not, strictly speaking, outcaste, but they ranked so low in caste that even the lowest class of Brahmans had to shun them as ritually unclean.

When the English first encountered Indic culture they did not fully grasp the nuances or implications of the caste system, but they could see the strict avoidance the Brahmans observed with regard to the *Paraiyar*. They thus drew their own conclusions, which did not differentiate between relatively low caste in a very elaborate and complicated hierarchy of positions and the true outcaste, a person outside the caste system. Some Brahmans extended the term *Paraiyar* as a general term for people of low caste status, but never applied it to those with no caste status.

Not all Hindus had to shun contact with the *Paraiyar*, but when the word *pariah* (spelled variously *Pareah, Piriawe, Bareier*, etc.) entered English in the early 17th century, it denoted 'someone to be shunned or avoided, a social outcast.' To most English speakers the connection with the Dravidian ethnic group and the meaning of its name remained unknown, a clear instance of semantic fading and generalization.

parlor

This turn-of-the-century term comes through Old French from the Late Latin word *parabolāre* 'to talk,' from the Greek *parabolē* a 'placing side by side; a comparison,' from which came the sense of a 'conversation; talking.' In 13th-century England, a *parlor* was a 'room set aside for talking,' later, a 'room in which to receive guests,' with a sense of conviviality and conversation understood.

As men and women assumed different household roles, the *parlor* became the preserve of the men, while women could withdraw from male company to the "(with)drawing room." In the 19th century, both men and women carried on social intercourse in the *parlor*.

Today, the term is commonly seen only in such phrases as *beauty parlor* or *ice cream parlor*, because the *parlor* at home has become the 'living room.'

pavilion

The Latin word *papiliō*, *papiliōnis* means a 'butterfly,' and the Old French form of the term was used in the Middle Ages in an extended sense to designate a 'tent without walls,' an area covered by a piece of cloth that flapped in the breeze like the wings of a butterfly. During the 12th and 13th centuries the word, in the sense of 'butterflylike tent' was borrowed from French into English, and it and its meanings have since undergone a number of changes. From 'canopy covering a military installation,' by the 17th century *pavilion* had come to designate a 'covered area for recreation,' often, but not always, with a canvas or cloth roof. Today, the temporary cover resembling a butterfly's wings has become a permanent structure.

peach

According to the Greek historian Herodotus, the Greeks derived *Persai*, the name of a group of Middle Eastern people, from *Perseus*, the legendary son of Zeus and Danaë, who rescued Andromeda from the dragon and slew the Medusa. It is not at all certain that this early etymology was correct, but there is no doubt that in Greek the adjective that described anything pertaining to these people or their country, later called *Persia* by the Romans, was *persikós*. One of the fruits indigenous to the region they called *persikòn mâlon*. *Mâlon* or *mêlon* (the Attic-Ionic form that gave the English *melon*) usually meant 'apple,' but sometimes referred to 'any fruit growing on trees.' The Romans borrowed this phrase as *persicum mālum*, and both Greek and Latin often shortened the phrase by dropping *mâlon* or *mālum* and localizing the entire meaning in the portion which had originally simply signified 'Persian.' This ellipsis became permanent by Late Latin.

The subsequent phonological and grammatical history of the word as it passed through later Latin into Old French includes a change of declension from *-um* (neuter) to *-a* (feminine), yielding *persica*; the loss of the inflectional ending itself, an assimilation of the *r* to *s*, and the loss of the *i*, giving first *persic*, then *pessic*, and then *pesc*; in the 13th century another *s* was lost, giving *pec*, and finally the *c* shifted to *ch*, to yield *pech(e)*. The area of the transmission can be identified as the southern part of France, since the northern dialect kept the *c*. By the late 14th century, when the word entered English, the geographical significance had long since faded as had the possible connection with the hero *Perseus*.

With the meaning centered on the fruit, connotations associated with the *peach* led to the semantic specialization 'the color of a *peach*,' or 'reddish yellow'; 'the aesthetic quality of a *peach*,' or 'good, desirable, providing pleasure, like a *peach*'; and, with generalization, simply 'good, desirable'—*peachy*—with the common adjectival suffix.

pedigree

To the clerks of the Middle Ages and early Renaissance, the curved three-line marks used by genealogists to signify lineage looked like bird tracks, and so they called them *pié* (or *pied*) *de grue*, literally 'crane's foot.' Various forms of this phrase, run together as *pedegrue*, *pedegrewe*, and *pedigrue*, among others, appear in English in the early 15th century. The French *pied*, which descends from the Latin *pedem*, the accusative case of *pēs* 'foot,' is a cognate of the English word *foot*. The Latin form of the root entered English in *pedestrian* 'one who goes on foot,' and a Greek cognate in *podiatrist* 'foot doctor.' The French *grue*, from Latin *gruem*, the accusative of *grus*, is an actual cognate of the English word *crane*.

Although knowledge of French was the norm among the English nobility from the Norman Conquest, 1066, until the middle of the 13th century, it became increasingly less general during the succeeding centuries. Consequently, many English speakers, not recognizing the three constituents of the word, mistook *degrue* for *degree* 'rank,' since a common purpose in tracing one's ancestry was to establish social position. Thus a partial phonological resemblance, correlating with a connotative association, reshaped the form of the word. The meaning, now changed, transferred from the form written on the page to what those written lines represented.

The word *degree* itself descends from the same Latin *de* (in its sense of 'down') that appears in *pié de grue*, plus some form of the Latin *gradus* 'step.' The phrase 'step down,' used of stairs or ladders, applies as well to one's position on the social ladder, or one's rank.

pen

The Latin word *penna* 'feather' descended via a different route from the same source as *feather*. The primary meaning remained side by side with later specializations from the 14th to the 19th century; in *Piers Ploughman* Langland refers to the "pennes of ye pecok."

The use of feathers sharpened at the end and slit to make nibs for applying ink caused the meaning to specialize, with a shift to the meaning 'writing implement.' "Subreption," the semanticist's term for the continued use of the same signifier even after the thing signified has changed, took place when materials other than feathers began to be used to apply ink. This significance continued through the use of *fountain pens* and *ball-point pens*, and now the meaning of those phrases has localized in the second element, so that we refer indiscriminately to both as *pens*.

person

The Latin word for 'mask' was *persōna*, which etymologists once analyzed as *per-* 'through' and *sōn-* 'sound,' or 'something through which sounds are projected.' This interpretation has been challenged on phonological grounds, some scholars maintaining that since the *o* of *persōna* is long, and not short, as might be expected if it were related to the Latin word for 'sound,' there must be another source for the term. It has been suggested by another group that the word represents a borrowing of some form of the ancient Etruscan word for 'mask' *phersu*.

Regardless of the source, the Latin *persōna* shifted its meaning from 'mask' to 'person wearing the mask,' another example of the familiar semantic process known as "transference." Later it generalized to mean 'the rôle one plays in the world.' It was in this sense that the word, shortened to *person*, finally reached English, via French, in the 13th century. Further generalization reduced its meaning to 'individual' or 'human being.'

It is in this sense that feminists urge substituting *-person* for the sexist "man" in such compounds as *chairperson, salesperson*, etc. Ironically, however, the Latin *persōna* was a feminine noun, and thus, it might be argued, the substitution is hardly nonsexist. (See also man.)

persuade

The English word *persuade* 'to induce the acceptance of a belief or position,' derives either directly or indirectly, via French, from the Latin *persuādēre*, which had much the same meaning. The word rests, however, on the intensive prefix *per-*, meaning 'very, or completely,' plus *-suād-*, a stem whose original meaning was 'sweet.' *Per-* is cognate with the English *fore-*, as, for example, in *forlorn* 'completely lost.' (See **forlorn hope**.) The word element *-suād-* is the exact cognate of the English word *sweet*, as well as of the *hēd-* of Greek *hēdús* 'sweet,' which entered English in *hedonist* 'one who lives for pleasure,' or, literally, 'one who likes everything sweet.' Thus *persuade*, or its Proto-Indo-European ancestor, probably meant 'to convince by making things very sweet.'

pester

This word is a shortened form of the Old French term *empestrer* 'to tether (an animal),' from an unattested Late Latin verb, **impastōriāre*, with essentially the same meaning. The Latin verb is formed from *in* 'in,' *pastōri(um)* 'of or belonging to a shepherd; a pasture,' and the productive verbal ending *-āre*. Thus it meant 'to fix animals with a device to restrain their movement when put out to pasture.'

The sense of the term as it entered English in the Middle Ages seems to have been a more general one, 'encumber,' not necessarily restricted to beasts of the field. Apparently a person could be *pestered*, as well as a cow or a sheep. The same holds true today, although the meaning of the word has changed somewhat over the years, coming to mean 'annoy, vex, plague.'

This more recent sense was influenced by the Latin *pestis* (French *peste*) 'plague, pestilence,' which entered English in the 16th century with that meaning. As the scourge of the Black Death abated, *pest* came to mean 'nuisance,' rather than anything stronger, and, in that weakened sense, affected the meaning of the phonetically similar *pester*.

phlegmatic

In ancient Greek, the stem *phleg-* meant 'burn' and, although there is a minor phonological puzzle regarding the vowel, is probably related to the Latin *flagrāre* 'to burn, blaze,' whose present participle lies behind the English loan word *flagrant*. This originally meant 'burning,' but later became 'shining forth,' and from this came to mean 'evoking notice,' 'glaring.' Oddly enough, a variant of the same Proto-Indo-European stem from which *phleg-* and *flag-* both derive also gave, via Germanic, the English word *black*, by following the semantic path 'burnt,' to 'burnt color,' to the specialization of its meaning to a 'particular burnt color.' An extension of the Greek stem yielded *phlégma*, *phlégmates* 'heat,' 'inflammation,' because the Greeks believed that heat caused *phlegm* or *mucus*, and the word became specialized in that meaning as well as in its basic sense. It is this deviation that gave rise to the word *phlegmatikós* 'pertaining to—or, later, abounding in—*phlegm*.' *Phlegm* was the name of one of the four basic humors, or fluids, of the body, according to the ancient physicians, and an excess of *phlegm* was believed to produce a calm, unexcitable temperament.

The word entered English in the 14th century as *phlegmatic*, together with other words relating to the theory of humors: *sanguine* (which see), *choler*, and *melancholy* (which see). As humors went out of fashion, the semantic focus of the word centered on the characteristic once believed to be a product of that humor, and a *phlegmatic* person is merely an unexcitable one.

picayune

In one of the southern dialects of French, a *picaillon*, or *picaioun* in Provencal, was 'a small copper coin of relatively little value.' The origins of the name of this coin are obscure. Some have suggested that *picaillon* is derived from a Proto-Romance word meaning 'small,' as attested in Italian *piccolo*, Spanish *pequeño*, and possibly French *petit*, to which the pejorative suffix *-ō*, *-ōnis* was added. Another hypothesis holds that the word comes from Latin *pecūnia* 'wealth,' which itself comes from *pecus* 'cattle,' and from which English *pecuniary* and *impecunious* are derived; but both etymologies are problematic.

Whatever its ultimate source, the word was transported to the New World and, in the French and Spanish territories of the southeastern United States, named a coin worth approximately half of a Spanish *real*. Its sense was extended to cover any 'small object of little value,' and, by the 19th century, a functional shift had taken place, resulting in the use of *picayune* as an adjective meaning 'paltry, petty,' with no monetary associations.

pickaninny

This term, which is now used pejoratively to designate a 'black child,' had its origins in the Portuguese and Spanish slave trade of the 17th century. Small West African children who were brought to the New World on Portuguese and Spanish slave ships were called, in Portuguese, *pequeninos*, and, in Spanish, *pequeñiños*, the two cognate terms being combinations of the word for 'small, little,' Portuguese *pequeno*, Spanish *pequeño*, plus a diminutive suffix, Portuguese *-ino*, Spanish *-iño*. Thus, a *pequenino*, or *pequeñiño*, was a 'little, little one.'

The term was adopted by the slaves as a word for 'child,' and was then passed on, in the specialized sense of 'black (slave) child,' to their white, English-speaking owners. Today, it has decidedly condescending, racist overtones, its generally neutral Iberian linguistic origin having been largely forgotten.

pilgrim

The Latin word *peregrīnus*, the ultimate ancestor of *pilgrim*, meant 'foreigner' or 'stranger.' By the classical period, the term had acquired a very technical legal sense for the Romans, involving property, voting, marital, commercial, and inheritance rights. It did not mean, simply, 'wanderer,' although it clearly derived from *per-* 'through,' *agr-* 'field' or 'territory' (cognate with the English *acre*), and *-in-* 'pertaining to,' thus 'pertaining to one who travels through fields or territories.' The *praetor peregrīnus*, for example, was the Roman magistrate who dealt with disputes or other problems involving foreigners residing in or passing through the home city. There was, however, a post-classical word, *pereger*, which signified 'one who is on a trip abroad or a journey away from home.' The Latin form from which English got *peregrination* 'wandering' shows this more generalized sense.

Peregrīnus, however, had a sharp legalistic ingroup-outgroup dichotomy lacking in the other two etymologically related terms. Its reversion to the meaning 'wanderer' probably started at about A.D. 212, when Emperor Caracalla granted Roman citizenship to most, if not all, inhabitants of the empire and thus obliterated the legal distinction between *peregrīnus*, on the one hand, and *cīvis* 'citizen' and *Latīnus* 'Latin,' on the other.

In its evolution to the Romance languages, the first of two consecutive *r*'s dissimilated to *l*, changing *peregrīnus* to *pelegrīnus*. (This change is not seen in *peregrination*, since that word entered English directly from Latin, rather than through French transmission.) The word first appeared in English around 1200 in the sense of 'traveler, wanderer,' but within decades the meaning became specialized to 'one who travels to a religious shrine or holy place,' probably because in the Middle Ages, when travel was difficult and dangerous, few undertook long journeys unless motivated by a wish to acquire heavenly credit to secure future joys or mitigate future punishments in the afterlife.

When the Puritans established their colony at Plymouth, Massachusetts, they too regarded themselves as travelers for religious purposes, although what they sought was the freedom to worship as they pleased rather than to pay devotion to religious relics. In 1630, accordingly, Governor Bradford referred to them as *pilgrims*, an epithet frequently repeated thereafter.

By the middle of the 19th century the distinction between the Puritans and other early settlers, many of whom came for economic rather than religious reasons, was often ignored, and they were all lumped together as founding fathers of the nation. Thus *Pilgrim*, now capitalized, was specialized to signify 'early settler' and generalized by dropping the religious signification altogether. Careful users of the language, however, still restrict the word *Pilgrim* to the Massachusetts settlers.

placebo

Placēbō is the first person singular future form of the Latin verb *placēre* 'to please, satisfy,' which is derived from the Proto-Indo-European root **pleΛk-* 'lie flat.' Germanic forms of this root appear in Modern English *flake* and *flag* (as in *flagstone*), while the Latin and Latinate forms have given *please*, *pleasant*, *plea*, and *placid*, as well as *Placebo/placebo*.

Placebo has two basic and quite distinct senses in English. The first, and earlier, which appeared in the 13th century, is a liturgical one, and refers to the 'vespers for the dead' in the Roman Catholic, Anglican, and Episcopalian services, where *Placēbō* is the first word of the antiphon of the first psalm of the Office for that ceremony: *Placēbō Dominō in rēgiōne vīvōrum* 'I will please the Lord in the land of the living.' Although the Christian service has for some time been held in the vernacular in English-speaking countries, its major sections are still referred to by the Latin words with which they begin: the *Te Deum, Laudamus, Benedictus,* and *Placebo.*

The second, and later, meaning of *placebo* has its origins in the 14th century when the word was still felt to have something to do with 'pleasing.' At that time, it was used in both English and French, to mean 'sycophant, flatterer,' a 'person who seeks to please.' This meaning, however, had all but disappeared by the late 17th century when it acquired a new use in English among members of the medical profession, most of whom were versed, to some extent, in Latin. Among the doctors, a *placebo* was a 'medicinal potion or pill with no intrinsic healing properties, given to patients to make them feel better,' or 'something to please, and perhaps thereby to cure, a patient.' This use is still current.

By extension, the term has come to designate any 'empty curative foisted upon the layman in the expectation that he or she will be pleased by it or take it for the genuine article.' Thus, politicians as well as doctors now offer *placebos* to the unsuspecting public, in hopes that everyone will think all is well and not ask too many questions.

plagiarism, plagium

Slavery was such a well-established and lucrative institution in ancient Rome, where captured enemy prisoners, debtors, and lawbreakers were all subjected to servitude, that in the first or second century B.C. it became necessary to pass the *Lex Fabia*, a statute designed to prevent the kidnapping of freemen and treating them as slaves. (See **serf.**) Additional enactments in succeeding centuries attest to the difficulty of curbing this crime, which was known as *plagium*, from the use of the *plaga* or 'hunting net' that might be used to capture the victims. The term *plagium* entered English in the 16th century, and continues in use as a technical term of civil law in its original sense of 'kidnapping.'

As long ago as the year A.D. 80 the Roman poet and epigrammist, Martial, employed the agent form *plagiarius* 'kidnapper' to describe 'one who steals or pretends to be the author of someone else's book.' Ben Jonson anglicized this word as *plagiary* in 1601, and two decades later the form was extended by adding *-ism*, creating the modern term for the 'appropriation of another's work or ideas as one's own.'

planet

In Greek, *plánēs*, from **plánēt-s*, meant a 'wanderer,' or 'vagabond,' and the phrase *plánētes astéres* meant 'wandering stars.' It was applied to those heavenly bodies whose evident motion contrasted with the relative immobility of the fixed stars. As frequently occurs, the meaning of the phrase as a whole became localized in its first element, and the word for 'star' was dropped. The shift to the meaning 'nonluminous body which revolves around and receives its light from a star' arose later, as astronomical science became more sophisticated.

When the word first entered English in the 11th century, first via Latin and then French, it carried the Ptolemaic concept of motion imparted by virtue of the fixation of the body in a sphere that rotated around the earth.

Plankton the 'drifting organic life of the ocean (and sometimes of fresh water)' represents a different extension of the same Greek stem, one which reached English in the 19th century via German.

poodle

The old vaudeville routine, "It's raining cats and dogs!" —"I know, I stepped in a poodle," is actually based on a real semantic relationship between *poodle* and *puddle*. *Poodle* is a 19th-century loan word for the German *Pudel*, itself a shortening of *Pudelhund* 'splash dog.' The corresponding German verb *puddel* still means 'to splash' or 'to paddle' in dialectal use, although in standard German the word has specialized as a metallurgical term, just as *lead puddling* has in English.

profanity

The Latin word *fānum* 'temple' or 'sanctuary' represents a specialization of the Proto-Indo-European root meaning 'speak' from the words or prayers uttered in the consecration of the site. (See also **fanatic**.) Expanded by the prefix *pro-* 'in front of, before,' this stem gave *profānus* 'in front of the temple.' By contrast with *fānum*, this came to mean 'not holy,' a connotative extension of the associations commonly assigned to religious sites. The initial expansion of meaning was probably a neutral one, signifying merely absence of sacred qualities, but eventually it intensified to mean 'wicked' or 'impious.'

A Late Latin addition to the stem gave *profānitās* 'state or quality of wickedness,' and its accusative case form, *profānitātem*, developed, via French, to the English *profanity*, borrowed with roughly the same meaning in the 16th century. Awareness of the earlier meaning of the *fān-* 'temple' word-element probably continued as long as *fānum* or its descendant persisted as a separate term, but faded either in Old French or during the passage of the word into English.

It is only in comparatively recent times that the word has started to restrict its meaning to 'wicked or blasphemous language,' a narrowing, or specialization, that almost brings it back full circle to the earliest meaning of the root. Incidentally, the *-phe-* of *blasphemous* represents the Greek development of the same Proto-Indo-European root.

prowess, proud, prude

All three of these words, with their varying degrees of positive connotations, come ultimately from the Latin verb *prōdesse* 'to be useful, advantageous, beneficial,' itself a compound from *prō* 'for' and *esse* 'to be.'

Prowess 'superiority in battle, superior ability,' is a 13th-century borrowing of the Old French *pro(u)esce* 'valor, bravery.' The Old French form, which represents a combination of Late Latin *prōde* 'advantageous, beneficial, useful,' and the qualitative noun-forming suffix *-esce* (English *-ess*), had already undergone some semantic changes. 'Useful' had come to mean 'useful in battle, brave' before the term was borrowed by English. English has kept the sense of 'bravery' and extended it to its present-day range of meanings.

Proud, either 'glorious' or 'vainglorious,' was also borrowed from Old French, but earlier, in the 11th century. The Late Latin *prōde*, Old French *prud/prod*, meant 'brave, superior in battle.' In English, however, *proud* has always had its double sense. It could mean not only 'gallant,' but also 'having an elevated opinion of oneself.' The progression went from 'brave' to 'worthy of esteem' to 'holding oneself in esteem,' the more common sense of the term today.

Prude, an 'overly righteous person,' is a later borrowing from French and has a more complex history. In French, a *pr(e)u de femme* was a 'good woman, woman worthy of esteem,' and a *pr(e)u d'homme* was a 'good man, man worthy of esteem.' *Pr(e)u* was the later French form of the Latin *prōde*, whose meaning had become generalized from 'brave' to 'good, estimable.' By processes known to etymologists as "back formation" and "localization," *pr(e)u de femme* became English *prude* and, by the 18th century, had come to mean a 'woman affecting great modesty or righteousness,' an extension with a pejorative sense of its original French meaning.

pumpkin

The Proto-Indo-European root **pekʷ* 'cook' has a large number of forms in English, all having to do with cooking. In Latin the initial **p* appears as *k* as the result of assimilation, giving *cook*, *concoct*, and *kitchen*; in Greek the form yields such words as *pepsin* and *peptic*, both referring to digestion. *Pumpkin* came into English through Latin and French, from an extended use of the same root in Greek.

In Greek, a *pépōn* is a 'variety of melon that is edible only when ripe,' where 'ripe' is the operative word of the definition and an extension of the original meaning 'cooked.' A similar extension in meaning gives the Hindi *pakkā* 'ripe,' which, as English *pukka*, has taken on the further extended sense of 'genuine, first-rate.' *Pépōn* was borrowed into Latin as *pepō*, yielding Old French *popon* and *pompon*, the forms which were borrowed into English in the 16th century. Almost immediately a number of variant pronunciations and spellings began to appear: *pompion, pompeon, pumpion*. By the end of the 17th century, the last of these variants had been made over to *pumpkin*, the *-ion* having been replaced by the diminutive suffix *-kin*.

During the Colonial period in New England, *pumpkin* was used in a now obsolete extended sense as an epithet applied by the British to their American cousins. Thus, Boston, Massachusetts, was sometimes called *Pumpkinshire*, and its residents, *Pumpkins*, a usage possibly influenced by the existence of the word *bumpkin* (which see).

puny, puisne

By the 12th century, the French phrase *puis né*, from *puis* 'after' and *né* 'born,' had coalesced into a single word meaning 'younger' or 'junior,' contrasting in legal terminology with *aisné* 'older,' a term based on *ainz* 'before' plus the same *né*. The first elements of these words descended ultimately from the Latin *post* or *ante*, while the *né* of both terms came from the past participle of the Latin verb *nascor* 'to be born,' the original root of which reflected a reduced variant of the stem that appeared in its fuller form as *genus* in Latin and as *kin* in English.

The *s* of both *puisné* and *aisné* disappeared during the 13th century (the Modern French *puîné* and *aîné* mark the lost *s* with a circumflex over the *i*). Thus, the French word *puisné* entered English twice, once before and once after this sound change, the form without the *s* coming to be spelled *puny*.

The earlier variant, *puisné*, appeared primarily in the sense of 'born later,' hence, 'being junior to' in the legal sense. In Medieval times this was a status of inferiority before the law, particularly with regard to inheritance rights. Later usage extended the meaning to signify 'appointed or enacted at a subsequent date,' with reference to judges or laws. A *puisne judge* was an inferior or junior justice, a sense now obsolescent in England itself, but one that survives in certain former British dominions. The earlier spelling fossilized in English orthography, but the actual later French pronunciation prevailed, since in 13th-century England most lawyers were fluent in French.

Outside of legal usage, the word in both spellings, as well as in some minor variations of these, came to mean 'inferior' in a variety of now highly technical senses. By Shakespeare's time, one sense of the term had developed to 'physically inferior,' that is, 'weak or feeble,' and the other meanings became obsolete.

The *puisne* alternate still survives, and it is pronounced the same as its doublet, *puny*. The French *aîné* likewise entered English, spelled variously as *aine*, *ayne*, or *aigne*, generally as a technical legal term which contrasts with *puisne* in its sense of 'younger' or 'junior.'

Q

queen, quean

These two terms represent one of the earliest cases of what semanticists call "radiation" in English. Both terms have as their source the Proto-Indo-European word *g^wen, which meant, simply, 'woman,' and is attested in Greek as *gynē̃, gynaikós* 'woman,' whence come *androgyne, gynecology,* and a host of other words having to do with women, and in Old Irish as *ben* 'woman,' from which English gets *banshee* 'fairy woman whose keening is a signal of impending death.' By the time the Old English form of *g^wen appears, the process of radiation and specialization seems to have begun. *Cwén* means 'wife of a king,' while *cwene* retains its original sense of 'woman.' It survives in the names *Guinevere* and *Gwendolyn.*

The meaning of *cwén,* Modern English *queen,* was slightly extended to mean not only 'wife of a king' but also 'female monarch,' and to this day has retained these two senses, to which has been added, in relatively recent times, that of 'effeminate male homosexual.' *Cwene,* Modern English *quean,* retains its original sense of 'woman' only dialectally, and with slight modification, at that, of 'young woman.' Elsewhere, *cwene* came to be used in Middle English in a pejorative sense, to designate an 'impudent woman.' In the 16th and 17th centuries this sense underwent further pejoration, with the result that *quean* came to be used as a synonym for 'whore.' Today the term is archaic in Standard English.

quick

The Proto-Indo-European stem *g^wHyH^w- is an algebraic reconstruction, devised to account for all the regular phonological correspondences whose precise pronunciation is irrelevant. It meant 'life,' and developed into such a diverse group of words, not only in different branches of the language family but even in the same branch, that a brief note may help to clarify the relationships.

In Greek the Proto-Indo-European $*g^w$ developed to b, d, or g, depending on what followed. If that were the semivowel i, the latter two sound elements became ζ (zeta), eventually rendered in English as z. Thus, one variant of the stem became *bios* 'life,' in Greek signifying 'mode or way of life,' rather than animal or organic life. Some of the compounds with *bio-* that reached English reflect this distinction, among them *biography*, a 17th-century loan; others, such as *biology*, a 19th-century loan, ignore it, although an early and now obsolete use of this term meant the 'study of man's life from the viewpoint of his character.'

In a second Greek development of the same stem, one in which the accent fell on the second syllable, $*g^wHy\acute{e}H^w$-, the form developed to *zôon* 'living creature, animal.' This variant had the neuter ending added; an adjectival variant, *zōós*, meant simply 'alive, or living.' This reached English in *zoology* or *zoo* (a shortening of *zoological garden*), among other words.

A third Greek development of the same stem, this one with the accent on the first syllable, $*g^w\acute{e}Hy H^w$-, became the *Dē-* of *Dēmétér*, the name of the goddess of fertility or vegetation, equated by the Romans with their own goddess *Ceres*, whose name appears in *cereal*. Since the latter part of *Dēmétér's* name was simply the Greek word for 'mother,' this goddess was the 'mother of life.' The derivative *Demetrius* rests on an expansion of this name.

The $*g^w$ became Latin v, and the stem became *vīv-*, which reached English in *vivacious* 'full of life, sprightly,' via Fench in the 17th century; *vivid*, also in the 17th century; and *vivisection*, in the 18th century, among other borrowed terms.

The direct Old English development of the stem, *cwicu-* 'live,' represents a reduplication or doubling of the form. This evolved to the modern word *quick*, which now has specialized to contrast with *slow*; but the earlier sense is still reflected in such phrases as *the quick and the dead*.

R

restive

The etymology of this adjective is complicated by the existence of two nouns, both spelled *rest*. The one, which means 'repose,' is attested from Old English times and comes from a Germanic root, **rast-*, which seems to have meant 'repose, relief from activity.' The other *rest* is a 16th-century borrowing from French, and means 'remainder.' The French form is derived from the Latin verb *restāre*, a combination of the prefix *rē-* 'back, again,' and the verb *stāre* 'to stand.' *Restāre* originally meant 'to stand back, stand firm, resist,' later coming to mean 'to remain,' the sense of the French *rester*.

Restive was borrowed from French in the 16th century. It was derived from an unattested Late Latin adjective, *restīvus*, a combination of the root of the verb *restāre* and the common suffix *-īvus*. Thus, one might have expected the original meaning to be something on the order of 'inclined to remain'; instead, the first attested meaning of the word in English is 'at rest, inert,' possibly as a result of filtering, confusion with the Germanic-based *rest*, or both.

By the following century, however, *restive* had acquired a slightly different sense, that of 'obstinate,' the principal meaning of Modern French *rétif* and one of the meanings of its Modern English cognate. It is not clear whether this shift in meaning reflected a harking-back to the Classical Latin sense of the verb or was simply the result of native specialization. In any case, it later underwent a further shift, from 'obstinate' to 'impatient, restless, especially when under some form of restraint.' Thus, in the space of four centuries, *restive* has come to mean the virtual opposite of its original English sense.

rival

In Latin, *rīvus* is a 'stream, brook,' and *rīvālis* 'of or pertaining to a stream or brook' is the adjective formed from that noun by adding the common suffix *-ālis*. In Roman times, *rīvālis*, used as a noun, came to mean, 'one who shares the (same) stream or brook; a neighbor.' In Late Latin, the term took on the additional sense of 'neighbor or person in competition with another; an adversary.' This seems to have been the primary sense with which the English associated *rival* when they borrowed the term from Old French in the 16th century, although the meaning 'associate, partner' is attested in Shakespeare's time: "... the rivals of my watch...."[*Hamlet*, I, i, 13].

rout

Proto-Indo-European **reup* seems to have meant both 'rip' and 'rip off,' in the sense of 'steal,' or so it would appear, on the basis of its Modern English descendants *rip*, *rob*, *rover* (in the sense of 'pirate'), and, less obviously, *rout*. *Rout* is a 13th-century borrowing from Old French, in which *route* 'military division' was derived from the Latin *rupta*, the feminine form of the past participle of the verb *rumpere* 'to break, tear, burst.' The specialized use of *rupta* 'broken (off)' in Old French to designate a military troop may be compared with the Modern English use of 'division' and 'detachment' to mean a 'group of soldiers,' all originating in the fact that such a military group is a 'detached portion or segment' of the army as a whole.

When *rout* was borrowed by English in the 13th century, it was with the sense of 'military division or company,' but it soon took on the connotation of 'rowdy, disordered company (of soldiers),' whether as a reflection of its original Latin sense of 'fragmentation and disorder' or as a gloss on the off-duty behavior of the military. It seems unlikely that the Proto-Indo-European sense of 'plunder, rob' was still present as a factor in this shift of meaning.

By the 14th century, *rout* had come to mean 'any (unruly) crowd of people,' and, by the 15th century, an 'uproar or riot' caused by such a crowd. Both of these senses are in use today. In the 16th century, the term acquired what is now its primary meaning, a 'disorderly retreat; utter defeat on the field of battle,' probably through the influence of the French *déroute* 'utter defeat', though there survives the somewhat less frequent sense 'formal gathering, ball'.

S

Sabbath, sabbatical

Sabbath is a 10th-century borrowing, either of Latin *sabbatum* or of its Old French form *sab(b)at*. The Latin term is itself a borrowing, possibly through Greek, of the Hebrew *shabat* 'rest, day of rest.' There is some disagreement among Semiticists as to the original sense of *shabatu*, which underlies *shabat*. The word my have meant 'rest,' then 'day of rest,' then 'seventh day of the week (on which rest is appropriate),' or the original sense may have been 'taboo,' then 'taboo associated with the end of each quarter cycle of the moon,' and then 'taboo associated with the seventh day of each week,' which would involve the avoidance of work, travel of any distance, the preparation of food, and so on. The biblical commandment to 'keep the Sabbath' in remembrance of the Lord's day of rest after the creation of the universe would, taking this sense, have had its origin in a lunar taboo.

In any case, *shabat* entered Greek, Latin, and Germanic as the 'Jewish day of rest (on the seventh day of the week).' Latin seems to have preserved both the meaning 'Jewish day of rest' and 'seventh day of the week,' while generalizing the meaning of *sabbatum* to cover other 'holidays.' Modern Spanish, French, and German, with slight phonetic variations, have taken the word in its sense of 'seventh day'; *sábado, samedi*, and *Samstag* all mean 'Saturday.' English seems to have borrowed the term in a more general sense; we speak of a *Witches' Sabbath* still as an annual midnight revel, and of the *Jewish* and *Christian Sabbaths* as the weekly days of rest and religious observance for those of the respective persuasions, the *Jewish Sabbath* celebrated on Saturday, the *Christian Sabbath* on Sunday. By extension of the 'seventh day' sense of *Sabbath*, *sabbatical* has come into English as a 'year of rest (following six years of work).' The original

163

Hebrew *sabbatical* year was one during which the fields were allowed to lie fallow. Today it is generally a year during which those in the academic profession are free of teaching duties.

sad

The Proto-Indo-European root *seA-* seems to have meant 'to satisfy,' and is the basis of Latin *satis* 'ample, sufficient,' from which comes Old English *sadian* 'to satisfy, fill,' probably with interference from the Latin *sate*. The past participle of Old English *sadian* appears as *sæd* 'sated,' which, by the 13th century, had extended its meaning in two different directions more or less simultaneously. On the one hand, it could mean 'solid, dense,' presumably because a person or thing that has been 'sated' or 'filled up' is in some sense 'solid.' On the other, *sæd* could also mean 'weary,' presumably because a person who has 'had enough' is 'weary' or 'lethargic.'

Sad in the sense of 'solid' was extended to metal products, as in *sad-iron*, in the 16th century, and to baked goods, as *sad bread* 'bread which has yet to rise,' in the 17th. In its sense of 'weary,' and possibly 'solid' as well, *sad* was extended to mean 'serious, grave' when applied to people in the 14th century. A further extension of this sense gave the contemporary meaning 'unhappy, sorrowful.'

salary

When the Roman army did not provide its soldiers with necessities, it gave them the money with which to purchase what they needed. Thus it paid out *argentum calcearius* 'shoe money,' *argentum vestiarum* 'clothes money,' and so forth. *Argentum* literally meant 'silver,' but this early Latin foreshadows the later development still seen in the Modern French use of *argent* in the sense of 'money.' *Argentum salārium* meant 'salt money.' *Sal-* is cognate with the English word *salt*, and with the Greek *hal-*, since *s-* becomes *h-* in Greek. This root entered English in various compounds, such as *halophyte* 'plant that tolerates salty soil,' and *halobiont*. In time, the meaning of the phrase *argentum salārium* became localized in its second element, and the word for 'silver' or 'money' was dropped.

By the 1st century A.D., the word had begun to generalize, acquiring the meaning of 'wages,' or 'regular payment for services,' whether or not the payment was intended for the purchase of salt. To the Romans, the original meaning remained self-evident, since they still used *sal* as an uncompounded form meaning 'salt.'

By the time the word reached English in the 14th century via French, the etymological significance of the root had faded. A later specialization narrowed the meaning to 'regular payments made for professional or white-collar services.' The word used for the remuneration of manual labor was, strictly speaking, *wages*, although this semantic distinction is not uniformly observed.

Although salt is no longer used as recompense for services rendered, such expressions as "He's worth his salt" reflect the same ancient practice preserved in the word *salary*.

sandwich

According to tradition, John Montagu, the 4th Earl of *Sandwich*, is to be credited with the invention of this staple. An inveterate gambler, the Earl had his evening meal served to him at the gaming table in a form that would allow him to continue to play and eat at the same time. The earliest *sandwiches*, then, were a combination of the foods that would normally have appeared on the nobleman's table, meat, greens, cheese, and onion, perhaps, all wedged between two slices of bread. Today a *sandwich* may contain virtually anything edible, the only requirement being that the contents be enveloped in bread. Even this requirement is not always observed, as in the case of the *open-face sandwich*, which may consist of anything edible atop a single slice of bread.

Metaphorically, the term is used to refer to something inserted, or *sandwiched*, between two other things, as a car *sandwiched* between two others in a parking lot, or even a social or business engagement *sandwiched* into a busy schedule.

sanguine

According to the physicians of ancient Greece, the health and disposition of an individual depended on the balance in his body of the four basic humors, or bodily fluids. An excess of yellow bile was believed to result in poor digestion and a disagreeable personality; an excess of black bile produced sadness and *melancholy* (which see); too much mucus, or phlegm (see *phlegmatic*), made for sluggishness; and a superabundance of blood was believed to be responsible for an energetic, optimistic, cheerful disposition.

Sanguine comes from the Latin word for 'bloody' *sanguineus*, which, in the early days of Roman medicine, came to be applied specifically to people whose energy was attributed to an excess of blood coursing through their veins. Today the term continues to be applied to optimistic and passionate or easily excitable people, although the theory of bodily humors has long since been disproved.

sarcophagus

Lithos sarcophágos 'flesh-eating stone' was the name given by the Greeks to a corrosive limestone, quarried at Assos in ancient Lycia, which they used to make caskets, precisely because of its capacity to dissolve the bodies buried in it. The phrase became attached to these caskets, and in time the first element of the phrase was dropped, leaving *sarcophágos* to carry the entire meaning. Even when noncorrosive stone replaced the stone that had evoked the name, the term continued, an illustration of what etymologists call "subreption." The word passed into Latin, and it was this form, with the customary Latin substitution of *-us* for *-os*, that entered English twice. First, in the early 17th century, it meant 'casket made of corrosive stone,' but when it entered for the second time in the early 18th century it was with the generalized meaning 'casket made of stone.'

scold

If, as is generally believed, the English word *scold* comes from Old Norse *skáld*, the history of this word constitutes one of the more dramatic examples of linguistic pejoration in our language. In Old Norse, a *skáld* was a 'poet,' while in Modern English a *scold* is a 'habitual fault-finder; a constant taker-to-task.'

The links in the chain of semantic change from 'poet' to 'fault-finder' seem to have been these. In Old Norse, a poet could be a specialist in versified lampooning; indeed, in Icelandic law, a special term, *skáldskapr*, was coined to refer to 'slander in verse form.' Whether by linguistic filtering or by the borrowing of *skáld* in its specialized sense of 'poet-lampooner' *scold* is first attested in English

in the 13th century as an 'abusive, libelous person,' the term soon
coming to refer especially to an 'abusive woman.' This sense was soon
extended to mean a 'quarrelsome, vituperative person (generally
female),' and, by the 15th century, a 'disturber of the peace by
constant harping.' Again, the word was primarily applied to the
female sex.

Today a *scold* may be either male or female, although the term is
still primarily associated with women.

senate

The Latin word *senātus*, ancestor of the English term, rested on the
root *sen-* 'old' and *-āt-* 'office of,' a specialization of the past participle
suffix. Thus, the Roman *senate* consisted of a select group of *senēs*
'old men,' who originally served as a purely consultative body for the
early rulers. This *sen-*, of course, is the same element seen in *senior*
'older,' which, via transmission through the Romance languages,
yielded English *sir*. An English cognate appears in the *sen-* of *seneschal* 'old retainer,' and, in Irish, in the *shan-* of *shanty* 'old house,'
earlier 'old roof.'

In Rome, the *senate* eventually acquired both legislative and
administrative functions, and it was in the sense of a council with
such duties that the word first entered English in the early 13th
century. Not until the 18th century did the meaning start to narrow
the responsibilities to the legislative function. Although in the United
States the required age for Senators remains greater than that for
Representatives, the basis for appointment to a *senate*, the quality of
being 'old,' has long since changed, and with it the meaning of the
word, although etymologically speaking, a "young *senator*" cannot
exist.

September, October, November, December

Since the early Romans regarded March as the first month of the year,
September was the seventh month, *October* was eighth, *November* the
ninth, and *December* the tenth. These names derive from the corresponding Latin numerals, all of which are the exactly the same as
their English counterparts.

Beginning in 153 B.C., however, the Roman political year began on January 1, the day the consuls took office; upon the introduction of the Julian calendar, still followed today, that starting point became official for the regular calendar. The change, of course, made *September* the ninth month, *October* the tenth, and so on, but the old names persisted, another example of what linguists call "subreption." The Romans, of course remained aware of the original significance of the names, but the "fading" of the sense, which left the terms without denotative content, probably took place after the French descendants of the words passed into English in the 10th and 11th centuries or whenever speakers with no knowledge of French used them.

serenade

Many etymologists regard Latin *serēnus* 'clear, fair, bright,' which is the direct ancestor of the English word *serenade*, as a cognate of the Greek *seirios* 'hot, scorching.' This yielded the name *Sirius*, via Latin transmission, for the brightest star in the sky. *Sirius* is also called the Dog Star because of its location in the constellation of *Canis Major* 'the Greater Dog.'

An expanded version of the Latin stem, probably a past participle, descended to the Romance languages in the sense of 'clear, cloudless weather,' and then 'open air.' A related transitional development appears in the phrase *luce serēnanti* 'in the bright, clear light,' or 'daylight,' employed by Cicero. One may postulate a semantic localization of the meaning of the phrase, with subsequent dropping of the accompanying noun (*luce* 'light,' *lux* in the nominative case). The phrase, however, shows the present participle rather than the past participle, which one must reconstruct for the Italian, Spanish, or Portuguese *serenata*. This word, *serenata,* then expanded its meaning to 'musical performance given in the open air,' probably through a second semantic localization—possibly with *cantata* as the word dropped.

The original Latin stem, *serēn-*, applied more properly to the day than to the evening, but the semantic component of 'brightness' faded. Then, since the performances described by the word occurred more frequently at night, the word came to mean 'evening song.' It was in this sense that the word entered French, becoming *sérénade*, and then passed into English in the 17th century.

The other Romance languages retained some of its other meanings, along with the later developments, and in the 18th century English borrowed the Italian version, *serenata*, to mean 'open air cantata.'

At about the same time, *serenade* started to occur without the 'evening' part of the meaning, although it is uncertain whether this development was a simple instance of semantic fading, or if it was an influence, called "contamination" by some linguists, from the related *serenata*.

The original Latin *serēnus*, or its neuter form, *serēnum*, developed the meaning now seen in the English derivative *serene*. In ancient Rome a bright sky or fair weather was regarded as propitious, portending good fortune, and, by personification, a reason for one to be glad, joyful, or *serene*.

serf

This word, which entered English in the 15th century from French, was the direct descendant of the Latin *servum* 'slave,' cited here in the accusative case. Gaius, the great Roman jurist of the 2nd century who was often cited as a prime authority in the 6th-century *Institutes* of Justinian, connected the word with the Latin verb *servāre* 'to preserve or save,' since Roman generals followed the practice of preserving and selling captives into slavery instead of executing them. Variants of this stem, such as *servile*, retain this derivative, specialized sense, while compounds such as *conserve* and *preserve* reflect the earlier meaning.

When the word first came into English it had the Latin meaning 'slave,' but this sense became obsolete. It was replaced near the beginning of the 17th century by a weakened version of the earlier meaning 'someone not quite so low as a slave, but existing in a state of semiservitude, bound or attached to land, and owing service to its owner.'

Since in Greek the Proto-Indo-European *s*- became *h*-, and the *w*- (written *v*- in Latin) disappeared, many etymologists believe that the same stem that gave Latin *servus* also yielded the Greek word *hérōs*, borrowed by English as *hero*. Here possibly the original meaning had been 'savior, one who saves others,' which makes it the exact antonym of the Latin cognate, 'one saved by others.'

sergeant

This term originally meant 'servant,' having come through Old French from Latin *serviēns*, the present participle (used substantively) of the verb *servire* 'to serve.' This itself produced the noun *servus* 'slave,' the basis for English *serf* (which see). While the sense of 'servant' remained associated with the English word *sergeant* well into the 16th century, the term gradually took on more and more respectable connotations, from 'servant' to 'servant of a knight' to 'person who, through noble service in the field, might be elevated to knighthood,' and thus 'a man of some authority,' albeit one still answerable to superiors in the chain of command.

Today an army or police *sergeant* is a middle- to high-ranking noncommissioned officer, while a *sergeant-at-arms* is an appointed officer in a nonmilitary organization whose duty it is to keep order. A *sergeant major* is a fish whose stripes are reminiscent of the "hash marks" worn on the sleeve of the highest-ranking military *sergeant* as a badge of office.

serpent

The Proto-Indo-European stem **serp-* meant 'to creep or crawl.' The Latin form of this word element, extended by the present participle *-ent-* gave *serpent* 'creeping,' a form applied to snakes. A development of the same *serp-* stem in Greek, where intitial *s-* becomes *h-*, gave *herpetón* a 'creeping thing, reptile, especially snake.' This entered English in the early 19th century in the compound *herpetology* the 'science that deals with reptiles.'

The Greek variant underwent another semantic specialization in medical usage, giving *hérpēs* 'the creeping disease,' or 'shingles.' This form entered English by the 14th century. A late 19th-century coinage on the base produced a different function for *herpetology* the 'science or study which deals with the skin disease.'

Another variant of the same Proto-Indo-European root gave the *rep-* of the Latin adjective *reptile* 'creeping,' which later came to be used as a noun in much the same sense as that now found in the English derivative.

shack

Two quite different etymologies have been proposed for the English word *shack*, a term closely associated with the American frontier in the 19th century. According to one derivation, the word comes from the southwestern Spanish *jacal*, a borrowing of the Aztec *xacatli* 'thatched cabin.' The term was applied to the hastily built dwellings erected on the land claimed by settlers in the West.

The other etymology derives *shack* from a dialectal variant of the English verb 'to shake' or its corresponding noun, to which the adjective *ramshackle(d)*, which shows the Scandinavian intensive prefix *ram-*, may be compared. Two plausible semantic modifications of the verb/noun *shake* are customarily cited in defense of this derivation. First, because the earliest *shacks* were of quick and careless construction, they could well be described as characteristically *shaky* 'wobbly.' Second, both the noun *shake* and its variant *shack* were current with the meaning 'chaff, fallen grain or nuts suitable for pig fodder.' A slight extension of this sense, 'leavings from a bale of marijuana,' is current among drug dealers in the United States. The application of a term meaning 'leftovers, chaff' might well have been applied to the *shacks* of the southwestern United States, made as they were from bits and pieces and intended for temporary shelter.

shambles

The Indo-European stem **skăp-*, with a long or short vowel depending on where the prehistoric accent fell, meant 'to support.' It appears in the ancient Greek *skēptron* (*skāp-tron* in West Greek dialects) a 'staff employed as a symbol of authority,' a semantic specialization that entered English as *scepter*. In Latin, the variant **skap-* with the short vowel combined with *-n-om* to give **skapnom*, later *scamnum*, a 'bench, stool, step,' or, in poetic usage, 'throne.'

A variation of this, *scamellum* 'little bench or stool' reached the early Germanic languages before the period of their separation. Modern German *Schemel* 'footstool' attests this loan, as does Old English *scamol* 'bench, stool.' This, however, evolved along a strange semantic path. Even within the Old English period the 'bench' started to serve as a 'table for displaying materials up for sale' or as a 'surface for counting out money.' This sense survived only to the end of the 13th century or the beginning of the 14th, by which time the articles

displayed came to be restricted to meat or fish. By the 15th century
the then central denotation 'table' started to fade, leaving the term
with the meaning 'place or market for the sale of meat or fish.' The
next state in the semantic development, during the 16th century, saw
an increasing emphasis on one connotation associated with this meaning, the fact that the animals were usually slaughtered in or near the
place where the meat was sold. Thus *shambles* eventually signified a
'slaughterhouse.' By the end of the century the term had generalized
to mean any 'place of carnage or bloodshed,' not only one where the
victims were animals.

In more recent times, the sense has passed to a 'place of devasta-
tion or ruin,' even without bloodshed, and even shading off to a
meaning of 'very untidy, extremely disordered, or messy,' as in "His
room is a complete *shambles*." Some purists object to this development, but it is well established in actual usage.

shampoo

The Hindi word *chāp* means 'pressure,' and the verb *chāmpnā*,
derived from that noun, means 'to press.' As well as these two forms,
one also finds the Hindi *chhāp* 'stamp, impression' and its corresponding verb *chhāpnā* 'to stamp, impress.' *Shampoo* comes from the familiar imperative, *chāmpo*, of the verb *chāmpnā*, with possible influence
from *chhāpnā* as well.

The kind of 'pressure' or 'stamp' associated with the word as it
was borrowed into English at the end of the 17th century was that of
a 'massage,' with its accompanying oils and soaps and its grand finale
of washing the hair. Until well into the 19th century, in fact, a
shampoo was a 'complete massage.' Only recently has *shampoo* come
to mean 'hair wash,' and, even more recently, 'product to be used in
washing the hair.'

shamus

This American English slang term for a 'detective, policeman' is in all
probability derived from the Yiddish *shammes* with linguistic interference from Irish Gaelic *Séamus*. The Yiddish term has the multiple
sense of 'temple sexton or beadle; candle used to light the other
candles of the menorah at Chanukkah; watchman, officer of the
peace.' It is derived from the Hebrew noun *shammash* 'servant; penis

(as the instrument of marital "service"),' which is itself derived from the verb *shammesh* 'to service; to perform one's marital duties.' The phallic association with the term as 'detective' is comparable to that of *dick* (said to be short for Richard).

Séamus is Irish-American for *'John'* (but Irish for *'James'*) *Séan* being the Irish Gaelic form of this common Christian name. During the period when *shamus* came into its slang use in English, both the Irish and the Jews were recent immigrants to the United States, and many of the Irish had found work as police officers, or *'cops'* (which see).

shanghai

The most important Chinese port of commerce, situated at the junction of the Wusung and Hwangpu rivers, takes its name from the Chinese words *shang* 'above' and *hai* 'sea,' because of its easy access to the ocean. During the 19th century shipowners often found it difficult to assemble the crew necessary to man the vessels bound for *Shanghai*, and they or their agents would drug or overpower seamen in coastal towns of the United States, drag them aboard ship, and press them into service. In nautical slang, then, the city's name underwent a functional shift from noun to verb, and, with what linguists call "connotative specialization," designated this practice. The term later generalized to mean using force or fraud to compel unwilling people to do anything at all, and its original signification meant nothing to speakers who knew no Chinese.

shantung, pongee, tussah

One of the Chinese provinces takes its name from *shan* 'mountain range' and *tung* 'eastern.' In this district, craftsmen wove a nubbly silken fabric, *pen chi* or *pon gee*, so called from the Chinese words for 'home loom,' possibly a shortening, with semantic localization, from a phrase that meant 'hand-loomed cloth.' This combination, *pongee*, entered English at the start of the 18th century as a name for the fabric, with the original sense filtered out in the transmission across linguistic boundaries. *Pongee* was woven of the silk produced from an indigenous worm, *Bombyx pernyi* or *Antheraea perynyi*, whose filaments received dyes readily, sometimes with cotton added for greater body.

However, the English also imported a similar fabric, or *tussah*, from India. *Tussah* (also spelled *tusser, tussor, tussure, tussur*), whose name derives from a Hindi or Urdu word meaning 'shuttle' (perhaps because the cocoon of the silkworm resembles a shuttle, or because a shuttle is used in the weaving), is made from the silk of a different worm, *Antheraea mylitta*, which is brownish in color and which does not readily accept dye. An understandable confusion occurred regarding the names of the two relatively similar fabrics, both imported from the Far East.

By the end of the 19th century, merchants had started to call the Chinese variety *Shantung pongee silk*, so as to avoid the ambiguity of *pongee* alone. The meaning localized in the first word, and subsequently *shantung* became the term for the cloth which might be dyed any color, while *pongee* remained the word for the uncolored fabric. The confusion of *pongee* with *tusser* persisted, however, leading to the occasional generalization of *pongee* as the name for the characteristic *tusser* color, a brilliant brown of reddish-yellow cast.

shanty

Three etymologies have been proposed for this word meaning a 'tumbledown house,' which first appeared in North America in the 19th century. The first derives *shanty* from Irish *sean* 'old' or *sion* 'storm,' plus *tig* 'house,' possibly through or influenced by Canadian French. The second derivation posits French *chantier* 'lumber camp, lumberjack's quarters' as the basis for the word. *Chantier* is derived from Latin *canterius* 'rafter, roof beam.' The third possibility, which is more fanciful than likely, is that *shanty* is derived from an unattested French form **chienté* 'doghouse.'

The most likely explanation for the origin of the term, given its geographical and temporal location, is that it was an Irish Gaelic borrowing into Canadian French, which made its way into Canadian-American English and thence back to the continent of Europe. In the 19th century lumberjacks in the woods of North America lived in makeshift dwellings, and it would have been appropriate to link the Irish *sean*, or *sion tig* 'old (storm) house' with the French *chantier* 'lumber camp' to refer to the quarters shared by workers chiefly Irish and French. Subsequently, when the hybrid term was borrowed by English speakers, it was applied to any 'rude, makeshift dwelling,' the sense it has today.

shibboleth

According to the Bible, following his victory over the Ammonites, granted to him by the Lord in return for the sacrifice of his daughter, Jephthah of Gilead warred successfully against the Ephraimites, his distant kinsmen. Having taken control of the fords on the river Jordan, the Gileadite warriors were faced with the problem of determining which of the men asking to cross were from their own tribe and which were from the tribe of Ephraim. This they did by asking each man to pronounce the word *shibboleth* (which of the term's two senses, 'ear of corn' or 'stream, current,' was intended is irrelevant, although the watery crossing makes the latter more likely in the view of certain scholars). The Ephraimites pronounced the word "*sibboleth*," thus giving away their identity, and Jephthah's men slew them. The Bible (Judges 12) says that "there fell at that time of Ephraim forty and two thousand," but fails to specify how many of these owed their doom to their inability to pronounce the *sh* sound.

The word first appears in English in John Wycliffe's translation of the Bible in 1382. Ironically enough, Wycliffe or his scribe spelled it "*sebolech*," thus failing the test himself. Later translations corrected the spelling. One may detect a further irony in the fact that the Council of Constance ordered Wycliffe's bones to be dug up and burned because of his alleged heresy, as the Ephraimites had threatened to burn Jephthah (Judges 12:1).

The original meaning, or meanings, of *shibboleth* were never apparent to anyone who did not know Hebrew unless they could be deduced from biblical annotations. In the 17th century the word acquired a new meaning from the function to which the Gileadites had put it: a 'word used as a device for detecting a foreigner or someone not a member of the group,' that is, a 'password.' It also came to mean, simply, a 'peculiarity of pronunciation.'

An additional development, a generalization that rested on dropping part of either of the foregoing senses, occurred in the 19th century, when *shibboleth* also came to mean any 'peculiarity, not necessarily linguistic, that distinguishes a particular group of people.'

shirt, skirt

The ultimate origin of this doublet is the Proto-Indo-European root *sker 'to cut,' from which English short, shear, and scissors are also derived. The original shirt/skirt was simply 'something cut; something made short.' By the time scyrte appeared in Old English and skyrta appeared in Old Norse, each had already become specialized in meaning. Old English scyrte, which underlies Modern English shirt, designated an 'undergarment of indeterminate length worn by both men and women,' while Old Norse skyrta, which underlies Modern English skirt, was a 'shirt, tunic.'

Scyrte came, as it were, out of the closet, and underwent a change in meaning from 'unisex undergarment' to something like its modern-day meaning, 'outer top garment worn (primarily) by men.'

Skyrta was then adopted into English and underwent a few changes of its own. At the time of its borrowing it designated a '(longish) outer garment covering the top of the body (with enough cloth left over to cover part of the lower body),' but came to mean a 'covering for the lower part of a (female) body.' Any sense of shortness had already been lost; indeed, petticoats 'small coats' and the skirts that covered them were probably the most voluminous articles of dress worn during the Middle Ages. It is, in fact, the generous size of the skirts of that era that gave rise to the extended sense of skirt as a verb meaning 'to avoid, go around the outer edge, cut and run.'

shroud

Like shirt, skirt, shrew, and shred, this word comes from the Proto-Indo-European root *sker 'to cut.' From this sense, it seems to have evolved the meaning of 'something cut,' and, specifically, 'something cut from cloth, suitable for wearing.' Indeed, when the word first appeared in Old English it was in the sense of 'attire, clothing,' possibly as a borrowing from Old Norse, in which skruð meant 'clothing, ornaments, gear.'

By the 16th century the term had become specialized to mean 'clothing worn by the dead about to be buried; winding sheet,' its primary meaning today. Further extensions of this meaning are attested from the 14th century on, however, suggesting that the sense of 'winding sheet' was current well before the 16th century. 'Veil,' 'screen,' and 'envelop(e),' both as nouns and as verbs, all made appearances in English as meanings of *shroud* between the 14th and 16th centuries.

Today a *shroud* is still essentially a 'winding sheet,' or, by extension, a 'means of concealment.' As a verb, it has come to mean 'to dress a corpse for burial,' in a curious throwback to the Old Norse term. A less macabre extension is 'to conceal, envelop.'

siesta

Sexta hōra, the 'sixth hour', as measured by the Romans, who divided the period of daylight into twelve segments, was what we now call "midday," or noon. In Spain this was the warmest part of the day, a period used for resting or sleeping. As commonly happens, the meaning of the phrase became localized in its second element, which evolved to *siesta* in Spanish. The connotation 'time for napping' extended the range of the meaning and then became its primary sense. There was some ambiguity as to whether the term applied to the time for the nap or the nap itself, and the sense extended to include the latter possibility. When the word entered English in the 17th century it was with this second meaning. See also **noon**.

silhouette

Three different theories purport to explain the way in which this 19th-century borrowing from French came to mean 'two-dimensional outline portrait in black' and, by extension, 'shadow.' All trace the word to the 18th-century politician, Étienne de *Silhouette*, but differ in their view of the nature of the connection between the man and the meanings associated with the term to which he gave his name.

Apparently a favorite of Mme. de Pompadour, Étienne de *Silhouette* was appointed Controller General in 1759 through her influence. After only nine months, however, he was forced out of office because of his unpopular policies. Two of the explanations for the linking of his name with 'shadow pictures' refer to his political career: the first likens the brevity of his tenure in office, a 'shadow of a career,' to the "abbreviated" nature of a *silhouette*, which shows only outline and is filled in in monochrome; the second refers to two of his more unpopular proposals, that there be a heavy land tax on nobles' estates and that government pensions be cut. Critics alleged that *Silhouette* wanted to reduce government expenditure to a 'shadow' of its former self, or, in other words, to *silhouette* it.

The third explanation for this etymology is more prosaic. *Silhouette* is said to have decorated his chateau at Bry-sur-Marne with outline portraits which he himself drew and painted as a hobby.

silk, serge

Both of these words derive ultimately from the Chinese *szŭ* or *szĕ* 'silk; people who produce silk,' which appears as Mongolian *sir-kek*, giving Old Slavonic *šelkŭ* and Greek *sēres*. The Old Slavonic term seems to have meant 'silk' and was passed into Old English in that meaning, with the form *seoluc*.

The Greek form, however, designated not the fabric but the people who produced it, although the derived adjective *sērikós* tended to be used as often in the sense of 'silken' as in the sense of 'Asian.' The Romans borrowed both the noun and the adjective from Greek and used them as the Greeks had, later adding a refinement that eventually resulted in Modern English *serge*. *Sērica lāna* 'Asian wool' was used to designate a less expensive, locally produced fabric made of wool but with the same weave as the much sought-after Eastern import. Eventually *sērica lāna* localized to *sērica*, as frequently occurs with such phrases, although in this case it had the advantage of suggesting that the fabric was better than it was.

Judging from the phonetic shape of the word, which is attested in English from the 16th century, *serge* was borrowed from Old French. It is not certain whether at the time it retained any exotic connotations, but by now they have faded completely.

silly

The Old English *sǣlig* meant 'happy, prosperous, fortunate,' a range of senses still displayed by the Modern German cognate *selig*. A colloquial use in German, with the meaning 'fuddled, confused in mind, tipsy,' shows a degeneration analogous to, but not exactly the same as, what happened to the English word. This passed through a progression of meanings, including 'spiritually blessed, blessed by God, holy, good, innocent or simple, lacking in guile,' to the modern 'lacking in judgment, foolish.'

A minor line of development, preserved only dialectally, includes 'weak in body,' and results, perhaps, in the semantic usage of Northern dialects of England, where *silly* is sometimes employed to mean 'unfortunate, pitiful,' a shift that completely reverses the word's earliest meanings.

sinister

This is a Latin term of ultimately obscure origin, meaning 'left, on the left-hand side,' and as such was borrowed into the terminology of English heraldry in the 15th century to denote 'something on the bearer's left side.' In Roman times, *sinister* had two other meanings: 'auspicious,' because Roman augurs, facing south, had the auspicious east to their left; and 'inauspicious,' because Greek augurs, facing north, had the inauspicious west to their left. The Greeks seem to have prevailed, since today *sinister* means 'inauspicious, ominous, evil,' a sense dating from the 16th century in English.

This specialization is, perhaps, not surprising, given the virtually worldwide bias against left-handedness shared by the right-handed majority of English speakers. Both *sinister* and *gauche*, from French *gauche* 'left,' have decidedly negative connotations in English, while *right, dextrous,* and *adroit,* all ultimately referring to right-handedness, are connotatively positive terms. Even those who are equally proficient with both hands are called *ambidextrous,* from Latin *ambo* 'both' and *dexter* 'right,' suggesting that the facility of the right hand is to be admired and the clumsiness of the left ignored.

sister, cousin

Kinship names for family members reflect a semantic fading of terms which once specified the functions performed by each member of the family rather than simple genetic relationships. *Sister,* from the Old English *swestor* or *suster,* is derived from the Proto-Indo-European root **sw-* or **su-* (*w* and *u* being consonantal and vocalic variants of the same Proto-Indo-European sound elements) plus the agent suffix meaning 'one who.' An accented version of the same root gave Old English *sēowian,* Modern English *sew.* Thus, *sister* originally signified the family 'seamstress.' This same Proto-Indo-European compound developed into the Latin *soror,* later borrowed by English in such forms as *sorority* or *sororal.* (The first *r* of *soror* replaces the second *s* of *sister*, since *s* between vowels regularly changed to *r* in Latin.) With different suffixes, Latin evolved the word that entered English as *suture*, and Sanskrit developed *sūtra* 'thread,' which specialized to 'string of rules, instructions, or aphorisms,' as in *Kāma Sūtra* 'love instruction.'

When joined to the prefix *com-* 'together,' the 'sew' root gave **com-swesr-īn-os*, the ancestor of Latin *cōnsobrīnus*, which developed, via French, into the word *cousin* 'offspring of sisters,' originally, 'offspring of those who sewed together.'

As the sound changes obscured the forms of the root and social customs changed, the earlier significance passed into oblivion and was replaced by a meaning that refers to biological rather than cultural relationships.

slogan, slew, charm

The word *slogan*, which now means a 'motto or catchphrase used in promoting a group, as a political party or fraternity, or in advertising a sales product,' was originally a battle cry of Celtic troops. It is derived from the Old Irish phrase *slóg*, which had a variant, *slúagh*, and *gairm*, later *ghairm*, literally 'troop, or host, call.' This entered English in the early 16th century by way of Scots Gaelic.

Slúagh 'host,' the variant of the first element of the phrase, also entered English as an independent word which survives in informal usage as *slew* or *slue*, meaning a 'large number,' as in "a slew of children." An Old Slavic cognate of this word, *sluga*, developed the meaning 'servant,' a specialization by connotative extension that probably reflects the same mass enslavement, in antiquity, of a defeated army or population that caused the word *slave* to develop from a variant of the word now preserved as *Slav*, whose original sense was 'glorious' or 'renowned.'

The second element of the phrase, *gairm*, represents the formation of a noun from the Old Irish verb stem seen in *gairid* 'he calls.' A Latin cognate of this form reached English in *garrulous* 'talkative.' An Old English cognate, *cierm* 'clamor,' or 'cry,' later became specialized to mean the 'mingled voices or singing of a group of birds or children.' Here the idea of 'singing' undoubtedly reflects a blending of the meaning of this term with one of the early senses of another word, *charm*, with which it partially merged thanks to a similarity of sound. That word, with which the earlier *cierm* coalesced completely in sound but only partly in significance, derives from the Latin *carmen* 'song' via French transmission. In ornithological usage, *charm* specialized to mean the 'singing of a group of finches,' rather than that of just any kind of bird. Subsequently the 'singing' part of the meaning was lost, probably at about the same time as the *charm* derived directly from *carmen* lost its sense of 'song.' This development left *charm* with the meaning a 'group or assemblage of finches.'(See also **charm**.)

smirk

In Old English, *smearcian*, the ancestor of Modern English *smirk*, meant simply 'to smile,' with no pejorative connotation. Once the word *smile* itself entered the English vocabulary, around 1300, and became well established, the stage was set for one or the other of the terms with the same semantic range either to differentiate or to disappear, since language tends to avoid true synonymy. In this case, the older word specialized, adding an overtone of in a 'sly, simpering, affected, or self-satisfied manner' to the previous meaning. The pejorative connotation was clearly well established by the 17th century, but evidence from citations and from the definitions of early lexicographers proves that the earlier, neutral signification coexisted with the new extension at least into the 18th century.

smock, smocking

Two etymologies have been proposed for the word *smock* and its derivative, *smocking*. According to the first, *smock* is derived from a Proto-Indo-European root **(s)meug*, which seems to have had the sense of 'wet, slippery.' A secondary meaning, 'to adorn, ornament' is then thought to have developed, possibly through a stage in which the root had the extended meaning of 'to make shiny or sleek.' A *smock* would then have been an 'adornment,' the original sense of the Yiddish cognate *schmuck*. Through specialization by connotative extention, the Yiddish term eventually came to refer to a particularly masculine adornment, the *membrum virile*. The progression from the sense of 'adornment' to the contemporary meaning of *smock* is presumably from 'adornment' to 'adornment of the body, a shirt, shift, or undergarment,' and thence to 'shirt or shift worn over the clothes to protect them.'

Smocking is an embellishment based on the wholly functional stitching on workers' *smocks* of the 19th century.

The other suggested derivation posits an etymology going back to a Proto-Germanic verb meaning 'to creep,' which appears in Old English, in that sense, as *sméogan*. A *smock*, then, would be a garment into which one would creep, as a hand creeps into a glove. The sense of creeping would have been lost, while the sense of 'garment' remained.

solar, helium, sun, south

The Proto-Indo-European stem meaning 'sun' reached English in several forms, some preserving the original sense and some not. One variant, *sōl*, which passed through Latin, appeared in English in the 15th century as the name of the sun personified, and had also specialized in the usage of medieval alchemists to mean 'gold,' as *lūna* 'moon' meant 'silver.' This usage is, of course, obsolete. A silver coin of Peru, which shows the sun on its face, acquired the designation *sol*, from the Spanish descendant of the Latin word. A Latin expansion of the basic stem, by adding the adjective-forming suffix *-ār-* gave the word that eventually reached English as *solar*.

The variant of that same Proto-Indo-European root that passed through Greek shifted the initial *s* to *h* and underwent the other sound changes usual for that branch of the language family. It became *hélios*, whence come such English terms as *heliocentric, heliotrope*, and *heliometric*. *Helium*, the inert gas which is the second element in the periodic table, rests on the same stem expanded by a Latin-derived *-um* suffix often used to denote chemical elements, as in *selenium, beryllium*, and so on. This coinage, which apparently dates from the year 1878, derives from the fact that the chemist Lockwood had ten years earlier inferred the existence of the substance from the presence of a line in the spectrum of the sun. Thus, when Ramsay first isolated the gas in 1895, a word already existed to describe it.

A variant of the *sol* stem expanded by an *-n* suffix came down through Germanic, which assimilated the *l* to the *n* and gave the Old English *sunne*, which became the Modern English word *sun* itself. A further Germanic expansion of this variant gave *sunth*, which eventually became the Modern English *south*. The sense of this word, historically based, as it was, on a stem meaning 'sun,' suggests that the ancient Germanic tribes must have inhabited a very northerly region, since they named the *southern* area from the fact that this was the direction from which the sun appeared to shine. The Germanic-based semantic development in *sun* may be compared with that preserved in two Latin-derived words, *orient* and *occident*, which also took the sun as a directional reference point. Their original meanings were, respectively, 'rising' and 'setting.'

The loss of the *n* before the *th*, in *south*, reflects a regular West Germanic sound change, well attested in numerous other words like the Germanic-derived *tooth* as compared with the Latin-based *dent-* stem of *dentist* or the Greek-based *odont-* of *periodontist*, both of which preserved the *n*.

Since the same *sun* stem gave rise to words of such diverse meanings, one may call the process "radiation"—in the semantic as well as the physical sense.

soothe

In Old English, *sōth* meant 'truth.' Thus, *forsooth* was an interjection much like Modern American English "for sure"; a *soothsayer* was 'someone who told the truth,' and specifically, the truth about the future; and to *soothe* was 'to tell the truth, or verify.'

By the middle of the 16th century, however, *soothe* had taken on the pejorative sense of 'cajole or flatter by pretending to believe that what a person says is the truth.' By the following century the term began to take on its modern sense to 'calm,' with accompanying loss of its negative connotations. Thus *soothe* had come full circle, from a more or less neutral term to a negative one and eventually to a verb with positive connotations.

sour

As with many terms used to describe sensory experiences, *sour* goes back to a Proto-Indo-European root whose precise original meaning is the subject of disagreement among etymologists. Some say that the original sense of the root was 'salty, bitter, acetic.' If this is the case, some narrowing of the meaning has occurred, since we no longer think of *salty* and *sour* either as similar tastes or as identical meta-phorical attributes. Others derive *sour* from a root meaning 'to scratch,' from the notion that a *sour* taste scratches the tongue. In either case, the meaning of *sour*, like that of *bitter*, has been extended to cover a variety of generally unpleasant sensations and their sources.

Sour first appears in English in the 12th century, in the sense of 'bitter, unpleasant-tasting.' By the following century it had become generalized in its application, referring not only to 'bitter or acetic' food or drink, but also to people who were 'querulous, bad-tempered,' or 'gloomy.' These literal and metaphorical senses of the word have remained with us to this day. See also **bitter**.

spaniel

Many of the common names for different breeds of animal, like the Bengal tiger, the Irish setter, and the Siamese cat, refer to the animal's actual or supposed place of origin. The *spaniel* seems to have come originally from Spain, or so it would appear from its name, which means 'Spanish' in Old French. While Chaucer still acknowledged the Spanish origin of the breed, it was not long before the use of *spaniel* as a noun facilitated the loss of the dog's Spanish identity, a loss underlined by the later names for such sub-breeds as the *Alpine spaniel*, *King Charles spaniel*, and *Norfolk spaniel*.

The most common variety of *spaniel* is the *cocker spaniel*. Two sources for the qualifier *cocker* have been suggested. One is that it comes from *cock*, the 'male bird,' a creature noted for its pugnacious-ness—an attribute that gave rise to the 13th-century use of the term *cocker* for a 'person looking for a fight.' *Spaniels* trained to hunt game birds were accorded this epithet. The other etymology for *cocker* derives the term from *woodcock*, a popular British game bird.

specious

The Proto-Indo-European stem **spek-* meant 'to look at, to see,' but the Latin *speciōsus* specialized to 'good to look at,' or 'beautiful, handsome, attractive.' The Sanskrit cognate *spaç-* 'see' reflects the earlier neutral sense, as do various Germanic cognates, like the Old Norse *speja* or Middle Dutch *spien*, from one of which English received the word *spy*, via French.

When *specious* reached English, which it had done by the early 15th century, either as a direct adaptation of the Latin or as a borrowing of its French derivative, it had no negative connotations but retained the generally favorable sense of the Latin word from which it came. By the early 17th century, however, it started to acquire a pejorative sense, 'seemingly attractive but actually devoid of attractiveness.' Both significations existed side by side for some centuries; the new development probably represented a specialized connotation acquired from some of the contexts in which the word frequently occurred. But by the 19th century the negative connotation had become part of the denotation, and the earlier sense became obsolete.

sphinx

This word comes from the Greek noun meaning 'strangler,' which is derived from the verb *sphingein* 'to tighten,' the same verb that gives us *sphincter*. The Greek *Sphinx* was a terrifying creature with the body of a winged lion and the breasts and head of a woman. This monster guarded the gate at Thebes and would strangle anyone who could not answer the riddle, "What goes on four legs at dawn, two at noon, and three at dusk?" Oedipus is credited with the correct answer, "Man," since man creeps on all fours as a baby, walks on two legs as an adult, and hobbles with a cane in old age. On hearing the correct answer, the *Sphinx* is said to have hurled herself off the wall at Thebes to her death.

Although Oedipus solved the riddle and the *Sphinx* was no more, to this day we still speak of a person who asks a seemingly unanswerable question or is inscrutable and mysterious as a *sphinx*; the sense of 'strangler' has faded. Moreover, *sphinx* is the word for the Egyptian monster that guards many of the tombs of the pharaohs, so called by the Greeks because it seemed to them that the beast with the body of a lion and the head of a pharaoh resembled the *Sphinx* of Thebes.

The Greek and Egyptian *sphinxes*, however, were quite different in function. Far from being a feared riddle-poser, the Egyptian *sphinx* was a source of information, and would answer any question asked of it by a passer-by. The most famous *sphinx*, at the pyramid of El-Gizeh, immortalizes the Pharaoh Cephren and depicts his facial likeness atop the body of an immense stone lion.

spinster

This term represents a combination of the Old English root *spin-*, from *spinnan* 'to spin,' and the agent suffix *-(e)stre*, giving a 'spinner; one who spins.' The form that underlies the suffix seems to have designated a specifically female agent, but became generalized in Old English and Dutch to mean an 'agent of either sex.' Later, *-ster* came to refer primarily to a 'male (or neutral) agent,' often with a pejorative sense. The corresponding feminine form, *-stress*, a combination of *-st(e)r* and the feminine agent suffix *-ess*, was then introduced to fill the gap.

Originally, then, *spinster* could refer to a 'spinner' of either sex, though its primary application was to females, since it was chiefly women who spun. By the 17th century the term had come to apply exclusively to women and had taken on the additional qualification of 'unmarried.' Indeed, it was at that time that it came to be used as a legal term designating an 'unmarried woman.' During the same period *spinstress* entered the language in the sense of 'woman who spins,' without any implication of marital status and presumably referring to a woman who spins for a living. Today a *spinster* is an 'old maid, unmarried woman old enough so that marriage is unlikely.'

spoon

The Old English word *spōn*, the ancestor of the modern form, signified any 'chip, shaving, or splinter of wood.' Not until the early 14th century did the term start to apply to those pieces of wood that had hollowed-out sections for use as culinary utensils. The new specialization, or narrowing of meaning, coincided almost exactly with the appearance in English of the word *chip*, which took over the function of the other term. The earliest attested citations are around 1330 for *chip*, and about 1340 for the new meaning of *spoon*, but actual occurrences may have started earlier. The use of the word continued, in a process linguists call "subreption," even when the utensil was no longer made of wood, a development well established by the early 16th century.

starve

The Old English *steorfan*, the ancestor of *starve*, meant simply 'to die,' without specification as to the cause, a meaning preserved in the German cognate, *sterben*.

Although occasional instances of the meaning 'to die of hunger' did occur in Old English times, the added meaning generally came from the context. By the early 12th century, however, the more specialized sense 'to die from lack of food' started to become general, eventually ousting the older meaning. A further functional specialization, 'to cause to die from hunger,' took place in the 16th century.

During this century the word has undergone a semantic weakening, coming to mean 'to be hungry,' as in "I'm starving for a hamburger." It has also been generalized to mean 'to suffer a deprivation of,' and hence 'to desire ardently,' as in "starved of love," "starved of education," and so on.

An additional semantic bypath from the original meaning, 'to perish of cold,' appeared frequently enough from the 17th to the late 19th century to deserve notice. This sense now appears to be obsolete, a linguistic fact that may reflect improved living conditions.

stigma

The Proto-Indo-European stem **stig-* meant 'point,' or 'be sharp,' as seen in the Greek *stígos* 'point' or the Sanskrit *tiga* 'be sharp, cause to be sharp.' When extended by **-mnt*, a suffix signifying 'result,' the form meant 'result of the point,' or a 'puncture, puncture mark.' In Greek, where the *n* of *-mnt* became *a*, and *t* in final position disappeared, this word, *stigma*, eventually specialized in a variety of senses, among them 'spot' and 'punctuation mark.'

The Romans borrowed the term and specialized it somewhat differently (according to one common connotative addition that reflected contemporary practices) as a 'mark burned into, or brand imposed upon, slaves or criminals.' Thus this mark, originally of an explicitly physical nature, also acquired the connotation of a 'badge of shame.'

The word first entered English in the 16th century in the physical sense. During the next century, the plural form, *stigmata*, applied to the wounds on the body of Jesus or to similar marks on the bodies of certain saints or holy persons, underwent an amelioration, losing the pejorative connotations. As the practice of branding as a form of punishment fell into disuse, *stigma* lost its physical denotation, and the former connotation became the primary general sense.

In biological terminology, however, the word reverted to a meaning close to its early significance, with subsequent specialization, possibly because many scholars of the 17th and 18th century studied Greek. Thus the term came to signify the small respiratory openings, also called "spiracles," of insects, and the points on the pistils of plants through which pollen enters.

In the 19th century, a *stigma* came to mean a 'point whose position in a plane depends upon that of another point,' in mathematical terminology, and in recent times nuclear physicists have used the term as the name for an extremely small unit of length, 10^{-12} meter, also known as a *bicron, micromicron, picometer*.

The English cognate of the unexpanded stem *stig-* is *stick*, a word which once probably referred to the sharp edge rather than to the entire piece of wood.

stirrup

Old English *stigrāp*, the direct ancestor of *stirrup*, consisted of *stig-* 'go up' or 'go down,' and *rāp* 'rope.' The second element developed into the different forms *-rup* or *rope* in the evolution to Modern English, according to whether it was unaccented, as in the compound, or accented, as it is when an independent word. *Stig-* is a variant of the stem seen in the Old English *stīgan*, which meant either 'to go,' with no vertical motion implied, or 'to go up, to mount, to ascend.' Both senses are semantically plausible, since a *stirrup* not only serves as a mounting and dismounting device, but is also used in riding horseback. Since today *stirrups* are commonly made of leather and metal, rather than rope, the *-rup* seems inappropriate if perceived in its original significance, but semantic fading and subreption of that early meaning have taken place.

street

The Latin word *strātum*, a past participle of *sternere*, first meant 'that which has been spread out,' and then specialized to such senses as 'bed, quilt, horse blanket,' acquiring connotations from the context. When employed as an adjective in agreement with the noun *via* 'way, road,' it came to mean 'paved.' Thus the combination *strāta via* meant a 'paved road.' By the post-classical period, the sense of the phrase had localized in the earlier element, *strāta*.

The Romans were the great roadbuilders of antiquity, and wherever they expanded their empire, their engineers paved the roads to make distant regions more accessible. Long before the future English language had separated from its West Germanic antecedents, the Germanic tribes had encountered the Roman legions and acquired the Latin term, which then evolved to Old English *strǣt* and finally to Modern English *street*. Modern German *Strasse* represents the High Germanic treatment of the same loan word. Although originally applied to military roads, the sense of *strǣt* had generalized, by the 10th century, to signify any road or pathway, whether paved or not. There are, however, occasional occurrences of Old English *strǣt* in the significance of 'bed' or 'couch,' a retention of one of the earlier Latin uses of *strātum*.

English cognates of the same stem include *strew* and *straw*. A Greek cognate, extended by a different suffix, followed a semantic development to 'mattress' or 'bed,' paralleling the Latin, and then reached English, via Latin, in a specialized medical usage. This was *stroma*, meaning the 'tissue bed or framework,' as opposed to the functional specialized parts of organs, glands, or other body structures.

stroke

The contemporary use of *stroke* in its medical sense, 'brain infarction' or 'apoplectic seizure,' reflects medieval and ancient medical theory which viewed illness as divine retribution for sinful conduct. A 16th-century medical handbook lists cinnamon water as a specific "for the stroke of Gods hande." The meaning of this phrase localized in the single word, and the remainder dropped off, but not in general usage until the 18th century. With the evolution of medical theory, the semantic focus of the term shifted from the supposed cause of the condition to the condition itself, and the original denotation faded. The development of *stroke* with this meaning parallels the similar history of *apoplexy*, which derives via French from a Greek word whose stem, *plēg-*, also meant 'blow' or 'stroke.'

swastika

The crooked cross, with its right-angle extensions, is today most often thought of as the Nazi symbol, associated with anti-Semitism and war; but the Nazis were only the most recent users of this ancient sign. The Sanskrit *svastika* is a compound of *su* 'good, well,' *asti* 'being,' and the suffix -*ka*, originally an adjective-forming suffix that later came to be used in forming nouns as well. The Sanskritic *svastika* was a symbol of well-being or good luck, derived, according to some scholars, from the stylization of the wheel of the god Vishnu's solar chariot.

In fact, the *swastika* appears in many different cultures all over the world, from ancient China to Mycenae to the British Isles (where it was known as the *fylfot* or *filfot*, arguably the 'one with four feet') to the New World. As a variant of the standard cross, it was used in the early Christian Church, where it was known as the *gammadion*, a figure made from four capital gammas. Wherever it appeared, the primary significance of the *swastika* was life-affirming, until the Nazis gave it a connotation quite at variance with its original one.

swindle

The Old High German verb *swintilōn*, the frequentative form of *swintan* 'to swoon, languish,' meant 'to be apt to swoon.' From this verb, or from one of its cognate forms in another Germanic dialect, was formed a noun designating a 'giddy person,' a 'person apt to swoon,' and it is this which entered English to form the basis of the noun *swindler* from which, by back-formation, the verb to *swindle* was created.

Swindler is said to have been introduced into English by German Jews toward the middle of the 18th century. By that time, *Schwindler*/*Swindler* meant not only a 'giddy person,' but had, as well, the extended sense of a 'person prone to making extravagant statements or predictions, especially about financial matters.' Such a person might have been called a *swindler* because of the giddiness of his predictions. From this sense soon evolved the idea of 'cheater, confidence man,' since such a person, who promised to make a fortune for another, might instead abscond with the money entrusted to him.

sycophant

The etymology of this term is controversial, not because its lexical underpinnings are unclear, but because it is by no means obvious why its original component parts were used to convey the meaning that they did. *Sycophant* comes from the Greek words *sŷkon* 'fig,' and *phaneîn* 'to show, to make appear.' The latter term appears in such English words as *phenomenon, phantasm, diaphanous*, and *fantastic*, since the root is a Proto-Indo-European term for 'light,' or by extension, 'appearance.'

In Greek, *sykophántēs* was an 'informer,' a 'slanderer.' From this sense evolved the Modern English meaning, 'flatterer,' a person who curries favor by saying nice things about a prospective patron or by saying nasty things about that patron's enemies—a tactic close to that of the informer who seeks a reward by betraying his associates to the authorities.

But what did 'fig-showing' have to do with being an informer? First, one who 'showed figs' may simply have been someone who was paid to shake the fig tree, causing the fruit to fall to the ground where it would be readily seen, collected, and shipped off to market. Second, this might have been a person who "uncovered" a plot to steal or smuggle figs, both crimes the Greeks wished to curtail. Third, one who 'showed figs' may have been a person who made the "sign of the fig" by making a fist and poking the thumb between the index and middle fingers in a bit of nonverbal communication still well attested to this day.

The "sign of the fig" seems to have been sexual in origin, since in the ancient world the fig was widely considered a symbol of female fertility and the sign was a stylized representation of the female genitalia with a penis inserted therein. Among its many functions, this sign at one time carried the meaning of the accusatory index finger, and the man who made the "sign of the fig" was literally "fingering" a wrong-doer, presumably in the hope of a reward.

Today, a *sycophant* is not so much an informer as a fawner or a toady, and its association with figs has been long forgotten.

syphilis

While many English terms for specific diseases come from Latin or Greek, either as borrowings of the folk nomenclature or newly minted from "scientific" Greek or Latin, *Syphilis* entered the language by a different route. It was the name of a swineherd, the protagonist in a didactic poem, *Syphilis, sive morbus gallicus* "Syphilis ('Pig-lover'), or The French Plague," written by Girolamo Fracastoro in the 16th century. In the poem, *Syphilis* suffered from what the Italians called the "French disease" (known in France as *le mal de Naples* 'the Neapolitan disease').

The term entered English in 1686, when Nahum Tate published his translation of Fracastoro's poem, and the name of the protagonist was soon lent to the disease from which he suffered.

syrup, sherbet, shrub, shrab

In Arabic, the triliteral root *sh-r-b* gives both the verb *shariba* 'to drink' and the noun *sharāb* 'beverage.' This term has been borrowed into English at several different points in history, each time from a different source language and with a slightly different meaning. *Sharāb* first appears in English as *syrup*, from Old French, which inherited it from Late Latin, into which it had been borrowed from the Arabic. This was in the sense of 'thick, sweet medicinal liquid,' a specialization of its original sense 'sweet beverage.' In more recent times, *syrup* has been regeneralized to mean a 'thick, sweet liquid,' not necessarily medicinal.

Sherbet entered English in the 17th century from Turkish, which had acquired the word from Persian, which had borrowed it from Arabic. This form had come to designate a 'sweet cooling drink' in Turkish, and it was borrowed into English in that sense. In British English, *sherbet* is still a beverage; the American *sherbet*, 'a frozen dessert made with a base of water, milk, or juice,' is called by its French name, *sorbet*, in England.

Shrub, first attested in English in the 18th century, may have come directly from Arabic or, more likely, may represent a slight phonetic modification of the Persian word *sharāb* 'wine,' attested as *sherab* and *sharab* in English in the 17th century. Whichever the case, *shrub* was, and remains, a 'sweet alcoholic beverage,' originally a 'sweet wine,' and later, a 'sweet drink made from sugar, fruit juice, brandy or rum,' each sense a specialization of the Arabic *sharāb* 'beverage.'

Shrab is the Hindustani reflex of Arabic *sharāb* and means 'wine, spirits.' It was borrowed into English in the 19th century, the heyday of British rule in India. It is virtually unknown in American English.

T

taboo, tabu

In the native languages of Melanesia and Polynesia, *ta* 'marked' and *bu* 'exceedingly' form a compound which is used in a specialized religious sense in the local cultures. The most common form of the term is *tapu* or *tambu* (Hawaiian *kapu*), but the first recorded contact that a native speaker of English had with the word was Captain Cook's, in 1777, when he encountered its Tongan form, *tabu*, in his travels.

The Malayo-Polynesians use the term adjectivally, to qualify objects marked as consecrated for the use of a god, king, priest, or chief. Since each object so qualified is sacred to or reserved for the use of a special individual, there is a strong sense of its being forbidden to anyone else. Thus the meaning of the term has been extended to refer to a thing forbidden, though not necessarily sacred. It may even be applied to a person under a special ban, someone who is not allowed to do something.

Cook and subsequent explorers carried home the word *tabu* with, at best, an imprecise sense of the range of its ritual and linguistic uses among the natives. They generalized its meaning to 'prohibited, prohibition,' the sense which it commonly has in English today, often with undertones of 'superstition.'

tandem

The various English meanings of this word descend ultimately from an etymological pun. One translation of the Latin adverb *tandem* was 'at length,' in the sense of 'finally, at last.' Certain 18th-century scholars, playfully transforming the temporal sense into a locative one, 'lengthwise,' applied the word to a carriage drawn by horses one behind the other. By the 19th century, *tandem* applied to the bicycle built for two or to a canoe with two paddlers, one behind the other.

More recently the use has extended to other units which operate together, such as the close sets of axles in trailer trucks. Each development after the word's entry into English represents a specialization by connotative extension.

The original Latin word represented a compound of *tam* 'thus,' a feminine extension of the Indo-European demonstrative that appears in many English words beginning with *th-*, as *the, this, then,* and *there,* among others, plus another emphatic element, *-dem.* Both of these particles did occasionally enter into locative use, so the humorous twist did have etymological precedents.

tariff

In Arabic, *'arafa* means 'to notify,' and a *ta'rif* is a 'notification, explanation.' During the 16th century, when trade by sea between the East and West was flourishing, the Turkish variant of the term came into English with the sense of a 'schedule of customs duties,' a specialization of its original Arabic meaning. This may have been the result of linguistic filtering between Arabic and Turkish.

Beginning in the 18th century, *tariff* was extended in English to cover any 'list of charges,' as a *hotel tariff*, or, later, a *railroad tariff*. Today, a *tariff* may, by further extension, refer to a 'charge or duty' itself, as in Spanish *tarifa* 'price list; fare.' (See also **fare**.)

tart¹, tart²

Historically there are two kinds of *tart* in English, one associated with 'bitterness,' the other, with 'sweetness.' *Tart¹* comes from a Proto-Indo-European verb root, **der,* which seems to have meant 'to flay, peel, skin,' and yields, in addition to *tart*, to *tear (apart),* and, through Greek, *dermatologist, epidermis,* and a number of other terms referring to the skin. Something *tart* was, then, either 'something torn,' or 'something used for tearing.' From this comes its English sense of 'sharp' and, by extension, in the 14th century, 'sharp or bitter to the taste,' the meaning of the term today.

Tart² comes from the Proto-Indo-European root **terkʷ* 'twist,' which appears in such Latinate forms as *torque* and *contort.* This *tart²* itself entered English from French in the 14th century as the name for a 'variety of pastry; a pie with a sweet filling,' to be compared with the later German borrowing, *torte*. The round or twisted shape of the edible *tart²* seems to have been the connection with its linguistic root.

Much as such terms as *sweetie pie, honey bun*, and *cupcake* have come to be applied to humans as terms of endearment, so *tart²*, with its agreeable taste associations, came to be used as an epithet for a dear one, usually female. But by the 19th century this term had come to refer specifically to a 'woman of loose morals; a prostitute,' a sense now obsolescent in American English.

In British usage, the verb to *tart up* is commonly used to refer to decorating a person or thing, especially in order to produce an impression of quality that does not, in fact, underlie a glossy exterior.

Tartar

The words we commonly use to designate specific peoples of the world in both polite and not-so-polite society constitute a rich and varied subset of the vocabulary of the English language. More often than not, these words are borrowings either from the language of the people named or from that of one of their close neighbors. Frequently the original sense of the borrowed term is lost or only dimly perceived in the course of the borrowing, laying the way for its subsequent application to people to whom the name did not originally apply.

Tartar and its sometime synonym *Hun* are cases in point. Both originally designated a 'person from Mongolia.' *Hun* is derived from Chinese *hsiung-nu* 'barbarian,' and *Tartar*, with some interference from Latin, from Persian *Tātār*, possibly a remaking of Chinese *Tahdzû*, a term of ultimately uncertain derivation and meaning. The *Tartars* or *Huns* became known in the Western world first in the 5th century and then again in the 13th with the invasion of Genghis Khan and his Mongol horde, a force of varied ethnic composition. The variety of its make-up is suggested by the word *horde* itself, which comes from the Turkish *ordī/ordū* '(military) camp,' and is the basis of *Urdu*, the 'language of the camp; Hindustani dialect spoken by Muslims.' The word *Hun* is also a borrowing from Turkish through Latin and Germanic, designating those Asiatic invaders joined by the Turks in the sweep across Asia and Eastern Europe. *Hun* retained something of its original Turkish sense until fairly recent times, when the term was appropriated to designate the Germans during the two world wars.

Tartar has a somewhat more colorful history. Saint Louis of France is said to have been responsible for changing Persian *Tātār* to *Tartare* in the 13th century, by equating the invaders with the denizens of hell (Latin *Tartarus*).

By the 17th century the meaning of *Tartar*, like that of *Hun*, had come to designate any 'fierce, uncivilized warrior,' giving rise to the saying *to catch a Tartar*, with the sense of 'to catch a tiger (wolf) by the tail, to bite off more than one can chew,' in other words, to enter an encounter in which one cannot win and from which one cannot escape.

task, tax

Both of these words come from the Late Latin noun *taxa* 'appraisal, assessment, assessed payment,' from the verb *taxāre* 'to evaluate, assess; to assess payment.' Two sources for the Latin verb have been suggested. The first is the Greek verb *tássein/táttein* (simple past *étaxa*) 'to arrange, to order; to fix payment' which may have been borrowed into Latin in its past form with the specific sense of 'assess payment.' The second possibility is that *taxāre* represents a form of the Latin verb *tangere* 'to touch' that had the meaning 'to touch again and again,' which might have been extended metaphorically to mean 'to assess or levy payment.'

In the Middle Ages, *taxa* (pronounced "taksa") changed to *tasca* ("taska") in certain Latin dialects, creating a doublet. The noun *task* entered English from Old French along with the verb *tax* in the 13th century. The verb seems to have come into English during the 14th century with the meaning 'to assess an amount (of payment),' a sense which evolved to 'to impose a compulsory payment.' At that time, the noun *tax* appeared in the language with essentially the contemporary sense of 'compulsory payment.' *Task*, meanwhile, had come to have the sense of 'obligatory labor (in lieu of monetary payment)'; that is, a *task* was a *tax* or tribute paid in work rather than coin.

By the 16th century, the noun *tax* had become fixed in its present sense, while *task* and the verb to *tax* had begun to become generalized. A *task* could be any 'obligatory labor or piece of work,' whether the obligation was imposed from without, by an employer or a teacher, or from within, by one's conscience. *Tax* as a verb came to refer not only to the imposition of a financial obligation to the king or local lord, but to more general demands as well, as in *tax the imagination* 'burden the imagination,' or *taxing labor* 'demanding, arduous work.' One might even refer to a *taxing task*, once the senses of *task* and *tax* had become sufficiently distinct and their single origin had been forgotten.

tattoo

This word is a remaking of *tap to(o)*, a 17th-century borrowing from the Dutch *tap toe* '(let the) tap (be) closed.' The *tap* in question was at the local tavern, and the exhortation to close it was the signal for military personnel to leave off drinking and return to quarters for the night. Thus a *tap toe* was a call to return to quarters, and was accompanied by drum beats, or, later, a bugle call.

It is not clear whether the English who borrowed the term fully understood its etymology, although Colonel Hutchinson of Nottingham ordered in 1644 that "if anyone shall bee found tiplinge or drinkinge in any Tavern, Inne, or Alehouse after the houre of nyne of the clock at night when *Tap Too* beates, he shall pay 2s, 6d." It is possible that this dictum reflects a grasp not so much of the literal meaning of the Dutch command as of the off-duty habits of the soldiery.

In any event, the *tap too*, or, later, *tattoo*, had as its earliest sense in English a 'call to quarters for the night,' the call emphasized by drumming. The drumming aspect of the meaning was subsequently extended, with fading of its military association, so that a *tattoo* or *devil's tattoo* is the 'drumming of the fingers of an impatient or distracted person.' Later, since the call to quarters could be accompanied or signaled by the bugle as well as by the drum, in the 18th century *tattoo* came to mean a 'military display featuring the drum and bugle corps.'

Finally, it is tempting to derive the American military call to quarters for the night, *taps*, from the Dutch *tap toe*, though most etymologists prefer to take that term from the *tap* of a drum beat rather than from the *tap* of a tavern.

tawdry

Aethelthryth, known in Old French as *Audrey*, wife of King Ecgfrith of Northumbria in the 7th century, nearly caused a war when she left her husband and fled for sanctuary to Wulfare, the ruler of the neighboring kingdom of Mercia. She founded an abbey at Ely, and devoted the rest of her life to pious works, her single worldly vice being a fondness for fine necklaces. When stricken by the cancer of the throat that killed her in 679, she saw her illness as punishment for her vanity. The city of Ely, however, which had received so much of her bounty, took her as its patron saint and celebrated her birthday every October 17th with a fair at which merchants sold fine silken scarves called *St. Audrey's laces* in memory of the royal abbess. Nine hundred years after her death, in 1579, Spenser wrote,

> Bind your fillets faste,
> And girde in your waste,
> For more finesse
> With a tawdrie lace.

At that time the connotations of *tawdry* were still entirely favorable, but eventually unscrupulous vendors allowed the quality of the scarves to deteriorate until the word *tawdry*, as associated with the products sold at the fair, came to signify 'gaudy, but of shoddy quality.' Later the word came to be used to describe anything that was cheap and lacking in refinement.

taxi, cab

These are alternate 20th-century abbreviations of *taxi-cab*, which is itself an abbreviation of the turn-of-the-century *taximeter-cab* 'a motorized coach for hire which is fitted with a device for measuring mileage and computing fares.' The *cab* of *taximeter-cab* is a 19th-century abbreviation of *cabriolet*, a term borrowed into English from French in the 18th century, and designating a 'two-wheeled coach drawn by a single horse.' *Cabriolet* is derived from the Italian verb *capriolare* 'to jump up in the air,' since that coach was known for its springy suspension.

Taximeter is a borrowing of the 19th-century French term *taxi-mètre*, a compound of *taxe* 'tariff, fare' and *mètre* 'meter,' a measuring device. The *i* was introduced either through the influence of Greek *táxis* 'assessment of tribute' or because of a felt need for a stronger linking vowel than the unstable French *e*. (*Taxameter* is also attested in English.) It is also possible that the strong tendency to make both parts of a compound created from classical components agree as to their source language may have played a part in replacing the French *e* and English *a* with *i*. *Mètre/meter* is a learned borrowing of Greek *métron* 'measure,' while *taxe/taxa* is Latinate.

Today, both *taxi* and *cab* may be used as verbs. To *cab* is 'to travel by (*taxi-*)*cab*.' To *taxi* can either mean 'to travel by *taxi-*(*cab*)' or, in reference to aircraft, 'to travel along a runway before take-off or after landing.'

test

In Latin, *testa* seems originally to have designated a 'shell, carapace.' This term was generalized, during the time of the Roman Empire, to mean a 'vessel,' that is, something concave like a shell, that could hold something. Working its way into the second and fourth declensions as *testum* and *testū*, respectively, this first-declension noun acquired two specific senses, each a rarification of the meaning '(earthen) vessel, pot.'

The first of these, attested in French but not in English, was 'head' (Modern French *tête*), presumably because of its shape and fragility. The Modern German *Kopf* 'head' has been similarly derived from the underlying form, which gives Modern English *cup*.

The second specialization of Latin *testa/testum/testū*, which is attested in English, was as a 'pot, cupel' which could be used to *test* coins for their content of valuable metal. Coins of dubious value would be melted down in such a pot so as to allow the components of the alloy to separate and be measured. From 'pot in which precious metals may be evaluated in their liquid state,' the sense of 'evaluation procedure for precious metals' evolved by transference and was subsequently generalized to mean 'evaluation procedure' of any sort. Thus *test*, originally a noun, came to be used as a verb in the sense of 'to perform an evaluation; evaluate.'

A related origin for *test* has also been proposed. This suggests that the Latinate earthen pot called a *testa* held lots which, when drawn from the vessel, would determine an individual's fate. Such lots and pots were standard at the oracles of Rome and Delphi and are highly suggestive of the contemporary practice of drawing lots from a hat. (See also **noggin**.)

testicle

Two etymologies compete for the origins of this word. One derives the term from the diminutive form of Latin *testis* 'witness; male reproductive gland,' while the other traces the English word back to the diminutive form of Latin *testa/testum/testū* 'vessel.' (See **test**.)

According to the first hypothesis, Latin *testis* comes from the Proto-Indo-European word for *three*, since three witnesses were generally required in Roman law in order to assure conviction of an alleged offender. Since his *testicles* are the most fundamental witnesses to his virility, so the argument goes, from the sense 'witness' came the specialized sense of 'witness(es) to manhood.' A slight variation on this etymology has it that it was customary in the ancient Near East for a man to swear an oath on his privates (often euphemized to his "knees" in ancient literatures of the region). Thus at one time to be a legal witness involved swearing on the genitalia—whence, perhaps, the sense of *testis* as 'witness.'

The derivation from *testa/testum/testū* simply traces meanings from a 'shell, carapace' to, by extension, a 'concavity suitable for holding things' and, later, a '(more or less globular) pot.' By extension of this last sense, the male reproductive glands would have acquired their name.

thigh, thumb

The Proto-Indo-European root *teu(H)* seems to have designated a 'swelling,' and is the source through Germanic of Modern English *thigh*, the 'swollen part of the leg,' *thumb*, the 'swollen finger,' and *thousand*, a 'swollen hundred.' The Latin outcome of this same root gives us *tumor* and, from Greek *boútyron* 'butter' (from *boûs* 'cow' plus *tyrós* 'cheese,' which is to say 'coagulated, "swollen" milk') we get *butter*.

While *thigh* has continued in its Old English sense of 'upper leg' following its early specialization, *thumb* has come to be used in a number of idiomatic expressions in extensions of its original meaning. Thus, a person who is *all thumbs* is 'clumsy,' while a person with a *green thumb* is an 'expert gardener.' *Thumbs up* and *thumbs down* are signals, dating from Roman times, for 'reprieve, or general favor' and 'condemnation, or general disfavor,' respectively. To be *under a person's thumb* is to be under that person's control. To *thumb your nose* at someone, in a gesture the French call *pied de nez* 'nose-foot,' is to show disrespect or defiance. It is also possible to *thumb a ride* 'hitchhike,' or *thumb through* 'leaf through' a book or periodical, or to follow a *rule of thumb*.

thing

The original meaning of this highly versatile word seems to have been an 'assembly of people,' more specifically, a 'gathering of people to decide legal matters,' as this is the earliest attested sense of the word in Old English and in such cognate forms as Old Frisian *ting*, Old High German *Ding*, and Old Norse *ping*. It is possible that the Germanic root underlying *thing* as well as *hustings*, originally a combination of 'house(hold)' and '*thing*,' was an extension of the Proto-Indo-European root **ten-* 'stretch,' which forms the basis of Latin *tenēre* 'to hold (together), grasp,' though the connection is obscure.

By the 11th century, the sense of *thing* in English had been transferred from 'legal assembly' to 'matter considered by a legal assembly,' a similar transfer having been made in at least some of the other Germanic languages as well. Soon the meaning of the word was extended to 'matter, affair' in general, and from that sense to 'entity' whether of thought or physical fact.

Today, *thing* generally designates a 'physical entity,' though it may also be used in a more general way to name any 'topic, matter, or item,' however intangible or imprecise in definition. Indeed, *thing* and its humorous compounds, *thingummy*, *thingumbob*, *thingamajig*, and so on, has become a convenient stand-in for virtually any object or idea whose common name is unknown to or escapes the speaker.

thug

This is a 19th-century borrowing from Hindi and comes from the Sanskrit verb root *sthag* 'to cover, conceal.' The Proto-Indo-European form which underlies *sthag* has also produced such English words as *thatch*, Old English 'cover for a house,' thus, 'roof'; *deck*, Dutch 'cover for a boat,' the 'platform extending from one side of a vessel to the other'; *shanty* (which see), Irish Gaelic 'cover for people,' thus, a 'house'; and the *-tect* of *detect and protect.* The Latin *tēctum* is a 'covered building, roof.'

In Hindi, a *ṭhag* is a 'cut-throat, robber,' on the order of the Near Eastern *assassin.* The Indian *thugs* or, as they were first known in English, *Thugs*, were a cohesive group that operated in gangs, pretending to be fellow-travelers until the opportunity arrived to rob, slaughter, and bury their victims. The burial was apparently carried out according to strict religious procedures, including consecration of the pickax and the ritual offering of sugar before the kill.

Actually, the *Thugs*, not all of whom were robbers, were members of a religious order in India. They claimed Muslim origins, while sacrificing to the Hindu goddess Kali. However, their association with robbery and killing led the British in India to eliminate the order, beginning in the 1830s. By 1879 the census listed only a handful of members for the sect, and today it is officially extinct.

By 1879, however, the word *thug* had already entered the English language with the meaning 'robber-murderer,' and without any accompanying sense of 'member of a religious sect.' From 'robber-murderer' has evolved the more general sense of 'hoodlum, tough guy' in use today. (See also **assassin.**)

timber

Proto-Indo-European **demH* meant 'dwelling, house,' and is the basis for both *domus* 'house, household,' from which we get such English words as *domicile, domain,* and *dominion,* and the Old English *timber,* which originally meant 'house.' (Cf. Modern German *Zimmer* 'room.') By the 10th century, *timber* had come to mean 'building material' as well as 'house,' and since the most common building material was wood, by the 12th century the sense of *timber* had become specialized to 'wood (for building).'

As the sense of 'house' faded, in the 14th century, the sense of 'wood' was generalized, so that the word came to mean 'wood in general,' whether hewed, sawed, and squared off or in its primitive form as a tree. By the 16th century, *timber* could mean 'trees; lumber; a beam,' all current senses today.

tire

Old French *attir(i)er* meant 'to order, arrange, equip,' and was borrowed into English with that range of senses in the 13th century. With the verb came a noun, *attire*, with the meaning 'equipment;' it could be used to designate the 'specific equipment worn or carried by soldiers.' By extension, in the following century, *attire* and its abbreviated variant, *tire*, came to refer to 'dress' in general, that is, the 'equipment with which an individual covers and adorns his or her body.' *Attire* is still used in this sense, although *tire* is not.

Tire came to have a specialized use in the 15th century, that of 'dressing for the wheels of a coach.' This dressing consisted of 'curved plating for the rim of a wheel.' In the 18th century, *tire* began to be used to designate a 'metal rim of a wheel,' its ornamental function having given way to that of lending structural support to the wheel. In the 19th century, *tires* came to be made of rubber, as they are today, to fit over the now metal rims of the wheels of a vehicle.

tithe

This word represents the regular phonetic outcome of the Old English combination of *ten* 'ten' and the ordinal-forming suffix *-oþa*, since in that language nasal consonants were commonly lost before such spirants. A *tithe* was originally a 'tenth part of something; a tenth.' This general sense continued until well into the 12th century, when the analogical form, *tenth*, began to gain currency. By that time, also, *tithe* had developed the specialized sense which has insured its continued use to this day. This specialized sense was a 'tenth of an individual's produce to be donated to the Christian Church for the support of its clergy.' The notion of such a donation was pre-Christian, the Jews having instituted the *ma'aser* 'tenth' in ancient times as a means of supporting both the Levites and the poor. The Levites, having been granted no land in the division of their country, were expected to live and teach in the territories occupied by the other ten tribes of Israel, and to be paid by the mandatory public donation of one-tenth of the landed citizenry's produce or income. With the destruction of the Temple and the collapse of the old tribal structure of Jewish society, the *ma'aser* became a voluntary gift.

The early Christians continued the practice of voluntary *tithing* until, in the 8th century, the financial needs of the church demanded that it be made obligatory. Thus by the 12th century the sense of *tithe* as an obligatory tenth to be given to the church was firmly established. Although the practice has not been observed in the mainstream Christian sects for three or four hundred years, largely as a result of the separation of church and state, certain fundamentalist sects continue to *tithe* their members.

By the 17th century *tithe* had become generalized, in common usage, to mean, on the one hand, any 'tax or levy,' and, on the other, any 'small amount,' this, presumably, as a gloss on the actual proportion of income freely given to the church once sanctions against giving less than a tenth were removed.

toast

The verb *toast* 'brown by heating' is a 14th-century borrowing of French *toster*, formed from the Late Latin *tostāre*, which itself goes back to the past participle, *tostus*, of the classical Latin verb *torrēre* 'to parch, dry out.' *Torrēre*, in turn, is derived from the Proto-Indo-European root **ters* 'dry,' which appears in English *thirst* and in a variety of words derived from Latin *terra* 'earth,' that is, dry land.

The noun *toast* 'bread browned by heating' is a specialized 15th-century derivative of the homophonous 14th-century verb. The noun *toast* 'individual honored by drinking to his or her health,' as in "the *toast* of the town," arose in the 17th century from a specialized use of *toast* 'bread browned by heating'; and the verb *toast* 'to drink someone's health' was then derived from the new noun. Thus the verb gave rise to the noun, which gave rise to what is in effect another noun which, in turn, gave rise to what is in effect another verb—even though they are all *toast*.

The connection between 'bread browned by heating' and 'person whose health is drunk' is that people used to flavor their alcoholic beverages by dunking spiced *toast* in them, as one might dunk a doughnut in coffee. The name of the person whose health was drunk was to flavor the drink as spiced *toast* might.

According to a piece by Richard Steele in the *Tatler* of June, 1709, the first *toast* drunk was proposed by a gentleman during the reign of Charles II, who scooped up a cup of a famous beauty's bathwater and drank her health with it, causing a friend to remark that he'd have been glad enough to do without the drink but would have been most happy to enjoy the *"toast"* floating in it.

toddy

While today we tend to think of a *toddy* as a hot drink made from brandy or rum, its original form seems to have been cool and nonalcoholic. The word is a souvenir of the British occupation of India, and comes from a palm tree. Sanskrit *tāla*, a word of uncertain descent, possibly from a Dravidian ancestor, meant 'palm tree.' By the time it entered the modern languages of northern India, it meant 'palm sap.' (Cf. Hindi *tārī*.) This sap, which ferments quickly, was a popular drink in northern India, and British sailors retained the Indian name for a tipple they concocted from the fermented juice of the sugar cane, or from brandy, and drank hot.

toilet

Toilette, a combination of French *toile* 'cloth' and the diminutive suffix *-et(te)*, originally meant 'little cloth.' When the word was borrowed into English in the 16th century, it was in the sense of 'laundry bag, cloth wrapper, container for clothing.' During the following century, however, the word was generally used in a different sense in both French and English, '(decorative) cloth covering for a (woman's) dressing-table.' These cloths were apparently large enough to double as 'shawls worn around the shoulders while the hair is dressed or make-up applied.'

In the 17th century, by transference from the sense 'dressing-table cover,' *toilet(te)* came to be used to designate both the 'articles used in dressing the hair and applying make-up' and the 'dressing-table' itself. *Toilet*, at that time, could also refer to the 'process of dressing or grooming oneself,' as it can today.

From 'dressing-table' the sense of *toilet* was extended in the early 19th century to 'dressing-room,' and, from there, to the room variously euphemistically termed the 'bathroom, lavatory, water closet, or w.c.,' and then, chiefly in the United States, to the 'apparatus for the disposal of human excreta' commonly found therein.

torpedo

The Proto-Indo-European stem *sterp- 'to become stiff' gave rise to a number of semantic lines, one of which, discussed under the entry for starve, passed through 'die' to 'die of hunger,' to 'be hungry.' Another line started with that variant of the stem which dropped the initial s, a phenomenon that often occurred with Indo-European words starting with s, since, when words followed one another in phrases, it was difficult to be sure if an s was the first consonant of the second word or the last consonant of the preceding one. The words steer and taurus 'bull' illustrate this variation involving the "s mobile" or "movable s," as some specialists in Indo-European linguistics call it. Thus one variant of the stem survived as the Latin torpēre 'to be stiff or numb.' A noun extension of the form gave the word torpedo, which basically meant 'stiffness' or 'numbness,' but transferred to cover certain fish, such as electric rays or crampfish, whose touch produces stiffness or numbness.

The word torpedo, then, reached English via Spanish or Portuguese transmission, in the early 16th century, referring to the 'family of fish characterized by a circular body and tapering tail, capable of emitting electrical discharges.'

In the late 18th century the term transferred to a type of explosive shell resembling these fish in appearance, but originally intended to be buried in the ground and detonated by the pressure of a footstep. These mines were also likened to "serpents." Later the term extended to floating mines, and also to the explosive mechanism invented by Robert Fulton for underwater attachment to enemy ships. Subsequently the device itself evolved to the more sophisticated self-propelled missile of today, a development that illustrates what linguists call "subreption," since the term remained although the artifact changed.

A very recent specialization of the word has occurred by transfer to a kind of sandwich (also called "a grinder, hero sandwich, or submarine") that resembles a torpedo in shape. An underworld slang specialization transfers the word to a 'gangster employed to commit violence.' This development represents first a generalization of torpedo as 'that which causes destruction,' dropping the sense that involves physical appearance, and then adding the connotation 'gangster.' (See also **starve.**)

torso

Greek *thýrsos* was a 'shaft, stock (of a plant),' and, by extension, the 'phallic staff carried by Dionysus.' Some have suggested that the more general meaning 'stock, shaft' is to be derived from the Dionysian vine-entwined staff with its pine-cone tip, but this seems unlikely. Others have wished to link the word with Greek *týrsis* 'tower' (cf. Latin *turris*), but this too is not without its difficulties. Most say that the origin of the term is obscure and let it go at that.

Whatever its ultimate origin, the word was borrowed into Latin with its original array of meanings, and survived into Italian, where it appears as *torso* 'stock, trunk, upper body (without head and arms) of a statue.' This last sense is a metaphorical extension of the vegetable reference, comparable to our use of the word *trunk* to designate that same part of the human body. It supplanted the other meanings as the word was passed from Italian to English in the 18th century, a time when Italian sculpture became popular all over Europe.

Today a *torso* is a 'human trunk,' while a *thyrse*, or *thyrsus*, a reborrowing of the Greco-Latin term, is, variously, a 'man-made vessel in the shape of a pine cone,' or a 'branching cluster of flowers at the end of a single stock,' as in the horse chestnut or lilac.

tragedy

The ancient Greek word *tragōidía*, from which the English *tragedy* derives, clearly meant 'goat song,' from the stems *tragos* 'goat' and *ōdé* 'ode, song,' but the precise significance of the compound has been disputed. The dramatic poetry of Greece originated with the worship of Dionysus, god of fertility and wine. Some scholars have attributed the *trag-* of *tragedy* to a goat sacrificed by worshipers of Dionysus. Others assert that a goat was one of the prizes for excellence in the poetic presentations that formed part of the revels. A third explanation holds that the first choric dancers wore goatskins.

Early *tragedy* dealt with serious actions by serious characters, but only when the word had reached English, in the 14th century, via Latin and French, did it come to imply a fatal conclusion to the drama, poem, or story. In the course of the following century it reverted to its original meaning, but by the early 16th century it had begun to be applied to calamitous events of real life as well as to fictional situations.

train

Both the noun and the verb come from the same unattested Late Latin verb *tragināre*, an extension of unattested **tragere*, a remaking of the Classical Latin verb *trahere* (past participle *tractus*), which meant 'to draw, drag, haul.' *Trahere* and its English cognates *drag* and *draw* came from the Proto-Indo-European root **dhragh-* 'draw, drag, haul.' To this day, the noun *train*, whether the *train* of a bridal gown, the *train* of people in a procession, or the *train* of a railroad, harks back to the notion of 'dragging' or 'hauling,' each being something 'hauled' behind someone or something.

Train as a verb retains only a metaphorically extended sense of the original root. From the 15th century on, one could *train* a plant to grow in a certain way, coaxing or 'dragging' it toward the desired direction of growth. From this usage arose the sense that higher forms of life could likewise be *trained* to grow in desired directions. If a rose could be *trained* on a trellis, a dog or child could be *trained* in analogous fashion through words or stronger coercive measures. By further extension, *train* has come to be used as a near synonym for *educate*.

treacle

The origin of this word is to be found in Greek *antidotos thēriakē* or *thēriakà phármaka*, a medicinal compound customarily served in a sweet liquid as an antidote to a poisonous bite. The adjective *thēriakós* means 'of or pertaining to a wild, venomous beast,' and is derived from the noun *thēr* 'beast; wild beast.' After the meaning of the phrases became localized in *thēriakē* or *thēriakà*, perhaps because animal parts were included in the antidote, the term passed into Latin and the Romance languages, at which point the spurious *l* found in the English form made its appearance. (Cf. Old French *triacle*.) From Romance, still in its sense of 'antidote to a poisonous bite,' the term made its way into English, maintaining its original sense well into the 19th century, although by then pharmacists had stopped putting animal matter into their cures. The pharmacological literature of the last century shows that *London Treacle* was composed of cumin seed, bayberries, germander, snakeroot, cloves, and honey. At about this time poor man's, or *"Common" Treacle* began to appear. This was nothing more or less than molasses. Today *treacle* is used in the sense of a 'cloying syrup.' It is also used metaphorically to describe unctuous speech or excessively sweet talk.

tribute

The earliest division of the Romans rested on three tribes or clans, the *Ramnes*, the *Tities*, and the *Luceres*. The Latin word *tribus* itself, meaning 'tribe,' derives from *tri-* 'three' plus *-bu-* 'clan.' *Tri-* is the exact cognate of the English word *three*, and *-bu-* the cognate of the Greek *phu-*, as in *phulon* 'stock or clan,' which entered English, via Latin, as *phylum*. Originally, the three tribes may have represented distinct genetic stocks, but as new groups joined the original clans and as the Romans split into more complicated subdivisions the original meaning of *tribus* faded, and the word came to mean simply a 'division of the people.' *Tributus*, which derives from *tribus*, originally meant 'that which was assigned to the three clans,' but came to signify 'that which was distributed to the clans,' no matter what their number, and then eventually meant 'anything distributed: payment; gift.'

As the Roman Empire grew through military conquest, subjugated nations were required to give 'enforced payments,' and *tributum*, a neuter form of the same word, specialized to mean 'payment from an inferior to a superior; tax.'

The Latin word entered English in the early 14th century with the latter meaning, and was applied to the payment made by vassals to their sovereign lord. Occasionally such contributions represented not merely acknowledgments of submission or the price of protection, or rent, but were expressions of esteem. Some time around the middle of the 18th century the meanings diverged, with one branch taking the signification of 'obligatory payment,' usually in concrete form, and the other that of 'freely given offering,' which might be abstract, as an expression of approval. This second meaning represents what etymologists call "amelioration."

tuxedo

P'tuksit 'he who has a round foot' was a common euphemism for 'wolf' among the Indians of eastern Massachusetts and western New York. European explorers encountered the word, which they heard as *tuxedo*, as a component in a number of place names, one of them present-day *Tuxedo Lake*, 25 miles or so north of New York City on the west bank of the Hudson River. Whether or not the early European settlers had any specific understanding of the meaning of the term (as might be suggested by the profusion of place names in the region with *wolf* in them) is not certain; but in any case, the original meaning soon faded in the areas where the Indian word was retained in the names of English plantations. In the early years of the 19th century a wealthy entrepreneur, Pierre Lorillard, bought *Tuxedo Lake* and its surrounding lands as a summer retreat. Having sold his holdings by 1880, he moved elsewhere, and the area was converted into an exclusive summer resort community. By the start of the 1890s the *Tuxedo Park Country Club* was established as a fashionable gathering-place for the privileged classes, and the men's dinner jacket known in America as the *tuxedo* became *de rigueur* there as evening dress.

There may be those who see a certain irony in referring to the formal attire of present-day males by a word that originally referred to a 'wolf.'

tycoon

This English word derives ultimately from the Chinese *tai* 'great' or 'exalted' and *kiun* 'lord; prince; ruler.' However, the title passed first into Japanese, and English speakers first heard it applied to the Shogun, the hereditary military leader who, prior to 1868, when the office became extinct, was the *de facto* ruling agent of the country, with powers actually surpassing those of the Mikado, or Emperor.

For all but well-educated Japanese who knew the Chinese language, the precise constituent meanings of the parts of the phrase probably began to fade as soon as it was transmitted to Japanese, but the use preserved the general sense both in Japanese and in English. Recently, however, the meaning has specialized in English to signify the leader of an industrial empire, an 'industrialist.'

V

vernacular

The Latin word *verna*, possibly of Etruscan origin, originally referred to a 'slave born in the house of his master,' but broadened its function from its use as a noun to that as an adjective, signifying anything 'domestic' or 'native.' *Vernus*, however, was homophonous with another word based on a stem meaning 'spring,' the season of the year. Consequently, an extension of the form meaning 'domestic,' *vernacula*, came into use to avoid possible ambiguity. Of course, this word could be employed with any noun. The grammarian Varro, a friend of Cicero, used it with *vocabula*, which generally meant 'designations, names, nouns.'

Apparently Renaissance scholars understood the phrase *vernacula vocabula* as 'native languages,' and localized its sense in the first element, dropping the second. Subsequently, they extended the word by an *r*, on the model of other Latin-derived terms. Thus, when *vernacular* entered English at the end of the 16th century or beginning of the 17th, its meaning had specialized to refer only to linguistic matters, in imitation of Varro's adventitious use of the word.

villain

In Latin, a *vīlla* was a 'country house,' and a *vīllānus* was a 'person belonging to a country household.' In English, *vīlla* appears both as *vill* 'feudal township' in the 16th century, and *villa* 'country house' in the 17th century and 'suburban residence' in the 18th. It also provides the basis for *village*, attested in English from Chaucer's time.

While *vill*, *villa*, and *village* all preserve elements of the 'country' and 'dwelling' components of the original Latin meaning, *villain* does not, although it did for a time. From 'person belonging to a country household' the sense of *villain* shifted in the Middle Ages to 'inhabitant of a *vill*; feudal serf.' This latter sense is preserved in the now-

213

archaic doublet *villein*. By extension of the sense of 'serf, peasant,' *villain* took on the meaning 'crude peasant, rustic,' and, subsequently, 'base person likely to commit evil acts,' a sense current by the 15th century.

Eventually the association of *villain* with rusticity and peasanthood faded entirely, leaving only the sense of 'one prone to do evil.'

virtue

The Latin *virtūs*, from which the English word descends through French transmission, rested on the stem *vir-* 'man' plus *-tūt*, an element employed to form qualitative abstracts from nouns or adjectives. Thus, the term meant the 'state or quality of manliness,' which included courage, strength, fortitude, power, and moral rectitude. Many of the derived meanings which radiated from this primary sense represent specializations that focus on one or another of these connotations, followed by generalizations caused by the fading and loss of the signification 'man,' or 'male.' This signification, implicit in the *vir-*, still survives in such terms as *virility*. An English cognate appears in the *were-* of *werewolf* 'man-wolf' and, with the normal change of Proto-Indo-European *w* to the Old Irish *f*, in the Celtic cognate, the proper name *Fergus*.

One specialization devoid of the 'male' element, gave 'power, efficacy,' attested in English by the 13th century in such phrases as 'the *virtue* of the medicine.' Another sense, attested for the same period, was 'moral rectitude.' The most extreme generalization ignored all of the connotations as well as the 'male' denotation, leaving only the sense of 'quality, characteristic,' the semantic function of the *-tut* stem alone.

A further specialization of the sense 'moral rectitude' applied it to the 'sexual purity' or 'chastity' of women. Many citations are ambiguous as to the precise nuances of meaning, but the signification 'chastity' had become established by Shakespeare's time.

W

wench

Wench is derived from a Proto-Indo-European root **weng* 'twist, bend,' and has come to be used to refer to a 'wanton woman.' The Old English form *wenćel* was, simply, a 'child' of either sex, presumably through an association with the malleability, inconstancy, or unreliability of youth. By the end of the 13th century *wench(e)* had come to be applied primarily to a 'female child,' and particularly a 'female servant child, female child of the peasant class.' By the 14th century it tended to designate a 'young female of low status or low morals,' much as *girl* is sometimes used today to designate a 'female servant or (young) female available for sport.'

By the end of the 16th century *wench* had also come to be used as a verb, meaning 'to consort with (loose) women,' as dialectal Modern English allows the use of *girl* or *go girling* to mean 'go in search of females for sport; cruise.' In both cases, the female is not a child but a 'young woman.' As far as the now obsolescent *wench* is concerned, this usage underlines the final change in meaning of the term; once a 'child,' it became a 'young woman' before evanescing from the language. (See also **tart²**.)

whisker

First attested in the English of the early 15th century, *whisker* originally appeared as the agent noun of the shorter noun *whisk* 'rapid sweeping movement.' This is the same form that appears in *whiskbroom* and in the phrase *in a whisk*. Thus *whisker* signified an object, such as a feather duster, small broom, switch, or a fan used to make such a quick motion.

The word was not applied to the hair growing on a man's face until the end of the 15th century, when it meant 'moustache,' possibly because of the resemblance of that entity to a small brush or broom—

an illustration of semantic transference. Later, *whisker* came to mean hair anywhere on the face except that over the lips; the word *moustache*, which had entered English in the 16th century, displaced it in that sense.

The historically earlier meaning, that referring to motion, appears in the nautical use of the word as a term for a lightweight, lateral spar used to move or spread the clew of the jib of a sailboat: *whisker pole*. Another nautical specialization which occurred in the late 19th century applied the term to the 'lever that explodes a torpedo.'

winter

Although the word *winter* has signified the 'cold season of the year' from its earliest appearance in English, its form suggests that it once referred to the 'wet season,' since the term is a nasalized variant of the same stem that gave the words *wet*, *water*, and *otter*, the 'water animal.' The Latin cognate *unda* 'wave,' a stem that eventually reached English in *undine*, *undulate*, and *inundate*, shows a reduced form of the same nasalized version. The Greek cognate, *húdor*, likewise entered English via Latin, either directly or through French, in such words as *hydrant*, *hydrophobia*, and *anhydrous*. A diminutive based on the Russian cognate *voda* 'water' became *vodka*; the Old Irish version of the stem, *visce* 'water' combined with the word for 'life,' giving *uisquebaugh*, which proceeded to localize the meaning in the first element and drop the second, leaving the word that entered English as *whiskey*. The semantic change from 'wet' to 'cold' season reflects a connotative extension with later fading of the original denotation; but one may also speculate on the possible shift in climate that evoked the semantic development in the millennia which separate the Proto-Indo-European language of 5000 B.C. (or earlier) from its descendants.

woodchuck

The animal known in Linnaean nomenclature as *Arctomys monax* 'lone bear-mouse' or *Marmota monax* 'lone mountain-mouse' is also known by the names *groundhog*, *whistlepig*, and, of course, *woodchuck*, all misnomers, since it is neither mouse nor pig, and its connection with wood and chuck is also unclear.

The Cree Indian word *otchek* 'marten, fisher' seems to have been the origin of *woodchuck*. Originally misheard, it was reanalyzed as if it were a compound of English *wood* and *chuck*, and then applied to the wrong animal. A vegetarian rodent popularly believed to predict a late or early spring by observing its own shadow, and better known, in that role, as a *groundhog*, the *woodchuck* is perhaps best known through the tongue-twister:

How much wood would a woodchuck chuck
If a woodchuck could chuck wood?
He'd chuck all the wood that a woodchuck could
If a woodchuck could chuck wood.

worship

King Alfred the Great employed the word *weorðscip*, 9th-century ancestor of Modern English *worship*, in the sense of 'honor' or 'renown.' The earliest Old English meaning of the first component of the term, now reduced to *wor-* in the compound but surviving independently as *worth*, was 'pecuniary value.' This pre-Germanic sense is attested by the cognate Latin verb *vertere* 'to turn,' whose stem reached English in such derivatives as *revert* and *convert*. The corresponding Old English verb *weorðan* meant 'to become,' having reached this meaning via an intermediate stage when it meant 'turn into.' The noun acquired its sense of 'value' or 'worth' from its use in the old barter system, where an object metaphorically 'became' or 'turned into' another which had the same exchange value or *worth*.

The word *worship* next generalized from 'monetary or fiscal value' to simply 'value,' gradually acquiring the sense of 'importance,' actually 'worthiness.' The shift probably received support from the fact that in ancient times people who owned great material wealth were held in high esteem. Thus a man of *worth*, that is, having many possessions or much wealth, became a man deserving of honor or respect. A trace of this sense still survives in Great Britain, where individuals of great dignity or honor may still be addressed as "Your Worship."

The modern specialization of the word to refer to 'veneration or honor as a sacred or supernatural object' did not arise until the 12th century, when the term was used in ecclesiastical rites or ceremonies. Pastoral letters of the late 15th century could still refer to "places of worship" in the sense of 'towns of importance,' rather than 'churches or other sites of religious assembly.' Likewise, Malory's *Morte d'Arthur*, written at this period, preserves the earlier meaning, 'honor.' When King Arthur or Sir Launcelot says that he seeks great *worship*, he means 'reputation,' not religious veneration.

It is not unlikely, however, that present nonecclesiastical usage in the meaning 'to hold in great respect,' as in "he *worships* her," represents a slight weakening of the religious use, rather than a simple continuation of the earlier sense, since the meaning carries connotative overtones suggesting veneration akin to that accorded a deity.

wretch

The Old English verb *wracian* meant 'to be in exile' and a noun *wræcca* (whose Kentish dialectal form, *wrecca*, is the direct ancestor of *wretch*), which corresponded to it, meant 'exile, stranger.' To the English, anyone in exile was unhappy or miserable, so the meaning became extended by this connotation. Even within the Old English period the original sense began to fade, generalizing the meaning to 'unhappy or unfortunate person.' An old view that an individual's destiny was a direct consequence of his actions led to one specialization, 'mean or despicable person,' and this sense coexists with the judgmentally neutral sense ('poor wretch').

The German cognate *Recke* 'valiant warrior' or 'hero' suggests a possible meaning of the stem, 'to be away from one's native land.' This may have preceded the earliest attested English sense, with the semantic split that separated the High and Low German derivatives (German and English respectively) depending on whether or not the sojourn abroad came about through the individual's choice. Thus, a knight errant, traveling by choice, could be denoted by the word in its sense 'hero,' whereas an exile, whence the meaning 'unhappy person,' traveled as a consequence of compulsion or misfortune.

Y

yarn

The meaning of such cognates as Old Norse *garnr* (plural of *görn*) and Lithuanian *žárna* suggests that the original sense of Old English *ʒearn* 'thread, wool,' the ancestor of modern *yarn*, was 'guts' or 'intestines.' Greek *khordḗ*, a descendant of the same Proto-Indo-European root (extended by the *-d-* suffix rather than by the *-n-*) eventually reached English as *cord* by the beginning of the 14th century, via Latin and French; *chord*, later in that same century, shows the probable semantic route. This was a specialization from 'guts' to 'string made of gut' and then to 'string.'

Once the Old English *ʒearn* had come to signify 'string' or 'thread,' from one of the uses to which men put animal guts, the word retained this sense when the material used for the thread shifted to wool, and descendants of the word retained the same meaning even when artificial fibers replaced wool. It is impossible to tell whether the extension is a simple instance of what linguists call "proreption," or if the word represents the localization of an adjectival modifier in a phrase, part of which has been dropped.

During the 18th and 19th centuries, sailors spent hours at sea spinning out *yarn* into heavy ropes for shipboard use. As they worked, they gossiped or told stories, and by the beginning of the 19th century *to spin a yarn* had come to mean 'to tell a story,' and the noun *yarn* came to mean a 'story, tale.'

Z

zany

The most common first name for a man in practically all the languages of Europe is, perhaps, John—Jean, Sean, Johann, Ivan, Juan, Jan, Giovanni, Yanis—and as such it is frequently used to designate any male, whatever his actual given name may be. *John Barleycorn* is the masculine personification of the grain from which whiskey is made; *John Bull* is the prototypical Englishman, while *John Doe* is the prototypical anonymous American male; a *Johnny-come-lately* is any latecomer; *Johnny Reb* was a Confederate soldier; and *a john* is a prostitute's client.

A similarly generalized use of the name in dialectal Italian gave rise to its application to a stock character in the 16th-century commedia dell'arte. *Zan(n)i* 'John(n)y' was the buffoonlike valet who aped the antics of his master to ridiculous effect. When the popular Italian drama with its traditional cast of characters entered England toward the end of the 16th century, and *zany* entered the language, it was not as 'John' but as a 'buffoon-like valet.' Subsequently, the term was used in English to denote any 'attendant' or a 'buffoon,' both senses current in the 17th century. By the 18th century the 'servant' aspect of the meaning had faded, and a *zany* was simply a 'fool.'

In more recent times *zany*, as a noun, has acquired a flavor of 'craziness'; today a *zany* is a 'person whose antics border on the insane,' usually applied with an affectionate connotation. As an adjective, *zany* is used to mean 'buffoonish, crazy,' by extension of the sense of the noun with functional shift.

221

Appendix I

Appendix I

academy
Fading
Generalization
Specialization by Connotative
Extension

albatross
Fading
Generalization by Connotative
Extension
Restructuring by Folk
Etymology
Semantic Reshaping by Folk
Etymology
Transference

Alcatraz
Fading
Generalization by Connotative
Extension
Restructuring by Folk
Etymology
Semantic Reshaping by Folk
Etymology
Transference

alchemy
Radiation
Semantic Restructuring by
Folk Etymology
Specialization by Connotative
Extension
Transference

alcohol
Fading
Generalization by Connotative
Extension
Localization

alcove
Generalization by Connotative
Extension
Partial Fading
Semantic Restructuring by
Folk Etymology

algebra
Fading
Generalization by Connotative
Extension
Specialization by Connotative
Addition

algorism
Transference

algorithm
Transference

alibi
Connotative Extension
Connotative Extension
Connotative Extension
Fading

aloof
Generalization

Specialization by Connotative
 Extension
Transference

amethyst
Fading

amine
Fading

amino acid
Fading

ammine
Fading

ammonia
Fading

apron
Radiation
Specialization

arena
Generalization
Specialization by Connotative
 Extension

arrive
Generalization by Connotative
 Extension

arrowroot
Fading
Restructuring by Folk
 Etymology
Semantic Reshaping by Folk
 Etymology
Transmissional Filtering

assassin
Fading
Generalization
Specialization by Connotative
 Extension

atone
Fading
Localization

attic
Fading
Fading
Functional Shift
Localization
Specialization
Transference

auburn
Fading
Restructuring by Folk
 Etymology
Semantic Reshaping by Folk
 Etymology

auction
Fading
Localization of Phrasal
 Meaning
Specialization

auspices
Fading
Transference

average
Filtering Across Linguistic
 Boundaries
Generalization by Connotative
 Extension
Partial Fading
Phonetic Restructuring by
 Suffixion
Transference

basilisk
Fading
Generalization Through Trans-
 missional Filtering
Generalization by Connotative
 Extension
Restructuring by Folk
 Etymology
Semantic Reshaping by Folk
 Etymology

bead
Generalization
Transference

belfry
Fading
Restructuring by Folk
Etymology
Semantic Reshaping by Folk
Etymology
Specialization by Connotative
Extension
Transference

beriberi
Fading
Specialization

bevy
Fading
Generalization
Localization
Specialization by Connotative
Extension

bizarre
Fading
Filtering Across Linguistic
Boundaries
Specialization by Connotative
Extension
Transference

blackmail
Fading
Specialization

blanket
Fading
Specialization by Connotative
Extension

bless
Fading
Generalization

Specialization by Connotative
Extension
Subreption

bonfire
Fading

boondocks
Transmissional Filtering

botulism
Fading
Specialization by Connotative
Extension

bread
Generalization
Localization
Specialization

bridal
Fading
Generalization by Connotative
Extension

broach
Generalization
Specialization by Connotative
Extension
Subreption

brocade
Fading by Filtration Across
Linguistic Boundaries
Generalization
Specialization by Connotative
Extension
Subreption

brochure
Fading by Filtration Across
Linguistic Boundaries
Generalization
Specialization by Connotative
Extension
Subreption

bromide
  Fading
  Localization
  Specialization by Connotative
    Extension

brooch
  Fading by Filtration Across
    Linguistic Boundaries
  Generalization
  Specialization by Connotative
    Extension
  Subreption

buccaneer
  Fading
  Specialization by Connotative
    Extension
  Transference

bugle
  Fading
  Localization
  Proreption

bumpkin
  Fading
  Generalization by Connotative
    Extension
  Pejoration
  Transference

bust
  Back Formation
  Fading
  Filtering Across Linguistic
    Boundaries
  Specialization by Connotative
    Extension
  Transference

buxom
  Fading
  Specialization by Connotative
    Extension

cab
  Functional Shift
  Localization
  Transference
  Truncation

cabal
  Fading
  Specialization by Connotative
    Extension
  Transference
  Transmissional Filtering

cad
  Fading
  Pejoration
  Radiation
  Specialization by Connotative
    Extension

caddie
  Fading
  Pejoration
  Radiation
  Specialization by Connotative
    Extension

cadet
  Fading
  Pejoration
  Radiation
  Specialization by Connotative
    Extension

canal
  Fading
  Filtering Across Linguistic
    Boundaries
  Generalization by Connotative
    Extension
  Restructuring by Folk
    Etymology
  Semantic Reshaping by Folk
    Etymology

cancel
Fading
Generalization
Specialization by Connotative
Extension
Transference

cancer
Fading
Generalization
Specialization
Transference

candidate
Generalization
Specialization by Connotative
Addition

candy
Generalization
Specialization by Connotative
Extension

cane, canister, cannibal
Fading
Filtering Across Linguistic
Boundaries
Generalization by Connotative
Extension
Restructuring by Folk
Etymology
Semantic Reshaping by Folk
Etymology

cannon
Fading
Specialization by Connotative
Extension

canopy
Fading
Filtering Across Linguistic
Boundaries
Radiation

Restructuring by Folk
Etymology
Semantic Reshaping by Folk
Etymology
Specialization by Connotative
Extension

cant
Fading
Pejoration
Specialization by Connotative
Extension

canter
Fading
Localization

canvas
Fading
Functional Shift
Specialization by Connotative
Extension
Transference

canvass
Fading
Functional Shift
Specialization by Connotative
Extension
Transference

canyon
Fading
Filtering Across Linguistic
Boundaries
Generalization by Connotative
Extension
Restructuring by Folk
Etymology
Semantic Reshaping by Folk
Etymology

carcinoma
Fading
Generalization

Specialization
Transference

carpet
Proreption
Specialization
Transference

catena
Localization
Radiation
Transference

catsup
Fading
Filtering Across Linguistic
Boundaries

cave
Generalization by Connotative
Extension
Radiation
Specialization by Connotative
Extension

cemetery
Fading
Specialization by Metaphorical
Extension

censor
Generalization
Specialization

center, centre
Fading
Generalization by Connotative
Extension
Transference

cephalic
Filtering Across Linguistic
Boundaries
Specialization

chagrin
Fading

Specialization by Connotative
Extension
Transference

chain
Localization
Radiation
Transference

chap
Generalization

chapel
Fading
Transference

charm
Fading
Fading
Generalization
Specialization by Connotative
Extension
Specialization with Semantic
Blending

chauffeur
Connotative Extension
Generalization
Subreption

chauvinist
Fading
Specialization by Connotative
Extension
Transference

cheap
Fading
Localization
Transference

cheat
Fading
Functional Shift
Pejoration
Radiation

Specialization by Connotative
　Extension

check
　Fading
　Functional Shift
　Generalization by Connotative
　　Extension
　Radiation

checker
　Fading
　Functional Shift
　Generalization by Connotative
　　Extension
　Radiation

cheer
　Fading
　Filtering Across Linguistic
　　Boundaries
　Functional Shift
　Localization
　Specialization by Connotative
　　Extension
　Transference

chemistry
　Radiation
　Semantic Restructuring by
　　Folk Etymology
　Specialization by Connotative
　　Extension
　Transference

cheque
　Fading
　Functional Shift
　Generalization by Connotative
　　Extension
　Radiation

chequer
　Fading
　Functional Shift

Generalization by Connotative
　Extension
Radiation

chess
　Fading
　Functional Shift
　Generalization by Connotative
　　Extension

chignon
　Localization
　Radiation
　Transference

chowder
　Transference

circle, circus
　Partial Fading
　Radiation
　Specialization by Connotative
　　Extension

cithara
　Connotative Extension
　Specialization
　Subreption

cleric
　Fading
　Generalization by Connotative
　　Extension
　Radiation
　Specialization by Connotative
　　Extension

clerk
　Fading
　Generalization by Connotative
　　Extension
　Radiation
　Specialization by Connotative
　　Extension

club
　Partial Fading

Proreption
Radiation
Specialization by Connotative
    Extension
cobalt
    Fading
cockatrice
    Fading
    Radiation
comet
    Fading
    Localization
    Specialization
companion
    Fading
    Specialization by Connotative
        Extension
constable
    Amelioration
    Fading
    Subreption
cop
    Pejoration
    Specialization
copper
    Fading
    Localization
coquette
    Fading
    Filtering Across Linguistic
        Boundaries
    Functional Shift
    Generalization by Connotative
        Extension
    Specialization by Connotative
        Extension
corn
    Fading

Specialization by Connotative
    Extension
cousin
    Fading
cove
    Fading
    Generalization by Connotative
        Extension
    Semantic Restructuring by
        Folk Etymology
cummerbund
    Transference
cynosure
    Connotative Extension
    Fading
    Generalization
Cyprus
    Fading
    Localization
dactyl
    Radiation
    Specialization
    Transference
December
    Fading by Filtration Across
        Linguistic Boundaries
    Subreption
decimate
    Fading
    Generalization by Connotative
        Extension
delirium
    Fading
    Specialization by Connotative
        Extension
derrick
    Fading
    Proreption

Transference

domino
Fading
Proreption
Specialization by Connotative
Extension
Transference

dreary
Fading
Specialization

dromedary
Fading by Filtration Across
Linguistic Boundaries
Localization

dunce
Fading
Pejoration
Specialization by Connotative
Extension

electric, electron
Fading
Specialization

eleven
Fading

entomology
Fading by Filtration Across
Linguistic Boundaries
Localization
Specialization

equip
Fading
Filtering Across Linguistic
Boundaries
Generalization by Connotative
Extension
Specialization by Connotative
Extension

ether
Fading

Proreption
Specialization by Connotative
Extension
Subreption

faint
Fading
Radiation
Specialization by Connotative
Extension

fanatic
Fading
Generalization
Specialization

fare
Fading
Functional Shift
Generalization by Connotative
Extension
Radiation
Specialization by Connotative
Extension
Transference

feint
Fading
Radiation
Specialization by Connotative
Extension

felon
Generalization by Connotative
Extension
Specialization by Connotative
Extension

forlorn hope
Filtering Across Linguistic
Boundaries

fornication
Fading
Specialization by Connotative
Extension

frank
Fading
Functional Shift
Generalization by Connotative
Extension
Radiation
Transference

furlong
Fading
Proreption

furnace
Fading
Specialization by Connotative
Extension

furtive
Generalization
Specialization by Connotative
Extension

gable
Filtering Across Linguistic
Boundaries
Specialization

galosh
Localization
Proreption
Transference

gamut
Fading
Generalization
Semantic Localization

garble
Fading
Generalization
Specialization

gargoyle
Fading
Specialization by Connotative
Extension
Transference

gasket
Fading
Radiation
Specialization by Connotative
Extension

giddy
Connotative Extension
Fading
Localization
Specialization
Specialization by Connotative
Extension

glamour
Generalization
Specialization by Connotative
Extension

God
Amelioration
Connotative Extension
Fading
Localization
Subreption

goodbye
Contextualization
Fading

gorilla
Fading
Filtering Across Linguistic
Boundaries
Transference

gossamer
Fading
Generalization by Connotative
Extension
Transference

gossip
Fading
Generalization by Connotative
Extension

Pejoration
Radiation
grammar
  Generalization
  Specialization by Connotation
    Extension
grog
  Localization
  Transference
groggy
  Localization
  Transference
groom
  Fading
  Generalization by Connotative
    Extension
  Localization
  Transference
grotesque
  Fading
  Generalization by Connotative
    Extension
guitar
  Connotative Extension
  Specialization
  Subreption
hack
  Fading
  Generalization by Connotative
    Extension
  Localization
  Pejoration
hackney
  Fading
  Generalization by Connotative
    Extension
  Localization
  Pejoration

hag
  Fading
  Generalization by Connotative
    Extension
  Pejoration
  Radiation
haggard
  Fading
  Generalization by Connotative
    Extension
  Pejoration
  Radiation
handkerchief
  Fading
  Generalization by Connotative
    Extension
harlequin
  Fading
  Filtering Across Linguistic
    Boundaries
  Functional Shift
  Generalization by Connotative
    Extension
  Transference
harlot
  Fading
  Filtering Across Linguistic
    Boundaries
  Specialization by Connotative
    Extension
harridan
  Fading
  Generalization by Connotative
    Extension
  Transference
hassock
  Radiation
  Subreption
  Transference

Specialization

iodine
Fading
Localization
Specialization

jade¹
Fading
Generalization by Connotative
   Extension
Pejoration
Specialization by Connotative
   Extension
Transference

jade²
Fading
Filtering Across Linguistic
   Boundaries
Localization
Phonetic Restructuring by
   Grammatical Misanalysis
Subreption

javelin
Filtering Across Linguistic
   Boundaries
Specialization

jingo
Connotative Extension
Fading

jingoism
Connotative Extension
Fading

jovial
Generalization by Connotative
   Extension
Fading

jubilee
Fading
Generalization by Connotative
   Extension

Specialization by Connotative
   Extension
Transference

juggernaut
Fading
Generalization by Connotative
   Extension
Transference

jumbo
Fading
Filtering Across Linguistic
   Boundaries
Localization
Transference

jungle
Fading
Generalization by Connotative
   Extension

junk
Fading
Pejoration
Specialization by Connotative
   Addition
Specialization by Connotative
   Extension

ketchup
Fading
Filtering Across Linguistic
   Boundaries

labyrinth
Fading
Radiation
Specialization by Connotative
   Extension

lace
Fading
Radiation
Specialization by Connotative
   Addition

Transference

laconic
Fading

last
Fading
Specialization by Connotative
Extension

latent
Fading

left
Fading
Specialization by Connotative
Extension

lemur
Filtering Across Linguistic
Boundaries

lethargic
Fading

lewd
Fading
Pejoration
Specialization by Connotative
Extension

licorice
Fading

lilac
Fading
Localization
Transference

lumber
Fading
Restructuring by Folk
Etymology
Semantic Reshaping by Folk
Etymology
Specialization by Connotative
Extension
Transference

lunatic
Fading
Specialization by Connotative
Extension

macabre
Fading
Functional Shift
Transference

machine
Specialization

mackinaw
Fading
Localization
Radiation
Specialization

madrigal
Fading
Localization
Specialization by Connotative
Extension

magazine
Partial Fading
Radiation
Specialization by Connotative
Extension

mail¹
Fading
Localization
Specialization by Connotative
Extension

mail²
Fading
Localization
Specialization

man
Fading
Pejoration

manure
Pejoration

Specialization

map
Radiation

marshal
Amelioration
Fading

marshmallow
Radiation
Subreption

martyr
Generalization
Specialization by Connotative
Extension

mathematic, mathematics
Fading
Radiation
Specialization

maudlin
Fading
Functional Shift
Pejoration
Radiation
Transference

meat
Localization
Specialization by Connotative
Extension

meerschaum
Fading
Localization

megrim
Fading
Specialization by Connotative
Extension

melancholy
Generalization
Specialization
Subreption

meretricious
Pejoration
Specialization by Connotative
Extension

migraine
Fading
Specialization by Connotative
Extension

mile
Fading
Localization
Subreption

mint
Radiation
Specialization by Connotative
Extension

money
Radiation
Specialization by Connotative
Extension

muscle
Fading

mustard
Fading
Transference

napkin
Radiation
Specialization

nausea
Generalization
Shift of Semantic Frame

nemesis
Fading
Transference

nest
Fading

nice
Amelioration

Fading
Specialization by Connotative
Extension

nickel
Fading

nickname
Fading
Localization of Phrasal
Meaning
Specialization

nicotine
Fading
Functional Shift
Localization
Transference

nidus
Fading

noggin
Fading
Radiation
Transference

noon
Localization
Subreption

November
Fading by Filtration Across
Linguistic Boundaries
Subreption

nun
Fading
Specialization by Connotative
Extension

October
Fading by Filtration Across
Linguistic Boundaries
Subreption

orang-utan
Fading

Filtering Across Linguistic
Boundaries
Transference

ostracism
Generalization
Weakening

pagan
Fading
Radiation
Specialization by Connotative
Extension

pain
Fading
Generalization
Specialization by Connotative
Extension

pajamas
Fading

palace
Fading
Generalization
Specialization by Connotative
Extension
Transference

pandemonium
Fading
Radiation

pander
Fading
Functional Shift
Pejoration
Radiation
Transference

pane
Fading
Radiation
Specialization by Connotative
Extension

panel
Partial Fading
Radiation
Specialization by Connotative
Extension

panic
Fading
Localization

pants
Fading
Proreption
Transference

parasite
Generalization
Pejoration
Specialization by Connotative
Extension

pariah
Fading
Generalization

parlor
Fading
Filtering Across Linguistic
Boundaries
Transference

pavilion
Fading
Specialization by Connotative
Extension

peach
Fading
Generalization
Localization
Specialization

peasant
Fading
Radiation
Specialization by Connotative
Extension

pedigree
Fading
Semantic Restructuring by
Folk Etymology
Transference

pen
Localization
Specialization
Subreption

person
Generalization
Transference

persuade
Fading

pester
Fading

phlegmatic
Fading
Specialization
Subreption

picayune
Fading
Functional Shift
Pejoration

pickaninny
Partial Fading
Pejoration
Specialization

pilgrim
Generalization
Specialization
Subreption

placebo
Fading
Functional Shift
Specialization by Connotative
Extension
Transference

plagiarism, plagium
Fading
Specialization
planet
Fading
Localization
Subreption
pongee
Fading by Filtration Across
Linguistic Boundaries
Generalization
Localization
Transference
poodle
Fading
Localization
profanity
Fading
Specialization by Connotative
Extension
proud
Fading
Functional Shift
Localization
Pejoration
Specialization by Connotative
Extension
Transference
prowess
Fading
Functional Shift
Localization
Pejoration
Specialization by Connotative
Extension
Transference
prude
Fading
Functional Shift

Localization
Pejoration
Specialization by Connotative
Extension
Transference
puisne
Generalization
Specialization by Connotative
Extension
pumpkin
Fading
Restructuring by Folk
Etymology
Semantic Reshaping by Folk
Etymology
Specialization by Connotative
Extension
puny
Generalization
Specialization by Connotative
Extension
pyjamas
Fading
quean
Fading
Pejoration
Radiation
Specialization by Connotative
Extension
queen
Fading
Pejoration
Radiation
Specialization by Connotative
Extension
quick
Fading
Specialization

restive
    Fading
    Filtering Across Linguistic
        Boundaries
    Restructuring by Folk
        Etymology
    Semantic Reshaping by Folk
        Etymology
    Specialization by Connotative
        Extension
rival
    Fading
    Functional Shift
    Specialization by Connotative
        Addition
    Specialization by Connotative
        Extension
rout
    Fading
    Pejoration
    Specialization by Connotative
        Extension
sabbath
    Partial Fading
    Specialization by Connotative
        Extension
    Transference
sabbatical
    Partial Fading
    Specialization by Connotative
        Extension
    Transference
sad
    Fading
salary
    Fading
    Generalization
    Localization
    Specialization

sandwich
    Fading
    Proreption
    Transference
sanguine
    Fading
    Specialization
    Subreption
sarcophagus
    Fading
    Localization
    Subreption
    Transference
scold
    Fading
    Filtering Across Linguistic
        Boundaries
    Pejoration
    Specialization by Connotative
        Extension
Scotist
    Fading
    Pejoration
    Specialization by Connotative
        Extension
senate
    Fading
    Proreption
September
    Fading by Filtration Across
        Linguistic Boundaries
    Subreption
serenade
    Fading
    Localization
    Specialization by Connotative
        Extension
    Subreption

serf
  Radiation
  Specialization
  Weakening
serge
  Fading
  Localization
  Specialization by Connotative
    Extension
  Transference
sergeant
  Amelioration
  Fading
serpent
  Fading
  Specialization
shack
  Filtering Across Linguistic
    Boundaries
  Pejoration
  Specialization by Connotative
    Extension
shambles
  Fading
  Generalization
  Pejoration
  Specialization by Connotative
    Extension
shampoo
  Specialization by Connotative
    Extension
shamus
  Fading
  Specialization by Connotative
    Extension
shanghai
  Fading by Filtration Across
    Linguistic Boundaries
  Functional Shift

  Generalization
  Specialization by Connotative
    Extension
shantung
  Fading by Filtration Across
    Linguistic Boundaries
  Generalization
  Localization
  Transference
shanty
  Filtering Across Linguistic
    Boundaries
  Specialization by Connotative
    Extension
sherbet
  Radiation
shibboleth
  Generalization
  Meaning Acquired by Func-
    tional Use
shirt
  Proreption
  Radiation
  Specialization
  Transference
shrab
  Radiation
shroud
  Fading
  Specialization by Connotative
    Addition
  Transference
shrub
  Radiation
siesta
  Localization
  Specialization by Connotative
    Extension
  Transference

silhouette
   Fading
   Transference
silk
   Fading
   Localization
   Specialization by Connotative
     Extension
   Transference
silly
   Degeneration
   Radiation
sinister
   Fading
sister
   Fading
   Subreption
skirt
   Proreption
   Radiation
   Specialization
   Transference
slew
   Fading
   Generalization
   Specialization with Semantic
     Blending
slogan
   Fading
   Generalization
   Specialization with Semantic
     Blending
smirk
   Pejoration
   Specialization
smock
   Specialization by Connotative
     Extension
   Transference

smocking
   Specialization by Connotative
     Extension
   Transference
solar
   Localization
   Radiation
   Specialization
soothe
   Amelioration
   Fading
   Pejoration
   Specialization by Connotative
     Extension
sour
   Generalization
   Specialization
south
   Localization
   Radiation
   Specialization
spaniel
   Fading
   Localization
Spartan
   Fading
specious
   Ameliorative Specialization
   Pejorative Specialization
sphinx
   Fading
   Proreption
   Specialization
spinster
   Fading
   Radiation
   Specialization by Connotative
     Addition

spoon
  Subreption
starve
  Generalization
  Specialization
  Weakening
stigma
  Fading
  Radiation
  Specialization by Connotative
    Extension
  Subreption
stirrup
  Fading
  Subreption
street
  Fading
  Generalization
  Localization
  Specialization by Connotative
    Extension
stroke
  Fading
  Localization
  Subreption
sulcate
  Fading
  Generalization
  Proreption
  Specialization
sun
  Localization
  Radiation
  Specialization
swastika
  Fading
  Pejoration
  Proreption

swindle
  Back Formation
  Fading
  Pejoration
  Specialization by Connotative
    Extension
sycophant
  Fading
  Specialization by Connotative
    Extension
syphilis
  Fading
  Transference
syrup
  Radiation
taboo, tabu
  Transmissional Filtering
tandem
  Pun
  Specialization by Connotative
    Extension
tariff
  Fading
  Filtering Across Linguistic
    Boundaries
  Specialization by Connotative
    Extension
tart¹, tart²
  Pejoration
  Specialization by Connotative
    Extension
Tartar
  Generalization by Connotative
    Extension
  Restructuring by Folk
    Etymology
  Semantic Reshaping by Folk
    Etymology

task
Partial Fading
Radiation
Specialization by Connotative
Extension

tattoo
Fading
Filtering Across Linguistic
Boundaries
Functional Shift
Phonetic Restructuring
Specialization by Connotative
Extension

tawdry
Generalization
Pejoration

tax
Partial Fading
Radiation
Specialization by Connotative
Extension

taxi
Functional Shift
Localization
Transference
Truncation

test
Fading
Functional Shift
Transference

testicle
Fading
Specialization by Connotative
Extension

thigh
Fading
Radiation
Specialization by Connotative
Extension

thing
Fading
Transference

thug
Fading
Filtering Across Linguistic
Boundaries
Specialization by Connotative
Extension

thumb
Fading
Radiation
Specialization by Connotative
Extension

timber
Fading
Specialization by Connotative
Extension
Transference

tire
Fading
Specialization by Connotative
Extension
Transference

tithe
Partial Fading
Specialization by Connotative
Extension

toast
Fading
Functional Shift
Radiation
Specialization by Connotative
Extension
Transference

toddy
Fading
Specialization by Connotative
Extension

Subreption
Transference
Transmissional Filtering

toilet
Fading
Specialization by Connotative
  Extension
Transference

torpedo
Generalization
Specialization by Connotative
  Extension
Transference

torso
Fading

tragedy
Fading
Specialization by Connotative
  Extension

train
Fading
Generalization
Generalization by Metaphorical
  Extension

treacle
Fading
Localization
Proreption
Subreption

tribute
Amelioration
Fading
Generalization
Radiation
Specialization

tussah
Fading by Filtration Across
  Linguistic Boundaries
Generalization

Localization
Transference

tuxedo
Fading
Filtering Across Linguistic
  Boundaries
Localization
Transference

twelve
Fading

tycoon
Specialization by Connotative
  Extension

vernacular
Generalization
Specialization by Localization

villain
Fading
Pejoration

violet
Fading
Localization
Specialization

virtue
Fading
Generalization
Radiation
Specialization by Connotative
  Extension

wench
Fading
Pejoration
Specialization by Connotative
  Extension

whisker
Radiation
Specialization
Transference

Appendix II

Appendix II

Appendix II

Amelioration
constable
God
marshal
nice
sergeant
soothe
tribute

Ameliorative Specialization
specious

Back Formation
bust
swindle

Connotative Extension
alibi
chauffeur
cithara
cynosure
giddy
God
guitar
henchman
jingo
jingoism
winter
zither

Contextualization
goodbye

Degeneration
silly

Fading
academy
albatross
Alcatraz
alcohol
algebra
alibi
amethyst
amine
amino acid
ammine
ammonia
arrowroot
assassin
atone
attic
attic
auburn
auction
auspices
basilisk
belfry
beriberi
bevy
bizarre
blackmail
blanket
bless
bonfire
botulism
bridal

bromide
buccaneer
bugle
bumpkin
bust
buxom
cabal
cad
caddie
cadet
canal
cancel
cancer
cane
canister
cannibal
cannon
canopy
cant
canter
canvas
canvass
canyon
carcinoma
catsup
cemetery
center
chagrin
chapel
charm
charm
chauvinist
cheap
cheat
check
checker
cheer
cheque
chequer
chess
cleric

clerk
cobalt
cockatrice
comet
companion
constable
copper
coquette
corn
cousin
cove
cynosure
Cyprus
decimate
delirium
derrick
domino
dreary
dunce
electric
electron
eleven
equip
ether
faint
fanatic
fare
feint
fornication
frank
furlong
furnace
gamut
garble
gargoyle
gasket
giddy
God
goodbye
gorilla
gossamer

gossip
groom
grotesque
hack
hackney
hag
haggard
handkerchief
harlequin
harlot
harridan
heathen
heir
hen
henchman
hint
hippopotamus
hobby
hobbyhorse
hulk
hypocrite
hysterics
inaugurate
iodine
jade¹
jade²
jingo
jingoism
jovial jubil
jubilee
juggernaut
jumbo
jungle
junk
ketchup
labyrinth
lace
laconic
last
latent
lethargic

lewd
licorice
lilac
lumber
lunatic
macabre
mackinaw
madrigal
mail¹
mail²
man
marshal
mathematic
mathematics
maudlin
meerschaum
megrim
migraine
mile
muscle
mustard
nemesis
nest
nice
nickel
nickname
nicotine
nidus
noggin
nun
orang-utan
pagan
pain
pajamas
palace
pandemonium
pander
pane
panic
pants
pariah

parlor
pavilion
peach
peasant
pedigree
persuade
pester
phlegmatic
picayune
placebo
plagiarism
plagium
planet
poodle
profanity
proud
prowess
prude
pumpkin
pyjamas
quean
queen
quick
restive
rival
rout
sad
salary
sandwich
sanguine
sarcophagus
scold
Scotist
senate
serenade
serge
sergeant
serpent
shambles
shamus
shroud

silhouette
silk
sinister
sister
slew
slogan
soothe
spaniel
Spartan
sphinx
spinster
stigma
stirrup
street
stroke
sulcate
swastika
swindle
sycophant
syphilis
tariff
tattoo
test
testicle
thigh
thing
thug
thumb
timber
tire
toast
toddy
toilet
torso
tragedy
train
treacle
tribute
tuxedo
twelve
villain

violet
virtue
wench
winter
wretch
zany

Fading by Filtration Across
　Linguistic Boundaries
　brocade
　brochure
　brooch
　December
　dromedary
　entomology
　insect
　November
　October
　pongee
　September
　shanghai
　shantung
　tussah

Filtering Across Linguistic
　Boundaries
　average
　bizarre
　bust
　canal
　cane
　canister
　cannibal
　canopy
　canyon
　catsup
　cephalic
　cheer
　coquette
　equip
　forlorn hope
　gable

gorilla
harlequin
harlot
indri
jade[2]
javelin
jumbo
ketchup
lemur
orang-utan
parlor
restive
scold
shack
shanty
tariff
tattoo
thug
tuxedo
zany

Functional Shift
　attic
　cab
　canvas
　canvass
　cheat
　check
　checker
　cheer
　cheque
　chequer
　chess
　coquette
　fare
　frank
　harlequin
　hint
　macabre
　maudlin
　nicotine
　pander

picayune
placebo
proud
prowess
prude
rival
shanghai
tattoo
taxi
test
toast
zany
Generalization
academy
aloof
arena
assassin
bead
bevy
bless
bread
broach
brocade
brochure
brooch
cancel
cancer
candidate
candy
carcinoma
censor
chap
charm
chauffeur
cynosure
fanatic
furtive
gamut
garble
glamour
grammar

heathen
henchman
hulk
martyr
melancholy
nausea
ostracism
pain
palace
parasite
pariah
peach
person
pilgrim
pongee
puisne
puny
salary
shambles
shanghai
shantung
shibboleth
shrew
slew
slogan
starve
street
sulcate
tawdry
torpedo
train
tribute
tussah
vernacular
virtue
worship
wretch
yarn

Generalization Through Transmissional Filtering
basilisk

Generalization by Connotative
　Extension
　　albatross
　　Alcatraz
　　alcohol
　　alcove
　　algebra
　　arrive
　　average
　　basilisk
　　bridal
　　bumpkin
　　canal
　　cane
　　canister
　　cannibal
　　canyon
　　cave
　　center
　　check
　　checker
　　cheque
　　chequer
　　chess
　　cleric
　　clerk
　　coquette
　　cove
　　decimate
　　equip
　　fare
　　felon
　　frank
　　gossamer
　　gossip
　　groom
　　grotesque
　　hack
　　hackney
　　hag
　　haggard

handkerchief
harlequin
harridan
heir
hen
hypocrite
hysterics
jade[1]
jovial
jubilee
juggernaut
jungle
Tartar

Generalization by Metaphorical
　Extension
　　train

Localization
　alcohol
　atone
　attic
　bevy
　bread
　bromide
　bugle
　cab
　canter
　catena
　chain
　cheap
　cheer
　chignon
　comet
　copper
　Cyprus
　dromedary
　entomology
　galosh
　giddy
　God
　grog

groggy
groom
hack
hackney
helium
hobby
hobbyhorse
hussy
insect
iodine
jade²
jumbo
lilac
mackinaw
madrigal
mail¹
mail²
meat
meerschaum
mile
nicotine
noon
panic
peach
pen
planet
pongee
poodle
proud
prowess
prude
salary
sarcophagus
serenade
serge
shantung
siesta
silk
solar
south
spaniel

street
stroke
sun
taxi
treacle
tussah
tuxedo
violet
yarn

Localization of Phrasal Meaning
auction
nickname

Meaning Acquired by Functional Use
shibboleth

Partial Fading
alcove
average
circle
circus
club
magazine
panel
pickaninny
sabbath
sabbatical
task
tax
tithe

Pejoration
Scotist
bumpkin
cad
caddie
cadet
cant
cheat
cop
dunce
garbel

gossip
hack
hackney
hag
haggard
hussy
jade¹
junk
lewd
man
manure
maudlin
meretricious
pander
parasite
picayune
pickaninny
proud
prowess
prude
quean
queen
rout
scold
shack
shambles
smirk
soothe
swastika
swindle
tart¹, tart²
tawdry
villain
wench

Pejorative Specialization
specious

Phonetic Restructuring
tattoo

Phonetic Restructuring by Grammatical Misanalysis
jade²

Phonetic Restructuring by Suffixion
average

Proreption
bugle
carpet
club
derrick
domino
ether
furlong
galosh
hulk
pants
sandwich
senate
shirt
skirt
sphinx
sulcate
swastika
treacle
yarn

Pun
tandem

Radiation
alchemy
apron
cad
caddie
cadet
canopy
catena
cave
chain
cheat
check
checker

chemistry
cheque
chequer
chignon
circle
circus
cleric
clerk
club
cockatrice
dactyl
faint
fare
feint
frank
gasket
gossip
hag
haggard
hassock
helium
hint
labyrinth
lace
mackinaw
magazine
map
marshmallow
mathematic
mathematics
maudlin
mint
money
napkin
noggin
pagan
pandemonium
pander
pane
panel
peasant

quean
queen
serf
sherbet
shirt
shrab
shrub
silly
skirt
solar
south
spinster
stigma
sun
syrup
task
tax
thigh
thumb
toast
tribute
virtue
whisker

Restructuring by Folk Etymology

albatross
Alcatraz
arrowroot
auburn
basilisk
belfry
canal
cane
canister
cannibal
canopy
canyon
lumber
pumpkin
restive
Tartar

Semantic Localization
   gamut

Semantic Reshaping by Folk
  Etymology
   albatross
   Alcatraz
   arrowroot
   auburn
   basilisk
   belfry
   cannibal
   canopy
   lumber
   pumpkin
   restive
   Tartar

Semantic Restructuring by Folk
  Etymology
   alchemy
   alcove
   canal
   cane
   canister
   canyon
   chemistry
   cove
   pedigree

Shift of Semantic Frame
   nausea

Specialization
   apron
   attic
   auction
   beriberi
   blackmail
   bread
   cancer
   carcinoma
   carpet
   censor

cephalic
cithara
comet
cop
dactyl
dreary
electric
electron
entomology
fanatic
gable
garble
giddy
guitar
helium
henchman
hulk
inaugurate
insect
iodine
javelin
machine
mackinaw
mail²
manure
mathematic
mathematics
melancholy
napkin
nickname
peach
pen
phlegmatic
pickaninny
pilgrim
plagiarism
plagium
quick
salary
sanguine
serf

serpent
shirt
skirt
smirk
solar
south
sphinx
starve
sulcate
sun
tribute
violet
whisker
yarn
zither

Specialization by Connotative
  Addition
  algebra
  candidate
  junk
  lace
  rival
  shroud
  spinster

Specialization by Connotative
  Extension
  academy
  alchemy
  aloof
  arena
  assassin
  belfry
  bevy
  bizarre
  blanket
  bless
  botulism
  broach
  brocade
  brochure

bromide
brooch
buccaneer
bust
buxom
cabal
cad
caddie
cadet
cancel
candy
cannon
canopy
cant
canvas
canvass
cave
chagrin
charm
chauvinist
cheat
cheer
chemistry
circle
circus
cleric
clerk
club
companion
coquette
corn
delirium
domino
dunce
equip
ether
faint
fare
feint
felon
fornication

furnace
furtive
gargoyle
gasket
giddy
glamour
grammar
harlot
heathen
hen
hint
hobby
hobbyhorse
hypocrite
hysterics
jade[1]
jubilee
junk
labyrinth
last
lewd
lumber
lunatic
madrigal
magazine
mail[1]
martyr
meat
megrim
meretricious
migraine
mint
money
nice
nun
pagan
pain
palace
pane
panel
parasite

pavilion
peasant
placebo
profanity
proud
prowess
prude
puisne
pumpkin
puny
quean
queen
restive
rival
rout
sabbath
sabbatical
scold
Scotist
serenade
serge
shack
shambles
shampoo
shamus
shanghai
shanty
shrew
siesta
silk
smock
smocking
soothe
stigma
street
swindle
sycophant
tandem
tariff
tart[1], tart[2]
task

tattoo
tax
testicle
thigh
thug
thumb
timber
tire
tithe
toast
toddy
toilet
torpedo
tragedy
tycoon
virtue
wench
worship
wretch
zany

Specialization by Localization
vernacular

Specialization by Metaphorical
Extension
cemetery

Specialization with Semantic
Blending
charm
slew
slogan

Subreption
bless
broach
brocade
brochure
brooch
chauffeur
cithara
constable
December

ether
God
guitar
hassock
hysterics
inaugurate
jade²
marshmallow
melancholy
mile
noon
November
October
pen
phlegmatic
pilgrim
planet
sanguine
sarcophagus
September
serenade
sister
spoon
stigma
stirrup
stroke
toddy
treacle
zither

Transference
albatross
Alcatraz
alchemy
algorism
algorithm
aloof
attic
auspices
average
bead
belfry

bizarre
buccaneer
bumpkin
bust
cab
cabal
cancel
cancer
canvas
canvass
carcinoma
carpet
catena
center
chagrin
chain
chapel
chauvinist
cheap
cheer
chemistry
chignon
chowder
cummerbund
dactyl
derrick
domino
fare
frank
galosh
gargoyle
gorilla
gossamer
grog
groggy
groom
harlequin
harridan
hassock
hen
hint

hobby
hobbyhorse
jade[1]
jubilee
juggernaut
jumbo
lace
lilac
lumber
macabre
maudlin
mustard
nemesis
nicotine
noggin
orang-utan
palace
pander
pants
parlor
pedigree
person
placebo
pongee
proud
prowess
prude
sabbath
sabbatical
sandwich
sarcophagus
serge
shantung
shirt
shrew
shroud
siesta
silhouette
silk
skirt
smock

smocking
syphilis
taxi
test
thing
timber
tire
toast
toddy
toilet
torpedo
tussah
tuxedo
whisker
yarn

Transmissional Filtering
   arrowroot
   boondocks
   cabal
   taboo
   tabu
   toddy
   woodchuck

Truncation
   cab
   taxi

Weakening
   ostracism
   serf
   starve
   worship

Index

Index

This Index contains all headwords, forms cited in italics, and glosses shown within single quotation marks, with references to the page numbers or alphabetic headword entries in which they appear. Also, types of linguistic change cited in the Foreword, Introduction, and Appendix II are shown in SMALL CAPITALS, with references to the pages in these sections where they can be found.

A

'abbreviated', silhouette.
'abounding in *phlegm*', phlegmatic.
'above', shanghai.
'abrasive cloth', chagrin.
abrown, auburn.
abrune, auburn.
abrune/abrown, auburn.
'absurd', grotesque.
'abusive', scold.
'abusive woman', scold.
Academus, academy.
academy, 1.
academy, academy; xxix.
accent, hen.
'accepted', cabal.
'acetic', sour.
acre, pilgrim.
'act', charm.

'acting like a fool', dunce.
'acting peculiarly because of the moon', lunatic.
'action-at-law', blackmail.
'active ingredient of *tobacco*', nicotine.
'activity', hobby.
'activity involving plaything', hobby.
'act of seizing', hint.
ad, arrive.
'additional', auction.
'additional name', auction.
'adorn', smock.
'adornment', smock.
'adornment of the body', smock.
'adorn with *lace*', lace.
adrīpāre, arrive.
adroit, sinister.

'adult', xxvii.
'adult hawk that can be trained to hunt', hag.
'adult man', nun.
'adult woman', hussy; nun.
'advance group of troops sent to the front lines', forlorn hope.
'advance troops sent on a dangerous mission', forlorn hope.
'advantageous', prowess.
'adversary', rival.
aḗr, ether.
'aesthetic quality of a *peach*', peach.
'affair', thing.
'affected', smirk.
'African idol', jumbo.
'after', puny.
'again', restive.
-*age*, average.
'agent of either sex', spinster.
'aggregation of people with shared interests', club.
agr-, pilgrim.
'agreeable', nice.
'agreement', blackmail.
aigne, puny.
aîné, puny.
aine, puny.
ainz, puisne.
air, ether.
Aira caespitosa, hassock.
aisné, puisne.
aīthein, ether.
aithḗr, ether.
akadḗmeia, academy.
Akadḗmeia, academy.
akimbo, buxom.
-*al*, bridal; mathematic.
al-, alchemy; alibi.
al, alchemy; alcohol; alcove; algebra; magazine.
A la recherche de temps perdu, maudlin.
'alarm', panic.
alba-, Alcatraz.
alba, auburn.
albatross, 1.
albatross, Alcatraz.
albatus, candidate.

albescent, auburn.
albino, auburn.
albumen, auburn.
alburnus, auburn.
albus, Alcatraz.
alca-, Alcatraz.
Alcatras, Alcatraz.
alcatraz, Alcatraz.
Alcatraz, 1.
alchemy, 2.
alchemy, alchemy.
alchymia, alchemy.
alcoba, alcove.
alcohol, 3.
alcohol, alcohol.
'alcohol derived from grain', parasite.
'alcoholic beverage made from malt', bridal.
'alcoholic beverage made with whiskey (and eggs)', noggin.
'alcohol-induced bravery', bumpkin.
alcohol of wine, alcohol.
alcohols, alcohol.
alcove, 4.
alcôve, alcove.
alcove, alcove.
ale, bridal.
algeber, algebra.
algebra, 4.
algebra, algebra.
algorism, 5.
algorism, algorism.
algorithm, 5.
algorithm, algorism.
Algoritmi, algorism.
Algoritmi de numero indorum, algorism.
alibi, 5.
alibi, alibi.
-*ālis*, rival.
-*alis*, bridal.
'alive', quick.
'alkaline air', ammonia.
'all', pandemonium.
allo-, alibi.
allomorph; allomerism, alibi.
'alloy consisting of precious and base metals', garble.

'alloy of gold and silver', **electric.**
all thumbs, **thigh.**
almacén, **magazine.**
aloof, 6.
a loof, **aloof.**
Alpine spaniel, **spaniel.**
al qādūs, **Alcatraz.**
al saggā, **Alcatraz.**
'also', **auction.**
'amber', **electric.**
ambi, **bust.**
ambidextrous, **sinister.**
ambo, **sinister.**
ambūrere, **bust.**
AMELIORATION, 253; xx; xxx.
AMELIORATIVE SPECIALIZATION, 253.
Ȧmen, **ammonia.**
Ȧmen-emhet, **ammonia.**
Ȧmenhotep, **ammonia.**
améthustos; a-, **amethyst.**
amethyst, 6.
amethyst, **amethyst.**
amine, 7.
amino, **ammonia.**
amino acid, 7.
ammine, 7.
ammine; amine, **ammonia.**
Ammon, **ammonia.**
ammonia, 7.
ammonia, **ammonia.**
ammoniakós, **ammonia.**
Ȧmon, **ammonia.**
'Amon is satisfied', **ammonia.**
'ample', **sad.**
an, **map.**
a napron, **map.**
an apron, **map.**
a naranj, **map.**
androgyne, **queen.**
a newt, **map.**
an ewt, **map.**
anhydrous, **winter.**
'animal', **quick.**
an napron, **map.**
'annoy', **pester.**
'annul or repeal', **cancel.**
an orange, **map.**
'answer', **hypocrite.**
ante, **puisne.**

Antheraea mylitta, **shantung.**
Antheraea perynyi, **tussah.**
'antidote to a poisonous bite',
   treacle.
antidotos thēriakḗ, **treacle.**
'anxiety', **chagrin.**
'anything light', **gossamer.**
'apathetic', **lethargic.**
'aphorisms', **sister.**
'apoplectic seizure', **stroke.**
apoplexy, **stroke.**
'apparently good but basically bad',
   xx.
'appearance', **sycophant.**
'appear dark', **lilac.**
'applaud', **cheer.**
'apple', **peach.**
'appointed officer of the peace',
   constable.
'appointed or enacted at a subsequent
   date', **puny.**
'apportion', **nemesis.**
'apportioned or divided', **nemesis.**
'apportionment', **nemesis.**
'appraisal', **task.**
'appropriation of another's work or
   ideas as one's own', **plagiarism.**
apron, 118.
apron, **map.**
'apt to swoon', **swindle.**
-ār-, **solar.**
'Arabic', **algorism.**
ᵓ*arafa,* **tariff.**
arc, **arrowroot.**
arcaduz, **Alcatraz.**
arch, **arrowroot.**
'arch', **fornication.**
archer, **arrowroot.**
'arching', **fornication.**
Arctomys monax, **woodchuck.**
arcus, **arrowroot.**
-ard, **hag.**
'arduous work', **task.**
-āre, **pester.**
'area', **pandemonium.**
arena, 7.
arena, **arena;** xx.
arenilitic, **arena.**

arenose, arena.
argent, salary.
argentum, salary.
argentum calcearius, salary.
argentum salārium, salary.
argentum vestiarum, salary.
'argument', alibi.
ar(h)we, arrowroot.
'arid', jungle.
arithmós, algorism.
**ark^w*, arrowroot.
Arlecchino, harlequin.
Arlette, harlot.
arlotus/erlotus, harlot.
'arrange', task; tire.
*arrīpāre, arrive.
arrive, 8.
arrive, arrive.
ar(r)iver, arrive.
arriving, xvii.
arrow, arrowroot.
'arrow', arrowroot.
arrowroot, 8.
arrowroot, arrowroot.
'articles used in dressing the hair and
    applying make-up', toilet.
artillerie, xxix.
artillery, xxix.
'art of setting bones', algebra.
aru-aru, arrowroot.
'ascend', stirrup.
'Asian', silk.
'Asian wool', silk.
'aspirer to office', xxvii.
assassin, 9.
assassin, assassin; thug.
'assemble', club.
assemblee bevee, bevy.
'assembly', club.
'Assembly of Hundreds', censor.
'assembly of people', thing.
'assess', task.
'assess an amount (of payment)',
    task.
'assessed payment', task.
'assessment', task.
'assessment of tribute', taxi.
'assess or levy payment', task.
'assess payment', task.

'assigned to the three clans', tribute.
'assistant to a coach-driver', cadet.
'associate', companion; rival.
'associated with caves or grottoes',
    xx.
'associate with whom one broke
    bread', companion.
astèr komḗtes, comet.
asti, swastika.
asylum, xx.
-āt-, senate.
'at', arrive.
Athens, attic.
'at last', tandem.
'at length', tandem; xxix.
atom, insect.
atone, 9.
at one, atone.
atone, atone.
'at rest', restive.
'attendant', constable; zany.
'attendant of the stable', constable.
'attend to the personal appearance',
    groom.
attic, 10.
attic, attic.
Attic, attic.
Attica, attic.
Attic order, attic.
Attic story, attic.
attire, tire.
'attire', shroud.
attir(i)er, tire.
'attractive', specious.
au-, inaugurate.
auborne, auburn.
auburn, 11.
auburn, auburn.
auction, 11.
auction, auction.
Audrey, tawdry.
**aug-*, auction.
augment, auction.
'aunt', nun.
'aura of wonder', glamour.
auspex, auspices.
'auspex', auspices.
auspice, auspices.

auspices, 12.
auspices, auspices.
auspicious, auspices.
'auspicious', sinister.
auspicium, auspices.
'austere', laconic.
auxesis, auction.
auxin, auction.
av-, inaugurate.
avarie(s), average.
'avenger', nemesis.
average, 12.
average, average.
average job, average.
averays, average.
averays/average, average.
aviary, inaugurate.
aviation, inaugurate.
avis, auspices.
'avoid', shirt.
'awārīya, average.
'away from one's native land', wretch.
awfully, xxii.
ayne, puny.

B

b, fanatic; quick.
b-, botulism; bugle.
babacoote, indri.
babakoto, indri.
'back', restive.
BACK FORMATION, 253.
bad, nice.
bad dude, nice.
'badge of shame', stigma.
'bad-tempered', sour.
'bag or pouch', mail.
'baked food', bread.
bake-meat, meat.
'ball', rout.
ball-point pens, pen.
bān, bonfire.
ban, fanatic.
-band, hussy.
band, cummerbund.
'banishment', ostracism.

'bank', arrive.
'bank or pawnshop', lumber.
banns, fanatic.
banshee, queen.
barbacóa, buccaneer.
'barbarian', Tartar.
barbecue, buccaneer.
'barge or ship that was towed', hulk.
'barrel', bumpkin.
'barter', cheap.
'base person likely to commit evil acts', villain.
basileús, basilisk.
basiliscus, basilisk.
Basiliscus, basilisk.
basilisk, 15.
basilisk, basilisk.
'basilisklike monster', cockatrice.
basiliskos, basilisk.
basilisks, basilisk.
bastard, hag.
basto, club.
'bat for striking a ball in sport', club.
'bathroom', toilet.
'be', prowess.
'be able', machine.
'beacon or point of reference', cynosure.
bead, 15.
bead, bead; xxiii.
beads, bead.
'beam', timber.
'bear', furtive.
'beard', bizarre.
'bearded person', bizarre.
'beast', treacle.
'beautiful', specious.
beauty parlor, parlor.
'became', heir; worship.
'become', worship.
'become lost', cheat.
'become reconciled', atone.
'become stiff', torpedo.
'becoming white', auburn.
'bed', street.
bedu, bead.
'beehive', cave.

'before', profanity; puny.
'beggar', harlot.
'be hungry', torpedo.
'being', swastika.
'being junior to', puny.
'be in ignorance, nice.
belfrey, belfry.
belfry, 16.
belfry, xxii.
bell, belfry.
'bell tower', belfry.
'belonging to a country household',
    villain.
'belonging to a shepherd', pester.
ben, queen.
'bench', shambles.
'bend', circus; wench.
'bend at the waist', buxom.
'bend(ing)', buxom.
beneath, nest.
Benedictus, placebo.
'beneficial', prowess.
'bent', buxom; circus.
Be of good cheer, cheer.
'be (or become) pregnant', auction.
ber-, belfry.
'bereft', heir.
berfrey, belfry; xxii.
berg, canter.
Berg, belfry.
beri, beriberi.
beriberi, 17.
beriberi, beriberi.
beryllium, solar.
'beside', parasite.
'be stiff or numb', torpedo.
'be strong', machine.
'between the radical and the
    conservative positions', center.
'between the two rivers',
    hippopotamus.
bevee, bevy.
'beverage', noon; syrup.
bevy, 17.
bevy, bevy.
be with you, goodbye.
b^h fanatic.
*b^heH; oin-,
*bhergh, belfry.

*bheug-, buxom.
bicron, stigma.
bid, bead.
'Bid him enter', bead.
'big or clumsy person', hulk.
'big turtle', mackinaw.
'bile', melancholy.
bio-, quick.
biography, quick.
biology, quick.
bios, quick.
'bird', auspices; inaugurate; xix.
'bird that sang in the morning',
    charm.
'bird-watcher', auspices.
'bit', bread.
'bitchy woman', gasket.
'bite off more than one can chew',
    Tartar.
bitter, sour.
'bitter', sour.
'bitterness', tart[1].
'bitter or acetic', sour.
bizar, bizarre.
bizarre, 17.
bizarre, bizarre.
'bizarre', grotesque.
bizarro, bizarre.
black, blackmail; phlegmatic.
'black', melancholy.
'black art', alchemy.
'black arts', cabal.
'black bile', melancholy.
'black bile condition', melancholy.
'black child', pickaninny.
'Black Earth', alchemy.
blackmail, 18.
blackmail, blackmail.
'black (slave) child', pickaninny.
'black yellow', melancholy.
blanca, blanket.
blank-, blanket.
blank, blanket.
'blank', blanket.
blanket, 18.
blanket, blanket.
blasphemous, profanity.
'blast of a trumpet', jubilee.

'blaze', phlegmatic.
'blazing', blanket.
bless, 19.
bless, bless.
'blessed', xxi.
'blessed by God', silly.
bletsian, bless.
blood, bless.
'blood', dreary.
'blood money', pain.
'bloody', dreary; sanguine.
'bloom', copper.
'blow', stroke.
'bluish', lilac.
'body of water', marshmallow.
bog, God; buxom.
'boisterous', circus.
bolt, pane.
Bombyx pernyi, tussah.
bomme, bumpkin.
bon-, bonfire.
bond, xviii.
bone, bonfire.
bone-fire, bonfire.
'bone of the cuttlefish', meerschaum.
'bone-setter', algebra.
'bone-setting', algebra.
bonfire, 19.
bonfire, bonfire.
boom, bumpkin.
boondocks, 20.
boondocks, boondocks; xxix.
boor, xxi.
boot, lace.
'booty', cheat.
'border', canter.
'boring', dreary.
'boring person', bromide.
'born', puny.
'born later', puny.
'born under the sign of Jupiter', jovial.
borough, belfry.
bōs, bugle.
botellus, botulism.
'both', sinister.
botulism, 20.
botulism, botulism.
botulismus, botulism.

botulus, botulism.
boucan, buccaneer.
boucane, buccaneer.
boucaniers, buccaneer.
'boundary', pagan.
boûs, thigh.
boútyron, thigh.
bovis, bugle.
bow, buxom.
'bow', arrowroot.
bow and arrow, buxom.
bowel, botulism.
'bows', xxix.
bow tie, buxom.
'boy', gasket; groom.
'braided rope', gasket.
'brain', gable.
'brain infarction', stroke.
'branch', gable.
'branching cluster of flowers at the end of a single stock', torso.
'branch of a tree used as a spear', gable.
'branch that forks off from the main stem', gable.
'brand', stigma.
'brandy or rum', syrup.
'brave', prowess.
'Brave People', cannibal.
'bravery', prowess.
bread, 21.
bread, bread.
'bread', companion.
'bread browned by heating', toast.
'bread which has yet to rise', sad.
'break', candy; rout.
'break a piece', bread.
'break *bread*', bread.
'break to bits', lumber.
'breast', cove.
'breastplate', cithara.
breeches, pajamas.
'bricklayer's mate', cadet.
bridal, 21.
bridal, bridal.
bridal(e), bridal.
bride, bridal.
'bride-ale', bridal.

bridegome, groom.
bridegroom, groom.
'bright', serenade.
'bright; clear light', serenade.
'brighten', xxix.
'brightness', serenade.
Brigit, canter.
'brine', catsup.
bring at one accord, atone.
'bring to a single state of agreement',
 atone.
'bring to shore', arrive.
broach, 22.
broach, broach.
brocade, 22.
brocade, broach.
*brocca, broach.
broccato, broach.
brocchus, broach.
brochure, 22.
brochure, broach.
brochures, broach.
'broken-down horse', harridan; jade.
'broken-down mare', jade.
'broken (off)', rout.
bromide, 23.
bromide, bromide.
bromides, bromide.
bromine, bromide; iodine.
brômos, bromide.
'brone', bizarre.
brooch, 22.
brooch, broach.
'brook', rival.
'brothel', fornication.
'brothers', nun.
brown, auburn.
'brown by heating', toast.
'brownie', hobby.
'brownish', auburn.
bru, bridal.
brúid, bread.
'brush and curry a horse', groom.
brúta, bridal.
brýd-ealu, bridal.
-bu-, tribute.
bu, taboo.
buccaneer, 23.
buccaneers, buccaneer.

buckaroo, bugle.
'bucket', Alcatraz.
būculus, bugle.
budget, xx.
'buffet', canvas.
'buffet verbally', canvas.
'buffoon', zany.
'buffoonish', zany.
'buffoon-like valet', zany.
bugle, 24.
bugle, bugle.
bugle horn, bugle.
bugles, bugle.
buhsum toward Gode, buxom.
'building material', timber; xix.
'building with complicated or
 convoluted passageways',
 labyrinth.
'bulky item', lumber.
'bull', bugle; torpedo.
bum, bumpkin.
bumble, bumpkin.
bumpkin, 24.
bumpkin, bumpkin; pumpkin.
'bumpkin humor', corn.
bundok, boondocks.
'burden the imagination', task.
burg, belfry.
'burial place', cemetery.
burig, canter.
'burn', bust; phlegmatic.
'burn around', bust.
'burning', phlegmatic.
'burning white hot', blanket.
'burnt', phlegmatic.
'burnt color', phlegmatic.
'burst', rout.
'business agent', chap.
bust, 25.
bust, bust.
bustum, bust.
butter, thigh.
'butter', thigh.
'butterfly', pavilion.
'butterflylike tent', pavilion.
'buttocks', bumpkin.
buvee, bevy.
buveur, bevy.

buxom, 25.
buxom, buxom; xviii.
'buy', cheap; cop.
'by', felon.
bye, goodbye.
'by God', jingo.
by golly, jingo.
by gosh, jingo.
by jingo, jingo.
'by *jingo*', jingo.
by the loving jingo, jingo.

C

c, peach.
cab, 200.
cab, taxi.
cabal, 27.
cabal, cabal.
cabala, cabal.
cabbala, kabala, cabal.
cabriolet, taxi.
cad, 28.
cad, cadet.
caddie, 28.
caddie, cadet.
cadet, 28.
cage, cave.
'cage (for birds or animals)', cave.
'cage for people', cave.
cal-, chowder.
calcātrix, cockatrice.
caldāria, chowder.
calfacere, chauffeur.
'call', slogan.
'call to mind', money.
'call to quarters for the night',
  tattoo.
'calm', soothe.
calopedia, galosh.
*calopia, galosh.
calopodes, galosh.
calorie, chowder.
'camel', gamut.
camelidae, dromedary.
'camel specially trained for riding',
  dromedary.
Camelus bactrianus, dromedary.

Camelus dromedarius, dromedary.
can-, charm.
canal, 31.
canal, cannon.
canapé, canopy.
canapeum, canopy.
canapium, canopy.
cancel, 28.
cancelli, cancel.
cancellus, cancel.
cancer, 29.
cancer, cancel; cancer.
'*cancer* in the body politic', cancer.
*cancerlus, cancel.
cand-, candidate.
'candid', frank.
candidate, 30.
candidate, xviii; xxvii.
candidatus, candidate; xxix.
'candidly', frank.
'candied', candy.
candy, 30.
cane, cannon.
cane, 31.
'cane', cove.
caned, cannon.
canere, cant.
can(e)vas, canvas.
canevas, canvas.
Caniba, cannibal.
canibales, cannibal.
Canibe, cannibal.
canine, cynosure.
canis, cannibal; cynosure.
Canis Major, serenade.
canister, 31.
canister, cannon.
*canmen, charm.
canna, cannon.
cannabis, canvas.
'cannabis', assassin.
cannibal, 31.
cannibals, cannibal.
cannon, 31.
cannon, cannon.
Canopus, canopy.
canopy, 32.
canopy, canopy.

'canopy covering a military installation', **pavilion.**
cant,   32.
cant,   **cant; canter; hen.**
Cant,   **cant.**
cantāre,   **cant.**
cantata,   **cant; serenade.**
canter,   33.
canter,   **canter; xxviii.**
Canterbury,   **canter.**
Canterbury gallop,   **canter.**
Canterbury pace,   **xxviii.**
Canterbury rate,   **canter.**
Canterbury trot,   **canter.**
canterius,   **shanty.**
canticle,   **cant.**
cantilation,   **cant.**
cantus,   **cant.**
Cant wara burig,   **canter.**
canvas,   34.
canvas,   **canvas.**
canvass,   34.
canvass,   **canvass.**
canyon,   31.
canyon,   **cannon.**
capdet,   **cadet.**
cape,   **chapel.**
'capital of Hell',   **pandemonium.**
capitellus,   **cadet.**
cappelani,   **chapel.**
cappella,   **chapel.**
capriolare,   **taxi.**
caput,   **cadet.**
'carapace',   **testicle.**
carcinoma,   29.
carcinoma,   **cancer.**
'carepace',   **test.**
Carex caespitosa,   **hassock.**
Carex paniculata,   **hassock.**
'Caribe',   **cannibal.**
carmen,   **charm; slogan.**
(carmen) matricālis,   **madrigal.**
caro/cara,   **cheer.**
carpe,   **carpet.**
Carpe diem,   **carpet.**
carpel,   **carpet.**
carpere,   **carpet.**
carpet,   34.
carpet,   **carpet.**

carpeta,   **carpet.**
carpets,   **carpet.**
carpetta,   **carpet.**
carphology,   **carpet.**
carpology,   **carpet.**
'carry',   **fare.**
'casket made of corrosive stone',
   sarcophagus.
'casket made of stone',   **sarcophagus.**
'catapaults',   **xxix.**
'catch',   **hag.**
catch a Tartar,   **Tartar.**
'catch a tiger (wolf) by the tail',
   Tartar.
catena,   44.
catena,   **chignon.**
catena patrum,   **chignon.**
catenary,   **chignon.**
catenation,   **chignon.**
catenionem,   **chignon.**
'cater to the baser lusts',   **pander.**
'cat-o',   **gasket.**
catsup,   35.
catsup,   **catsup.**
'cattle',   **picayune; xvii.**
cauldron,   **chowder.**
caup-,   **chap.**
caupō,   **chap; cheap; cop.**
cauponārī,   **chap.**
caupōnis,   **cop.**
caupōnis,   **cheap.**
'cause blood to flow',   **bless.**
'causes destruction',   **torpedo.**
'cause to be sharp',   **stigma.**
'cause to die from hunger',   **starve.**
cave,   35.
cave,   **cave; cove.**
'cave',   **grotesque.**
cavea,   **cave.**
caveola,   **cave.**
'cavern',   **cave; grotesque.**
'caviling purely for the sake of
   arguing',   **dunce.**
cavity,   **cave.**
cavus,   **cave.**
čēap,   **cheap.**
cemetery,   36.
cemetery,   **cemetery.**

cĕna,   pain.
censor,   37.
censor,   censor.
census,   censor.
Cent-,   censor.
center,   37.
center,   center.
'center of a circle',   center.
centrists,   center.
centrum,   center.
centum,   censor.
centurion,   censor.
century,   censor.
cephalalgia,   gable.
cephalic,   73.
cephalic,   gable.
cereal,   quick.
Ceres,   quick.
ch-,   melancholy.
ch,   peach.
'chaff',   shack.
chafing-dish,   chauffeur.
chagrin,   38.
chagrin,   chagrin.
chain,   44.
chain,   chignon.
chairman,   man.
chairperson,   person.
chamberlain,   xxi.
chāmpnā,   shampoo.
chāmpo,   shampoo.
chancel,   cancel.
chancellors,   cancel.
chant,   cant; charm; hen.
'chanted',   cant.
chantier,   shanty.
chap,   38.
chāp,   shampoo.
chap,   chap.
'chap',   cove.
chapel,   39.
chapel,   chapel; xxviii.
chapels,   chapel.
chaplains,   chapel.
chapman,   chap.
'charachteristic',   virtue.
'charge or duty',   tariff.
'charge (to repel someone or
    something)',   junk.

'charge to the owner of shipped
    goods',   average.
charm,   39; 180.
charm,   slogan.
charme,   charm.
'chastity',   virtue.
chaudière,   chowder.
chauffeur,   40.
chauffeur,   chauffeur.
chaunte,   charm.
Chauntecleer,   charm.
chauvinisme,   chauvinist.
chauvinist,   40.
chauvinist,   chauvinist.
chauviniste,   chauvinist.
cheap,   41.
cheap,   chap; cheap.
cheapen,   cheap.
cheat,   41.
cheat,   cheat.
cheater,   cheat.
'cheater',   swindle.
cheating,   cheat.
check,   42.
check,   check; chess.
'Check',   check.
checked,   check.
checker,   42.
checkmate,   check.
cheer,   43.
cheer,   cheer.
cheer a person (up),   cheer.
cheer one's comrades (on),   cheer.
'cheese',   thigh.
cheîn,   alchemy.
chēmia,   alchemy.
Chēmia,   alchemy.
'chemical or hormone promoting
    growth',   auction.
chemist,   alchemy.
chemistry,   2.
chemistry,   alchemy.
chemists,   alchemy.
-chemy,   alchemy.
cheque,   42.
cheque,   check.
chequer,   42.
chequer,   check.

chequers, check.
cher/chère, cheer.
chess, 43.
chess, chess.
'chessboard', check.
'chess piece', check.
cheumeîa, alchemy.
chhāp, shampoo.
chhāpnā, shampoo.
chief, handkerchief.
*chienté, shanty.
chignon, 44.
chignon, chignon.
chih, catsup.
child, gossip.
'child', pickaninny; wench.
'child's toy', hobby.
'child's toy horse', hobby.
chip, spoon.
'chip', spoon.
'chisel employed by stonemasons',
  broach.
chlorine, iodine.
chol-, melancholy.
choler, phlegmatic.
chord, yarn.
Chorea Maccabaeorum, macabre.
chowder, 45.
chowder, chowder.
'Christian clergy', cleric.
Christian Sabbaths, Sabbath.
chuck, woodchuck.
'churches or other sites of religious
  assembly', worship.
churl, xxi.
chymeîa, alchemy.
cierm, slogan.
circle, 45.
circle, circus.
'circle', circus.
'circling hawk', circus.
'circular arena for athletic contests',
  circus.
'circular intersection of roadways',
  circus.
circulus, circus.
circus, 45.
circus, circus.
cithara, 46.

cithara, cithara.
cither, cithara.
'citizen', pagan; pilgrim.
citole, cithara.
city, cemetery.
cīvis, pilgrim.
cīvitās, cemetery.
'clamor', slogan.
'clan', pagan; tribute.
'clandestine; sinister-seeming group',
  cabal.
'clear', serenade.
'clear singer', charm.
cleric, 46.
cleric, clerk.
clerical, cleric.
clerk, 46.
clerk, clerk.
'cloak', domino.
'clog', galosh.
'closet', cove.
Clostridium botulinum, botulism.
'cloth', map; toilet.
'clothed in white', candidate.
'clothes money', salary.
'clothing', pajamas; shroud.
'clothing worn by the dead about to
  be buried', shroud.
'cloth waved as a starting signal for
  racersin the circus', map.
'cloth wrapper', toilet.
'cloudless weather', serenade.
'cloying syrup', treacle.
club, 47.
club, club.
'club', club.
club, to, club.
'clue', hint.
clump, club.
'clumps or tufts of grass', hassock.
'clumsy', hulk; thigh.
'clumsy ship', hulk.
'coach for hire', hackney.
'coagulated 'swollen' milk', thigh.
coat of mail, mail[1].
cobalt, 48.
cobalt, cobalt; nickel.
'cobwebs', gossamer.

Cocarde tricolore, La, chauvinist.
cocātrix, cockatrice.
cock, spaniel.
'cock', coquette.
cockatrice, 48.
cockatrice, cockatrice.
cocker, spaniel.
cocker spaniel, spaniel.
cofa, cove.
'coin', money.
'coih money', money.
'cold', winter.
'cold season of the year', winter.
'collect', club.
'collection of (appointed or selected) people', panel.
'collection of houses', cemetery.
'colorful water bird', harlequin.
'color of a *peach*', peach.
com-, sister.
'combine', club.
'come again', jingo.
comes, constable.
comes stabulī, constable.
comet, 49.
comet, comet; xxiii.
comēta, comet.
'come to harmony or concord', atone.
'come to shore', arrive.
Comitia Centuriata, censor.
comitis, constable.
'commit suicide', bumpkin.
'common draft horse', hobby.
'common drudge', hackney.
'common people', lewd.
"Common" Treacle, treacle.
'Common Treacle', treacle.
'community of people', cemetery.
companie bevee, bevy.
companion, 49.
'companion', meat.
compāniōnem, companion.
'comparison', parlor.
'completely', persuade.
'completely lost', persuade.
'complete massage', shampoo.
'compliant', buxom.
'compulsory payment', task.

*com-swesr-īn-os, sister.
conapeum, canopy.
concatenate, chignon.
'concavity suitable for holding things', testicle.
'conceal', shroud; thug.
'conceive of', feint.
concoct, pumpkin.
'condemnation', xxiii.
'condemnation, or general disfavor', thigh.
'condition', botulism; melancholy.
'condition in which the fingers or toes are joined', dactyl.
'conduit', Alcatraz.
'confection', candy.
'confidence man', swindle.
'confused in mind', silly.
connotation, xxvii.
CONNOTATIVE EXTENSION, 253; xix.
conopeum, canopy.
'consecrate', bless.
conserve, serf.
cōnsobrīnus, sister.
'consort with (loose) women', wench.
constable, 50.
constable, constable; xxx.
'construction for confining birds and animals', cave.
'container', cannon.
'container for clothing', toilet.
'container for powder and shot for a cannon', cannon.
'container (of spirits)', noggin.
CONTEXTUALIZATION, 253; xxiii.
contort, tart[1].
'contract', blackmail.
'contrivance', machine.
'conversation', parlor.
convert, worship.
'convince by making things very sweet', persuade.
cook, pumpkin.
'cook', pumpkin.
'cooked', pumpkin.
cop, 50.
cop, cop.
cop a piece of goods, cop.

cop a plea, cop.
copor, copper.
copper, 51.
copper, cop; copper.
'*copper*', cop.
'copper-nickel', nickel.
cops, shamus.
'*cops*', shamus.
coq, coquette.
coquet, coquette.
coquette, 52.
coquette, coquette.
cord, yarn.
'*cord*', lace.
corn, 52.
corn-, corn.
corn, corn.
corn liquor, corn.
'*corn liquor*', corn.
'corpse', macabre.
'correspondence', mail.
corset, lace.
'cost', pain.
'costly bargain', cheap.
'couch', canopy; street.
count, constable.
counterpane, pane.
'count (or tally) one's prayers', **bead**.
'country', villain.
'country house', villain.
'countryman', pagan.
'countryside', pagan.
cousin, 179.
cousin, sister.
couvre, handkerchief.
cove, 53.
cove, alcove; cove.
'cover', handkerchief; thug.
'covered area for recreation',
 pavilion.
'covered building', thug.
'covered circular arena', circle.
'covered couch', canopy.
'cover for a boat', thug.
'cover for a house', thug.
'cover for people', thug.
'covering', canopy.
'covering for the lower part of a
 (female) body', shirt.

'covering worn on the head',
 handkerchief.
cow, bugle; xxvii.
'cow', bugle; thigh.
'cowardly', feint.
'cowboy', bugle.
'coy', nice.
crab, xxxi.
'crab', cancel; cancer.
'cradle', cemetery.
crafty, xxi.
crane, pedigree.
'crane', derrick.
'crane's foot', pedigree.
cranium, megrim.
craw, gargoyle.
crayfish, xxx.
'craziness', zany.
'crazy', zany.
'creature that seizes its prey', **hag**.
'creep', smock.
'creeping', serpent.
'creeping disease', serpent.
'creeping thing', serpent.
'creep or crawl', serpent.
cribellum, garble.
'cripple', lumber.
'criticize', canvas.
'crooked', circus.
crotesque, grotesque.
crotto, grotesque.
'crude peasant', villain.
'cruise', wench.
'cry', slogan.
crypt, grotesque.
crypta, grotesque.
cū, bugle.
cum, constable.
cummerbund, 53.
cūna, cemetery.
cunning, xxi.
cup, test.
'cup', noggin.
cupcake, tart[1].
'cupel', test.
cupēre, copper.
Cupid, copper.
cupidity, copper.

Cupīdo, **copper**.
'cup or mug of liquor',   **noggin**.
cupreum aes, **copper**.
cuprum, **copper**.
curchief, **handkerchief**.
curfew, **handkerchief**.
'current', **shibboleth**.
curve, **circus**.
'curved', **circus**.
'curved plating for the rim of a
  wheel',   **tire**.
curvus, **circus**.
'cushions',   **hassock**.
'customer',   **chap**.
'custom or law',   **nemesis**.
'cut',   **shirt; shroud**.
'cut and run',   **shirt**.
'cut in, or notched; animals',   **insect**.
'cut or carve',   **glamour**.
'cut-throat',   **thug**.
cwén,   **queen**.
Cwén,   **queen**.
cwene,   **queen**.
cwicu-,   **quick**.
cynosura,   **cynosure**.
cynosure,   53.
cynosure,   **cynosure**.
Cyprus,   51.

D

d,   **dactyl; lewd; nest; quick**.
-d-,   **yarn**.
dactyl,   55.
dactyl,   **dactyl; xxx**.
dactylitis,   **dactyl**.
daimōn,   **pandemonium**.
dak-,   **dactyl**.
dáktulos,   **dactyl**.
'damaged goods',   **average**.
'damaged or lost cargo',   **average**.
'dance of the Maccabees',   **macabre**.
Danse macabrée,   **macabre**.
Danses macabrées,   **macabre**.
'date',   **dactyl**.
daughter,   **gossip**.
'daughter-in-law',   **bridal**.
Daunce of Machabree,   **macabre**.

'day',   **jovial**.
'daylight',   **serenade**.
'day of rest',   **Sabbath**.
'daytime sky',   **jovial**.
de-,   **delirium**.
de,   **pedigree**.
Dē-,   **quick**.
'dealer at market booths',   **chap**.
'deal made under the influence of
  liquor',   **bumpkin**.
'dear',   **cheer**.
dear cheap,   **cheap**.
'deceive',   **cheat**.
December,   167.
December,   **September**.
decimāre,   **decimate**.
decimate,   56.
decimate,   **decimate**.
decimus,   **decimate**.
deck,   **thug**.
deer,   xix.
de facto,   **tycoon**.
'defraud',   **cheat**.
DEGENERATION,   253.
degree,   **pedigree**.
degrue,   **pedigree**.
deîma pānikón,   **panic**.
'deity',   **jingo**.
'Deity',   **God**.
'Deity who enjoys the sacrifice',
  God.
'delicate',   **gossamer**.
dēlīrāre,   **delirium**.
delirium,   56.
delirium,   **delirium**.
-dem,   **tandem**.
'demanding',   **task**.
Dēmétēr,   **quick**.
Demetrius,   **quick**.
*demH,   **timber**.
'demon king',   **harlequin**.
'denise',   **feint**.
denotation,   xxvii.
DENOTATIVE SHIFT,   xix.
'dense',   **sad**.
dent-,   **solar**.
dentist,   **solar**.
'department store',   **magazine**.

*_der_, **tart**[1].
de rigueur, **tuxedo**.
dermatologist, **tart**[1].
déroute, **rout**.
derrick, 57.
derrick, **derrick**; xix; xxix.
Derrick, **derrick**.
_de se_, **felon**.
'desert', **heathen**.
'desert land', **jungle**.
'deserve (a portion or share)',
   meretricious.
'designations', **vernacular**.
'desirable', **peach**.
'desire', **copper**.
'desire ardently', **starve**.
'despondency', **migraine**.
'destroy a large part of', **decimate**.
'destructive force', **juggernaut**.
'detached portion or segment', **rout**.
'detachment', **rout**.
detect and protect, **thug**.
'detective', **shamus**.
deus ex machinā, **machine**.
'device for hoisting', **derrick**.
'device for hurling destructive
   missiles', xxix.
'device for masking faulty work',
   bumpkin.
'device or means for applying force or
   power', **machine**.
'devil', **nickel; pandemonium**.
devil's tattoo, **tattoo**.
dexter, **sinister**.
dextrous, **sinister**.
*_dheigh_, **feint**.
*_dhragh-_, **train**.
diaphanous, **sycophant**.
dick, **shamus**.
'die', **starve; torpedo**.
'die from lack of food', **starve**.
'die of hunger', **starve; torpedo**.
diēs, **jovial**.
diet, **jovial**.
Ding, **thing**.
discern, **garble**.
'discuss', **hypocrite**.
'discuss thoroughly', **canvas**.
disease, xxi.

'disentangle', **carpet**.
'disgust', **nausea**.
'dismal', **dreary**.
'disordered company (of soldiers)',
   rout.
'disorderly gathering or event',
   circus.
'disorderly retreat', **rout**.
'dispenser of divine retribution',
   nemesis.
'disreputable woman', **jade**.
'dissembler', **hypocrite**.
'distributed: payment', **tribute**.
'distributed to the clans', **tribute**.
'distribution', **nemesis**.
'district', **pagan**.
'disturber of the peace by constant
   harping', **scold**.
diurnal, **jovial**.
'divide', **nemesis**.
'divide into tenths', **decimate**.
'divine justice', **nemesis**.
'divine or prophetic sign or omen',
   auspices.
'divine retribution', **nemesis**.
'division', **rout**.
'division of the people', **tribute**.
'dizzy', **giddy**.
dobbin, **hobby**.
Dobbin, **hobby**.
dobby, **hobby**.
Dobby, **hobby**.
'Doctor Subtilis', **dunce**.
dodecahedron, **eleven**.
dōdeka, **eleven**.
'dog', **cannibal**.
'doghouse', **shanty**.
dōm, xxiii.
domain, **timber**.
'domestic', **vernacular**.
domicile, **timber**.
dominion, **timber**.
domino, 57.
domino, **domino**.
Domino, **domino**.
'_Domino!_', **domino**.
dominoes, **domino**.
dominus, **domino**.

domus, timber.
doom, xxiii.
'dormitory', cemetery.
dough, feint.
'down', nest; pedigree.
'downtown focus of mercantile
   activity', center.
drag, train.
'drag', train.
'dragging', train.
'drag or tow', hulk.
'draught', noon.
draw, train.
'draw', train.
'drawing of a geographical projection',
   map.
dreary, 58.
drēor, dreary.
drēorig, dreary.
drēosan, dreary.
'dress', tire.
'dress a corpse for burial', shroud.
'dressing for the wheels of a coach',
   tire.
'dressing room', toilet; xxi.
'dressing-table', toilet.
'dressing-table cover', toilet.
'drifting organic life of the ocean',
   planet.
'drink', bevy; syrup.
'drinker', bevy.
'drinking', bevy.
'drinking group', bevy.
'drink someone's health', toast.
'driver', chauffeur.
dromad-, dromedary.
dromedarius, dromedary.
dromedary, 58.
dromedary, dromedary.
'drop', dreary.
dropena drēorung, dreary.
'dross', alchemy.
'drummers', pariah.
'drumming of the fingers', tattoo.
drunkard, hag.
'drunken', amethyst.
'dry', toast.
'dry out', toast.
dunce, 59.

dunce, dunce; xix; xxix; xxx.
Duns, dunce.
Duns learning, dunce.
Duns men, dunce.
Duns prelate, dunce.
Duns Scotus, dunce.
Dutch auction, bumpkin.
Dutch bargain, bumpkin.
Dutch courage, bumpkin.
dutchman, bumpkin.
Dutch treat, bumpkin.
Dutch uncle, bumpkin.
'duty', average.
'dwarf', nickel; nun.
'dwell', hussy.
'dwelling', timber; villain.
*dyēus, jovial.
*dyēus-pHter, jovial.

E

e, chess; henchman; spinster; taxi.
e-, eleven.
ēac, auction.
ēacian, auction.
'early settler', pilgrim.
'earn or acquire (a share)',
   meretricious.
'ear of corn', shibboleth.
'earth', toast.
'(earthen) vessel', test.
'earthenware pot', noggin.
'eastern', shantung.
'easy-going', buxom.
'eat', bread.
*Ecclesiastical History of the English
   People*, henchman.
échec, check; chess.
Échec, chess.
échecs, chess.
economy, nemesis.
-(e)d, lewd.
'(edible) flesh', meat
'edible portion of a nut or other fruit',
   meat.
educate, train.
'effeminate male homosexual', queen.

'efficacy', **virtue.**
'effort', **pain.**
eft, **map.**
eggnog, **noggin.**
'Egypt', **alchemy.**
'Egyptian couch covered with
  mosquito netting', **canopy.**
eidēs, **iodine.**
eight, **noon.**
eion, **pumpkin.**
éjade, **jade²**.
éjade, l', **jade²**.
eke, **auction.**
eke-name, **auction.**
'eke out a living', **auction.**
ekin, **pumpkin.**
el-, **alibi.**
'elaborately vaulted recess in a room',
  alcove.
elbow, **buxom.**
ēlectr-, **electric.**
electric, 63.
electric, **electric.**
electron, 63.
electron, **electric.**
electrons, **electric.**
ēlectrum, **electric.**
Ēlectrum, **electric.**
ēléktor, **electric.**
ēlektri, **electric.**
ēlektron, **electric.**
elektron, **electric.**
'elevated opinion of oneself',
  prowess.
eleven, 63.
eleven, **eleven.**
else, **alibi.**
elsewhere, **alibi.**
'elsewhere', **alibi.**
'embodiment of the spirits of their
  ancestors', **indri.**
'embossed', **broach.**
empestrer, **pester.**
en-, **gable.**
encephalo-, **gable.**
encephalogram, **gable.**
enchant, **charm.**
'enchantment', **glamour.**
'enclosure', **cave.**

'encourage one's comrades', **cheer.**
'encumber', **pester.**
endocarp, **carpet.**
'enforced payments', **tribute.**
'engage in trade or business', **chap.**
'engine of war', **machine.**
'enjoyer or consumer of that which
  has been poured forth', **God.**
énnea, **noon.**
-ent-, **serpent.**
'enthusiastic', **fanatic.**
'entity', **thing.**
éntoma zôa, **insect.**
entomo-, **insect.**
entomology, 98.
entomology, **insect.**
'entreaty', **bead.**
'envelop', **shroud.**
'envelop(e)', **shroud.**
eoh, **hippopotamus.**
epidermis, **tart¹.**
equestrian, **hippopotamus.**
equine, **hippopotamus.**
equip, 64.
equip, **equip.**
'equip', **tire.**
'equipment', **tire.**
'equipment worn or carried by
  soldiers', **tire.**
'equitably shared loss', **average.**
equus, **hippopotamus.**
-er, **ether; pander.**
Erithacus rubecula, **hobby.**
-eron, **map.**
'errand boy', **cadet.**
-esce, **proud; prowess.**
escheat, **cheat.**
'escheat', **cheat.**
eschete, **cheat.**
(e)skippare, **equip.**
-esque, **grotesque.**
esquiper, **equip.**
-ess, **spinster.**
-ess, **proud; prowess.**
esse, **prowess.**
'essentialism', **dunce.**
'essentialist', **dunce.**
'estimable', **prowess.**

'fuller's frame', cave.
'full of life', quick.
'full of sorrow', dreary.
fumée, buccaneer.
FUNCTIONAL SHIFT, 257.
'fundamental negative particle of an atom', electric.
funeral, bonfire.
'funeral pyre', bonfire.
'funereal', macabre.
funer(is), bonfire.
funus, bonfire.
für, furtive.
furh, furlong.
furhlang, furlong.
furlong, 72.
furlong, furlong.
furnace, 70.
furnace, fornication.
'furrow', delirium; furlong.
'furrow made by a plow', hulk.
furtive, 72.
furtive, furtive.
furtively, furtive.
furtivus;, furtive.
furtivus, furtive.
'fury', hag.
'(fussy or maternal) human female', hen.
fylfot, swastika.

G

g, licorice; melancholy; quick.
*g-, bugle.
g-, melancholy.
ga-, companion.
Gabel, gable.
gable, 73.
gable, gable.
gabul, gable.
gahlaiba, companion.
gaiole, cave.
gairid, slogan.
gairm, slogan.
gall, melancholy.
'gall', melancholy.
'gallant', prowess.

gallica, galosh.
gallicula, galosh.
'gallows', derrick.
galoche, galosh.
galosh, 74.
galosh, galosh.
galoshes, galosh.
galoshoes, galosh.
'galoshoes', galosh.
'game of kings and the king of games', chess.
gamma, gamut.
gammadion, swastika.
gamut, 74.
gamut, gamut.
gamut scale, gamut.
'gangster', torpedo.
'gangster employed to commit violence', torpedo.
garbel, garble.
garble, 75.
garbled, garble.
garble the coinage, garble.
garce, gasket.
garceta, gasket.
garcette, gasket.
garçon, gasket.
gargle, gargoyle.
gargouille, gargoyle.
gargoyle, 76.
gargoyle, gargoyle.
'garment', pajamas; smock.
'garment composed of metal links', mail.
garnr, yarn.
garrulous, slogan.
gasket, 76.
gasket, gasket.
gast-cofa, cove.
'gathering of people to decide legal matters', thing.
'gather together', club.
gauche, sinister.
'gaudy; but of shoddy quality', tawdry.
'Gaul', galosh.
'Gaulish sandal', galosh.
'gaunt', hag.

'gear', shroud.
'gelding', henchman.
gemæte, meat.
GENERALIZATION, 258; xix; xxviii.
GENERALIZATION BY CONNOTATIVE
EXTENSION, 258.
GENERALIZATION BY METAPHORICAL
EXTENSION, 259.
GENERALIZATION THROUGH TRANSMIS-
SION FILTERING, 258.
'general noise and confusion',
pandemonium.
gens, pagan.
gentile, pagan.
gentle, xxi.
'(genuinely) weak', feint.
'genuine', pumpkin.
genus, puisne.
'get', cop.
ghairm, slogan.
gharbala, garble.
'ghastly', macabre.
ghirbāl, garble.
'ghosts', indri.
$*^{ghw}$-, fornication.
$*^{ghw}er$, fornication.
'gibberish', jumbo.
giddy, 77.
giddy, giddy.
'giddy person', swindle.
'gift', tribute.
'gigantic; oversized', jumbo.
gimel, gamut.
girl, wench; xxvii.
'girl', gasket.
gittern, cithara.
glamour, 78.
glamour, charm; glamour.
'glaring', phlegmatic.
'gleaming', electric.
'gloomy', dreary; sour.
'glorious', prowess; slogan.
glukús, licorice.
'gluttons', harlot.
glycose, licorice.
'go', constable; fare; stirrup.
'go around the outer edge', shirt.
'goat', tragedy.
'goat song', tragedy.

'go-between in affairs of the heart',
pander.
god, giddy.
'god', pandemonium.
God, 78.
God, God; goodbye; gossip; xxviii.
'God', God; jingo.
God be with you, goodbye.
'God be wi' you!', goodbye.
'God buy', goodbye.
'goddess of divine retribution',
nemesis.
'god from a machine or contrivance',
machine.
'god (God)', jingo.
'God-Kin', xix.
'go down', stirrup.
godsib, gossip; xix.
godsibs/gossips, gossip.
'go (forward)', fare.
go girling, wench.
'go in search of females for sport',
wench.
'gold', solar.
'golden brown', auburn.
-gome, groom.
'good', nice; peach; prowess; silly;
swastika.
goodbye, 79.
good cheap, cheap.
good cheer, cheer.
Good day, goodbye.
'good inexpensive bargain', cheap.
'good man', nice; prowess.
'good mood', cheer.
Good night, goodbye.
'good to look at', specious; xx.
'good woman', prowess.
'go on a journey', fare.
goose, gossamer.
goose-summer, gossamer.
goose-summer/gossamer, gossamer.
gorge, gargoyle.
gorilla, 79.
gorillas, gorilla.
'Gorillas', gorilla.
görn, yarn.
'gory', dreary.

gossamer, 80.
gossamer, gossamer.
gossip, 80.
gossip, gossip; xix.
gossips, gossip.
'go to sleep', cemetery.
'go up', stirrup.
'go well', fare.
'grab', cop.
gradus, pedigree.
grain, corn.
'grain', parasite.
grain of salt, corn.
gramaire, glamour.
grámma, glamour.
grammar, 78.
'grammar', glamour.
grámmata, glamour.
'grandfather', nun.
'grape', dactyl.
graph-, glamour.
*graph-ma, glamour.
'grasp', hint; thing.
'grasped', hint.
'grasping', hint.
grass, assassin.
'grating', cancel.
'grave', sad.
'gray', blanket.
'great', tycoon.
'great bargain', cheap.
Great cheap, cheap.
'Greater Dog', serenade.
'great meal', arrowroot.
'great weakness', beriberi.
green thumb, thigh.
*grH, corn.
grim, migraine.
'grinder', torpedo.
grog, 81.
grog, grog.
groggy, 81.
groggy, grog.
grogoran, grog.
grogram, grog.
grogran, grog.
Grog's mixture, grog.
Grog's ration, grog.
grom, groom.

groom, 81.
groom, groom.
'groom', henchman; xxi.
Groom of the Privy Chamber,
  groom.
Groom of the Stable, groom.
Groom of the Stole, groom.
groom one's hair, groom.
groom someone for office, groom.
'groove made with a pointed tool',
  hulk.
gros grain, grog.
grotesque, 82.
grotesque, grotesque; xx.
grotto, grotesque.
'grottolike painting', grotesque.
groundhog, woodchuck.
'group', bevy.
'group drinking', bevy.
'group of jurors', panel.
'group of soldiers', rout.
'group or assemblage of finches',
  slogan.
'grow or increase', auction.
'growth process', auction.
grætan, heir.
grue, pedigree.
gruem, pedigree.
'gruesome', macabre.
grupta, grotesque.
grus, pedigree.
'guiding star', cynosure.
Guinevere, queen.
guitar, 46.
guitar, cithara.
gulf, gargoyle.
gullet, gargoyle.
'gullet', gargoyle.
gurgle, gargoyle.
gurguliō, gargoyle.
'guts', yarn.
*g^w, quick.
*$g^w H^y éH^w$-, quick.
*$g^w H^y H^w$-, quick.
Gwendolyn, queen.
gyd-, giddy.
gydig, giddy.
gynaikós, queen.

gyné, queen.
gynecology, queen.

H

h, dactyl; hulk; hypocrite; solar.
'habitual fault-finder', scold.
hack, 83.
hack, hackney.
hackney, 83.
hackney, hackney.
Hackney, hackney.
hackney coach, hackney.
hackneyed phrase, hackney.
hackney horse, hackney.
hadda, chignon.
'had enough', sad.
haegtesse, hag.
hæþ, heathen.
hǣðen, heathen.
hag, 83.
hag, hag.
hagard, hag.
haggard, 83.
haggard, hag.
haggard hawk, hag.
hai, shanghai.
'hair of the head', comet.
'hairstyle featuring side-locks', gasket.
'hair wash', shampoo.
Hakenei, hackney.
hal-, salary.
halàs ammoniakós, ammonia.
'half the skull', migraine.
halobiont, salary.
halophyte, salary.
hamlet, cemetery.
Hamlet, rival.
'hand', aloof.
handkerchief, 84.
handkerchief, handkerchief.
'hand-loomed cloth', shantung.
'handsome', specious.
'hanging locks with *violets* and little
    roses', iodine.
'hangman', derrick.
'happiness', cheer.
'happy', buxom; jovial; silly; xxi.
'(happy) face', cheer.

hard, cancer.
'hard-shelled animal', cancer.
harena, arena.
haridelle, harridan.
harle, harlequin.
harlequin, harlequin.
Harlequin's, harlequin.
harlequin, 85.
harlot, 85.
harlot, harlot.
'harlot', hussy.
harlotry, harlot.
harlots, harlot.
harridan, 86.
harridan, harridan.
harvest, carpet.
'harvest life's fruits', carpet.
hashāsh, assassin.
hashāshīn, assassin.
hashish, assassin.
'hash marks', sergeant.
hassock, 87.
hassock, hassock.
hassuc, hassock.
'haul', train.
'hauled', train.
'hauling', train.
'having a share in the Christian
    ministry', cleric.
'having the characteristics of',
    grotesque.
'head', cadet; gable; handkerchief;
    noggin; test.
'headache', gable.
'headstrong', xx.
'healthy', buxom.
heap, forlorn hope.
'heat', chowder; phlegmatic.
heath, heathen.
heathen, 87.
heathen, heathen.
heaðorian, chignon.
'heathen', pagan.
'heaven', jovial.
'heaven-father', jovial.
'heavily', lumber.
'heavy-duty cloth made from hemp',
    canvas.

'he breaks', **bread.**
'he calls', **slogan.**
hēd-, **persuade.**
hedge, **hag.**
hedonist, **persuade.**
hēdús, **persuade.**
heir, 88.
heir, **heir.**
'heir', **heir.**
heirs, **heir.**
'he is a flirt', **coquette.**
'he is flirtatious', **coquette.**
heliocentric, **solar.**
heliometric, **solar.**
hélios, **solar.**
heliotrope, **solar.**
helium, 182.
helium, **solar.**
'Hell', **pandemonium.**
hēmi-, **megrim.**
hēmikrānia, **megrim.**
hemp, **canvas.**
'hemp', **assassin.**
'hemp users', **assassin.**
hen, 90.
hen, **cant; charm; hen.**
henchman, 90.
henchman, **henchman.**
hendecachord, **eleven.**
hendecasyllable, **eleven.**
héndeka, **eleven.**
hengest, **henchman.**
Hengest, **henchman.**
hengestmann, **henchman.**
hengist, **henchman.**
hengst, **henchman.**
Hengst, **henchman.**
Hengstmann, **henchman.**
hent, **hint.**
hentan, **hint.**
hent/hint, **hint.**
herba nicotiana, **nicotine.**
heredem, **heir.**
heredes sui et necessarii, **heir.**
'hereditary king', **basilisk.**
herem, **heir.**
heres, **heir.**
Herla Cyning, **harlequin.**
'Herla the King', **harlequin.**

herle, **harlequin.**
Herlequin, **harlequin.**
hero, **serf.**
'hero', **wretch.**
hérōs, **serf.**
'hero sandwich', **torpedo.**
hérpēs, **serpent.**
herpetology, **serpent.**
herpetón, **serpent.**
hesg, **hassock.**
'He's worth his salt', **salary.**
hetaxa, **task.**
'he who has a round foot', **tuxedo.**
'he *worships* her', **worship.**
'hidden one', **ammonia.**
'hide', **grotesque.**
hierle, **harlequin.**
'high', **canter.**
'high *jingo;* come again', **jingo.**
'high (place)', **belfry.**
'high place of security or protection',
 belfry.
'high-ranking official', **constable.**
'hill', **palace.**
Hinks, **henchman.**
hint, 91.
hint, **hint.**
hippo-, **hippopotamus.**
Hippocrates, **hippopotamus.**
Hippocratic oath, **hippopotamus.**
hippodrome, **hippopotamus.**
hippopotamos, **hippopotamus.**
hippopotamus, 92.
'hirsute African people discovered by
 Hanno', **gorilla.**
'His room is a complete *shambles*',
 shambles.
'hitchhike', **thigh.**
hlāf, **bread.**
hlaifa, **companion.**
Hob(b)in, **hobby.**
hobby, 92.
hobby, **hobby.**
Hobby, **hobby.**
hobbyhorse, 92.
hobbyhorse, **hobby.**
'holding oneself in esteem', **prowess.**
'hold in great respect', **worship.**

'hold (together)', **thing.**
holiday, xix.
'holidays', **Sabbath.**
holkás, **hulk.**
'hollow', **cave.**
'hollow area', **cove.**
'(hollow) enclosure', **cove.**
'hollow place in the earth', **cave.**
'holy', **silly.**
home, **cemetery.**
'home loom', **shantung.**
homo, **groom.**
HOMONYMY, xiii.
honey bun, **tart**[1].
'honor', **pain; worship.**
'hood', **domino.**
'hoodlum', **thug.**
hoop, **forlorn hope.**
hope, **forlorn hope.**
'hopeless enterprise', **forlorn hope.**
'hopeless undertaking', **forlorn hope.**
horde, **Tartar.**
hordome and harlotry, **harlot.**
'horizontal spar', **bumpkin.**
horn, xxii.
'horn', **cheer.**
'hors d'oeuvre', **canopy.**
'horse', **henchman; hippopotamus;**
    jade; marshal.
'horse blanket', **panel; street.**
'horse servant', **marshal; xxi.**
'host', **slogan.**
'hot', **fornication; serenade.**
hotel tariff, **tariff.**
hound, **cynosure.**
'house', **hussy; shanty; thug; timber.**
'house(hold)', **thing.**
'household', **hussy; timber.**
housewife, **hussy.**
housewives, **hussy.**
'How did it go for you?/It went well
    for me', **fare.**
How did you fare?/I fared well,
    fare.
'howitzers', xxix.
hsiung-nu, **Tartar.**
húdor, **winter.**
hulk, 93.
hulk, **hulk.**

'human', xxvii.
'human being', **person.**
'human being; person', **man.**
'human trunk', **torso.**
'humble or obedient', **buxom.**
Hun, **Tartar.**
hund, **censor.**
hundred, **censor.**
'hungry', **starve.**
Huns, **Tartar.**
'hunting net', **plagiarism.**
husband, **hussy.**
husbands, **hussy.**
hūsewíf, **hussy.**
hussy, 94.
hussy, **hussy.**
hustings, **thing.**
huta, **God.**
huta-bhug, **God.**
(h)ūtan, **orang-utan.**
hydrant, **winter.**
hydrophobia, **winter.**
hypocrite, 94.
(h)ypocrite, **hypocrite.**
hypokrínesthai, **hypocrite.**
hypokritḗs, **hypocrite.**
hystéra, **hysterics.**
hysterectomy, **hysterics.**
hysteria, **hysterics.**
hysteric passion, **hysterics.**
hysterics, 95.
hysterics, **hysterics.**
hysterikós, **hysterics.**
hýsteros, **hysterics.**

I

i, **giddy; henchman; nausea; nest;**
    pain; peach; puny; quick; taxi.
-ia, **melancholy.**
-ic-, **meretricious.**
iceberg, **belfry; canter.**
ice cream parlor, **parlor.**
ichneúmon, **cockatrice.**
'idle pastime', **hobby.**
'idle prattle', **gossip.**
'idle prattler', **gossip.**

ignite, God.
'ignorant', lewd; nice; xviii.
ijada, jade².
Il est coquet, coquette.
iliata, jade².
ilium, jade².
'illicitly', furtive.
'illiterate', lewd.
'illness with symptoms resembling
   seasickness', nausea.
immaculate, mail¹.
immaculate conception, mail¹.
'immediately', xxii.
'imp', nickel.
*impastōriāre, pester.
'impatiently active', xx.
impecunious, picayune.
'impious', profanity.
'importance', worship.
'impose a compulsory payment', task.
'impress', shampoo.
'impression', shampoo.
'improvement', xx.
'improve or train a person', manure.
'impudent woman', queen.
-in-, pilgrim.
-in, assassin.
in, pester.
'in', gable; pester.
'in a clandestine manner', furtive.
'in addition to', auction.
'in another place', alibi.
inaugurāre, inaugurate.
inaugurate, 97.
inaugurate, inaugurate.
inauguration, inaugurate.
'inauspicious', sinister.
in a whisk, whisker.
incantation, charm; hen.
'incapable of weighty or serious
   thought', giddy.
'inclined to remain', restive.
'inclined to swoon', feint.
'incongruous', grotesque.
'inconstant of mind', giddy.
'increase', auction.
'increase one's holdings with
   difficulty', auction.
'increase or growth', auction.

Indian corn, corn.
'Indian summer', gossamer.
indisposition, xxi.
'individual', person.
'individual honored by drinking to his
   or her health', toast.
indri, 97.
indri, indri.
'Indry!', indri.
'induce the acceptance of a belief or
   position', person.
'industrialist', tycoon.
-ine, bromide; iodine.
'inebriated by grog', grog.
'(inedible) concomitants of (edible)
   flesh', meat.
'inert', restive.
'inexpensive', cheap.
'infancy', madrigal.
'inferior', puny.
'inflammation', phlegmatic.
'inflammation of the finger', dactyl.
'informer', sycophant.
'in front of', profanity.
'in front of the temple', profanity.
'inhabitant of a *vill*', villain.
'inheritance', cheat; cleric.
'inheritance taken by the state',
   cheat.
'inherited', heir.
'inlet', cove.
'innkeeper', chap.
'innocent or simple', silly.
-ino, pickaninny.
-iño., pickaninny.
in one ear, xxviii.
in potestate, heir.
'insubstantial', gossamer.
'insane', giddy; lunatic.
insect, 98.
insect, insect.
insectum animale, insect.
'inspired by a god', fanatic.
Institutes, serf.
'insurmountable foe or rival',
   nemesis.
'intellect', man.
'interest', charm; hobby.

'intestine', botulism.
'intestines', yarn.
'in the power', heir.
inundate, winter.
'invent', feint.
'invent in a self-serving way', feint.
iode, iodine.
iōdēs, iodine.
iodine, 98.
iodine, iodine.
iōn, iodine.
īre, constable.
'irregular', bizarre.
-iscus, grotesque.
-ism, plagiarism.
isomer, meretricious.
'item', thing.
'items stitched or sewn with a needle', broach.
'itinerant pedlar', chap.
'it pleases Aton', ammonia.
-ium, pandemonium.
-ivus, restive.
'I will please the Lord in the land of the living', placebo.

J

jabr, algebra.
jacal, shack.
jade¹, 101.
jade², 101.
jade¹, harridan.
jade, jade¹; jade².
jaded, jade¹.
jadeite, jade².
jade, le, jade².
Jagannāth, juggernaut.
jagannātha, juggernaut.
jail, cave.
jail/gaol, cave.
jaiole, cave.
jamah, pajamas.
'James', shamus.
jangala, jungle.
javelin, 73.
javelin, gable.
'javelin', frank; gable.

javelot, gable.
Jeffrey, belfry.
'Jewish day of rest', Sabbath.
'Jewish day of rest (on the seventh day of the week)', Sabbath.
Jewish Sabbath, Sabbath.
jingo, 102.
jingo, jingo.
Jingoes, jingo.
jingoism, 102.
jingoism, jingo.
jingoist, chauvinist.
Jinko, jingo.
John, shamus.
'John', zany.
'John', shamus.
John Barleycorn, zany.
John Bull, zany.
John Doe, zany.
'John(n)y', zany.
Johnny-come-lately, zany.
Johnny Reb, zany.
'joint-footed animals', insect.
'jolly', buxom; jovial.
jong, junk.
jonquil, junk.
'journey', fare.
Jove, jovial.
jovial, 103.
jovial, jovial.
joviālis, jovial.
joviality, xix.
Jovis, jovial.
Jovius, jovial.
jovy, jovial.
jubilee, 104.
jubilee, jubilee.
judgment, xxiii.
juggernaut, 104.
juggernaut, juggernaut.
jumbo, 105.
Jumbo, jumbo.
'jump up in the air', taxi.
juncus, junk.
jungle, 105.
'jungle', orang-utan.
'junior', puny.
'junior military officer', cadet.

junk, 106.
junk, junk.
junket, junk.
Juno Moneta, money.
Jupiter, jovial.

K

k, dactyl; pumpkin.
-ka, swastika.
kabbala, cabal.
kaêná, pain.
*kagh, hag.
kâlon, galosh.
kalopódion/kalopódia, galosh.
kamarband, cummerbund.
Kāma Sūtra, sister.
*kan, hen.
kand, candy.
kánna, cannon.
kánnabis, canvas.
Kánōpos, canopy.
kapu, taboo.
kára, cheer.
karkinōma, cancer.
karkínos, cancer.
karpós, carpet.
kaufen, cheap; cop.
'keeping away', aloof.
'keep the Sabbath', Sabbath.
kef-i-daryā, meerschaum.
*kei, cemetery.
keîsthai, cemetery.
-ken, bumpkin.
kenteîn, center.
kéntron, center.
kephalē̆, gable.
*ker, cancer; cheer.
kerchief, handkerchief.
*ker-ker, cancer.
kernel, corn.
kernel of truth, corn.
ketchup, 35.
ketchup, catsup.
Khāns, cannibal.
k^haVnd, candy.
kheros, heir.
Khmi, alchemy.

khordē̆, yarn.
'kidnapper', plagiarism.
'kidnapping', plagiarism.
'kidney', jade.
-kijn, bumpkin.
-kin, bumpkin; map.
kind, xxi.
'kindle', ether.
'king', check; chess.
King Charles spaniel, spaniel.
'king dies', check.
kirkos, circus.
kirkos/kríkos, circus.
Kitab al-jabr w'al muqabala (The Book about Redintegration and Equation), algebra.
kitchen, pumpkin.
kithára, cithara.
kitharos, guitar.
kiun, tycoon.
klērikós, clerk.
klē̆ros, clerk.
klostr-, botulism.
knave, xxi.
'knave', harlot.
'knead', feint.
'knees', testicle.
'knife', frank.
Kobold, cobalt.
köe, catsup.
koh'l, alcohol.
kohl, alcohol.
koimân, cemetery.
koimētérion, cemetery.
kómē̆, comet.
komē̆tes, comet.
kōnopeîon, canopy.
kónōps, canopy.
Kopf, noggin; test.
krāni-, megrim.
kríkos, circus.
kryptē̆, grotesque.
krýptein, grotesque.
kuno, cynosure.
kunós oura, cynosure.
Kupfernickel, nickel.
Kuprîa, copper.
Kúpris, copper.

kuprismós, copper.
kúpros, copper.
Kúpros, copper.
$*k^{w}i$-; oi-,
k^{w}-, pain.

L

l, glamour; laconic; lilac; pilgrim; solar; treacle.
la, gamut.
lábrus, labyrinth.
labúrinthos, labyrinth.
labyrinth, 107.
labyrinth, labyrinth.
lace, 107.
lace, lace.
'Lacedaemonians', laconic.
lacere, lace.
'lacking in guile', silly.
'lacking in judgment', silly.
'lacking pigmentation', auburn.
'lack of ease', xxi.
'lack of order', xxi.
'Laconians', laconic.
laconic, 108.
laconic, laconic.
ladh, lethargic.
laicus, lewd.
laikós, lewd.
'lake', marshmallow.
Lakedaimónioi, laconic.
'lake or a pool', meerschaum.
Lákōnoi, laconic.
lame, lumber.
'land a boat', arrive.
lang, furlong.
'languish', swindle.
laós, lewd.
laqueus, lace.
'large number', slogan.
'large photographic print', panel.
'Larger Bear', cynosure.
'large reed', cane; cannon.
'lascivious', lewd.
lascivious behavior, lewd.
lasso, lace.

last, 56.
last, delirium.
latent, 109.
latent, lethargic.
'Latin', pilgrim.
'Latin grammar', glamour.
Latīnus, pilgrim.
'latter', hysterics.
'lattice', cancel.
Laudamus, placebo.
'laundry bag', toilet.
lavatory, xxi.
'lavatory', toilet.
'lay', lewd.
'lay minister who assists the parish priest', cleric.
'lay officer of the church', cleric.
'lay person', lewd.
'lay waste to', decimate.
lazo, lace.
'lazy', feint.
lb, delirium.
'lead', fare.
'leader', fare.
lead puddling, poodle.
'lead ram', jubilee.
'leaf through', thigh.
'learn', mathematic.
'leather', chagrin.
leave, eleven.
'leavings from a bale of marijuana', shack.
left, 109.
left, left.
'left', eleven; sinister.
'left after the count of ten', eleven.
'left-hand side', sinister.
'leftovers', shack.
'legal assembly', thing.
'legal suit', blackmail.
lemur, 97.
lemurs, indri.
length, xxix.
'lengthwise', tandem.
lethargic, 109.
lethargic, lethargic.
'lethargic', sad.
Lēthē, lethargic.

'letters', glamour.
'(let the) tap (be) closed', tattoo.
-lev-, eleven.
'lever that explodes a torpedo',
   whisker.
lewd, 109.
lewd, lewd.
'Lewd did I live and evil I did dwel',
   lewd.
'lewd woman', harridan.
Lex Fabia, plagiarism.
'libellous person', scold.
libra, delirium.
licorice, 110.
licorice, licorice.
'lie', cemetery.
'lie down', cemetery.
'lie flat', placebo.
'lie (hidden)', lethargic.
'life', quick; winter.
light, lunatic.
'light', serenade; sycophant.
'light ship', hulk.
'light up', ether.
'like a peach', peach.
lilac, 110.
lilac, lilac.
'linen used for any purpose; but
   usually for table use', map.
'line of poetry containing eleven
   syllables', eleven.
LINGUISTIC FILTERING, xxix.
lion, xx.
liquorice, licorice.
līra, delirium.
lira, delirium.
'list of charges', tariff.
'list of names', panel.
'literate person', cleric.
'literature', glamour.
lithos sarcophágos, sarcophagus.
'little', pickaninny.
'little bag', xx.
'little barrel', bumpkin.
'little bench or stool', shambles.
'little chief', cadet.
'little cloak', chapel.
'little cloth', toilet; xxi.
'little cock', coquette.

'little head', cadet.
'little mouse', muscle.
'little; (old)', nun.
'little one', pickaninny.
'little piece of cloth', panel.
'little tree', bumpkin.
'little woman', hussy.
'live', quick.
'live now!', carpet.
'living', quick.
'living creature', quick.
'living room', parlor.
loaf, bread; companion.
lobotomy, insect.
LOCALIZATION, 259; xxiii; xxviii.
LOCALIZATION OF PHRASAL MEANING,
   260.
'local resident in a university town',
   cadet.
'lodge', cemetery.
loef, aloof.
lōf, aloof.
'loin', cummerbund; jade.
loma, lumber.
Lombard, lumber.
Lombard-house, lumber.
Lombards, lumber.
lomra, lumber.
London Treacle, treacle.
'lone bear-mouse', worship.
'lone mountain-mouse', worship.
'long', furlong.
'long-haired', xxiii.
'long haired stars', xxiii.
lonja, noon.
loof, aloof.
'Look!', indri.
'look at', specious.
'lord', domino.
'lord;', tycoon.
lose, forlorn hope.
'lose', forlorn hope.
'lost', forlorn hope.
'lost heap', forlorn hope.
'lost inheritance', cheat.
'lost troop', forlorn hope.
'lot', cleric.
loud, lumber.

'loud noise of announcement',
  jubilee.
*louksmen, lunatic.
*louksnam, lunatic.
'love', belfry.
'love instruction', sister.
lovelorn, forlorn hope.
Love's Labour's Lost, goodbye.
'Love Song of Jo Alfred Prufrock;
  The', ether.
'lower', hysterics.
'lower air', ether.
'lower part of a woman's anatomy',
  hysterics.
'lowlife', harlot.
'low spirits', migraine.
luce, serenade.
Luceres, tribute.
luce serēnanti, serenade.
luf, left.
luff, aloof.
lumber, 111.
lumber, lumber.
'lumber', timber.
'lumber camp', shanty.
'lumberjack's quarters', shanty.
lumber room, lumber.
lūmen, lunatic.
luminōsis, lunatic.
luminous, lunatic.
lump, lumber; noon.
'lump', club.
'lump together', club.
lūna, lunatic; solar.
lunatic, 112.
lunatic, lunatic.
lūnāticus, lunatic.
lunch, noon.
luncheon, noon.
lux, serenade.
læwan, lewd.
lyft, left.
lyft-adl, left.

M

m, map; maudlin.
-m-, fornication.

maᵓaser, tithe.
Macaber, macabre.
macabre, 113.
macabre, macabre.
Macabré, macabre.
macabré(e), macabre.
Maccabee, macabre.
Maccabees, macabre.
macchabé, macabre.
machine, 113.
machine, machine.
Mackinac, mackinaw.
mackinaw, 114.
mackinaw, xxx.
Mackinaw, mackinaw.
Mackinaw boat, mackinaw.
Mackinaw coats, mackinaw.
mackinaws, mackinaw.
Mackinaw trout, mackinaw.
macula, mail¹.
maculate, mail¹.
'mad', fanatic; lunatic.
madeleine, maudlin.
Madeleine, maudlin.
'madness', delirium.
madrigal, 115.
madrigal, madrigal.
madrigals, madrigal.
mæl, blackmail.
magan, machine.
magasin, magazine.
magazine, 116.
magazine, magazine.
magazines, magazine.
Magdalen, maudlin.
Magdalena, maudlin.
Magdalene, xix.
'magical incantation', charm.
mahsan, magazine.
mail¹, 116.
mail², 117.
-mail, blackmail.
mail, blackmail; mail¹; mail².
mail bag, mail².
maille, mail¹.
mail of letters, mail².
'major attendant to a Highland chief',
  henchman.

'make a lattice (or something resembling one)', **cancel.**
'make amends or expiate', **atone.**
'make appear', **sycophant.**
'make heat', **chauffeur.**
'makeshift dwelling', **shanty.**
'make shiny or sleek', **smock.**
mākhaná, **machine.**
māl, **blackmail.**
malachite, **marshmallow.**
malákhē, **marshmallow.**
mal de Naples le, **syphilis.**
male, **mail²; xxx.**
'male', **virtue; xxvii.**
'male bird', **spaniel.**
male chauvinist, **chauvinist.**
'male child', **groom.**
'male domestic fowl noted for his 'singing', **hen.**
'male flirt', **coquette.**
'male fowl', **hen.**
'(male) glutton', **harlot.**
'male (or neutral) agent', **spinster.**
'male person', **groom.**
'male reproductive gland', **testicle.**
'male servant', **groom.**
'male servant in charge of the horses', **groom.**
'male supremacist', **chauvinist.**
malha, **mail².**
'malicious', **xxi.**
'malignant or deadly element', **cancer.**
malle, **mail².**
mallow, **marshmallow.**
mâlon, **peach.**
mālum, **peach.**
malva, **marshmallow.**
māmá-gyombō, **jumbo.**
man, **117.**
man, **chap; man; xxvii.**
'man', **canter; groom; orang-utan; person; virtue.**
'man about to be married or just married', **groom.**
'manage or administer', **manure.**
'manager of the royal household', **constable.**
'man clothed in white', **candidate.**

mándra, **madrigal.**
mandra, **madrigal.**
mandriālis, **madrigal.**
'man-eating native of the New World', **cannibal.**
maneuvre, **manure.**
'man from Chorasmia', **algorism.**
'man-made vessel in the shape of a pine cone', **torso.**
'man-made watercourse', **cannon.**
'manner of writing', **xx.**
'man of some authority', **sergeant.**
'man of the forest', **orang-utan.**
'mansion or building of great splendor inhabited by a ruler', **palace.**
manthánein, **mathematic.**
mantra, **meat.**
manure, **118.**
manure, **manure.**
'man-wolf', **virtue.**
'man worthy of esteem', **prowess.**
map, **118.**
map, **map.**
mapa, **map.**
mappa, **map.**
marah, **marshal.**
marahscalh, **marshal.**
Maranta arundinacea, **arrowroot.**
mare, **marshal; meerschaum; xxvii.**
'mare', **jade.**
'marijuana', **assassin.**
marine, **marshmallow; meerschaum.**
maritime, **marshmallow; meerschaum.**
'mark', **mail; stigma.**
'marked', **taboo.**
'marked by stakes', **pagan.**
'marked with furrows', **hulk.**
'mark of a contrasting color in a mineral', **mail.**
Marmota monax, **woodchuck.**
'marriage announcements', **fanatic.**
marsh, **marshmallow.**
marshal, **119.**
marshal, **constable; marshal; xxi.**
marshals, **marshal.**
marshmallow, **120.**
marsh mallow, **marshmallow.**

marshmallow, marshmallow.
marshmallows, marshmallow.
'marsh or fen', meerschaum.
'marten', worship.
mártur, martyr.
martúrion, martyr.
martyr, 121.
martyr, martyr.
'Mary of Magdala', maudlin.
'mask', domino; person.
'mass', noon.
'massage', shampoo.
'master', domino.
'Master!', domino.
Master of Glomery, glamour.
'Master of Grammar', glamour.
mate, meat.
materiāles, madrigal.
'material of a coarse grain', grog.
matheîn, mathematic.
mathematic, 121.
mathematic, mathematic.
mathematical, mathematic.
mathematics, 121.
mathematics, mathematic.
mathēmatikós, mathematic.
matricālis, madrigal.
'matter', thing.
'matter considered by a legal
   assembly', thing.
'mattress', street.
Maudelen, maudlin.
Maudeleyn, maudlin.
maudlin, 122.
maudlin, maudlin; xviii.
Maudlin, maudlin.
mauve, marshmallow.
may, machine.
mayl, mail².
mead, amethyst.
'meal', fare.
'meal of meals', arrowroot.
MEANING ACQUIRED BY FUNCTIONAL
   USE, 260.
'meaningless incantation', jumbo.
'meaningless object of worship',
   jumbo.
'mean or despicable person', wretch.

'means of accomplishing something',
   machine.
'means of concealment', shroud.
'measure', meat; taxi.
meat, 122.
meat, meat; xix.
meat and bone, meat.
meat and hide, meat.
meats, meat.
*med, meat.
mediate; modicum, meat.
meer, meerschaum.
meerschaum, 123.
meerschaum, marshmallow;
   meerschaum.
meerschaum pipe, meerschaum.
megrim, 125.
megrim, megrim; migraine.
megrims, migraine.
melan-, melancholy.
melancholia, melancholy.
melancholy, 124.
melancholy, phlegmatic; sanguine.
mêlon, peach.
melon, peach.
'member of an ecclesiastical order',
   domino.
'member of a religious sect', thug.
membrum virile, smock.
'memory', money.
-men, charm.
mēns, man.
mensch, man.
Mensch, man.
mental, man.
*mer-, meretricious.
mer-, meerschaum.
'merchant', chap; cheap; cop.
merē-, meretricious.
mere, meerschaum.
merērī, meretricious.
meretricious, 124.
meretricious, meretricious.
meretricius, meretricious.
meretrix, meretricious.
merit, meretricious.
meritum, meretricious.
mermaid, marshmallow; meerschaum.
méros, meretricious.

'mesh of a net', mail.
Mesopotamia, **hippopotamus.**
'messy', **shambles.**
'metal rim of a wheel', **tire.**
METAPHOR, xx.
mete, meat.
méthu, amethyst.
*methustos, amethyst.
METONYMY, xx.
'meter', taxi.
mètre, taxi.
Mètre/meter, taxi.
métron, taxi.
metronome, nemesis.
Mi, gamut.
micromicron, stigma.
'midday', siesta.
might, machine.
migraine, 125.
migraine, megrim.
mile, 125.
mile, xxviii.
milia, mile.
milia passuum, mile; xxviii.
'(military) camp', **Tartar.**
'military display featuring the drum
    and bugle corps', **tattoo.**
'military division', **rout.**
'military division or company', **rout.**
'military trainee', **cadet.**
milk-meat, meat.
mince-meat, meat.
mincemeat, meat.
mind, man.
'mind', man.
'mingled voices or singing', **slogan.**
'mingling', **alchemy.**
'minor official at the county level of
    government', **constable.**
mint, 126.
mint, money.
'mistress of a household', **hussy.**
mitchimakinak, mackinaw.
'mixture', **alchemy.**
-mnt, stigma.
*-mnt, stigma.
mobile, torpedo.
'mock horse used by morris dancers',
    hobby.

'mode or way of life', **quick.**
molgós, mail[2].
*mon, man.
monere, money.
Moneta, money.
'monetary or fiscal value', **worship.**
money, 126.
money, money.
'money', salary.
'money to pay for a trip', **fare.**
mono-, man.
monocle, man.
monomania, man.
mononuclear, man.
mōns, palace.
Mōns Palātīnus, palace.
'mood', cheer.
'moon', lunatic; solar.
'moonstruck', lunatic.
moquém, buccaneer.
'moral rectitude', **virtue.**
'(more or less globular) pot', **testicle.**
*mori, marshmallow.
'mortars', xxix.
Morte d'Arthur, worship.
'mosquito', canopy.
mother, gossip.
'mother', madrigal; quick.
'Mother Church', madrigal.
'mother of life', quick.
'mother tongue', madrigal.
'motto or catchphrase ', **slogan.**
mount, palace.
'mount', stirrup.
'mountain', belfry; boondocks;
    canter.
'mountain range', **shantung.**
'mourn', heir.
'mouse', muscle.
moustache, whisker.
'moustache', whisker.
'movable s', **torpedo.**
'movable siege tower', **belfry.**
'move clumsily', **lumber.**
'move heavily', **lumber.**
mucus, phlegmatic.
'mug', noggin.
mukém, buccaneer.

mumbo-jumbo, **jumbo**.
mus, **muscle**.
muscle, 126.
muscle, **muscle**.
muscles, **muscle**.
musculus, **muscle**.
'musical performance given in the
    open air', **serenade**.
'musical setting of a secular poetic
    text', **madrigal**.
must, **mustard**.
mustard, 127.
mustard, **mustard**.
mustard seed, **mustard**.
mustum, **mustard**.
'my lord', **goodbye**.
mynet, **money**.
mynetian, **money**.

N

n, **auction; cancel; cancer; charm;
    felon; lilac; map; nemesis; solar;
    stigma**.
N, **average**.
-n, **solar**.
-n-, **fornication; yarn**.
n', **map**.
'nag', **harridan; jade**.
'nail', **broach; center**.
namaycush, **mackinaw**.
'names', **vernacular**.
Nana, **nun**.
nanny, **nun**.
nánnos, **nun**.
nape, **map**.
naperon, **map**.
napery, **map**.
napkin, 118.
napkin, **map**.
'napkin', **map**.
napron, **map**.
nāranja, **map**.
NARROWING, xxviii.
nascor, **puisne**.
'native', **vernacular**.
'native languages', **vernacular**.
'natives of the *Canibe* , **cannibal**.

Natural History, **labyrinth**.
nau-, **nausea**.
nausea, 129.
nausea, **nausea; xxviii**.
nausia, **nausea**.
naut-, **nausea**.
naútēs, **nausea**.
nautía, **nausea**.
naval, **nausea**.
navy, **nausea**.
nè, **puisne**.
ne-, **nest**.
-nea-, **nest**.
'Neapolitan disease', **syphilis**.
'near', **parasite**.
'needle', **broach**.
nehmen, **nemesis**.
'neighbor', **rival**.
'neighbor or person in competition
    with another', **rival**.
neke-name, **auction**.
némein, **nemesis**.
nemesis, 129.
nemesis, **nemesis**.
Nemesis, **nemesis**.
*nem/*nom, **nemesis**.
nénna, **nun**.
nénnos, **nun**.
néos, **noon**.
nephrite, **jade²**.
nephrós, **jade²**.
nescire, **nice**.
nescius, **nice; xviii**.
nest, 130.
nest, **nest**.
nether, **nest**.
nether regions, **nest**.
'netting', **canopy**.
new, **noon**.
'new', **noon**.
'new or fresh wine', **mustard**.
*ni, **nest**.
ni, **nest**.
nice, 131.
nice, **nice; xviii**.
'nice', **nice**.
nice bit of flim-flam, **nice**.
nice distinction, **nice**.

nickel, 131.
nickel, nickel.
nickname, 11.
Nickname, auction.
nicotine, 131.
nicotine, nicotine.
nidus, 130.
nidus, nest.
nil, lilac.
nila, lilac.
nilak, lilac.
nine, noon.
'nine', noon.
'ninth', noon.
*nisdos, nest.
noble, xxi.
nog, noggin.
noggin, 132.
noggin, noggin.
noigean, noggin.
'noise', lumber.
-n-om, shambles.
-nome, nemesis.
nómos, nemesis.
-nomy, nemesis.
non, noon.
nona, noon.
'nonadult', xxvii.
nona hora, noon.
'nonbeliever', pagan.
'non-Christian', heathen; pagan.
'noncleric', lewd.
none shemch, noon.
'nonhuman', xxvii.
nonna, nun.
nonnus, nun.
'nonordinary', bizarre.
noon, 132.
noon, noon.
'noon cup or drink', noon.
'noose', lace.
Norfolk spaniel, spaniel.
'nose-foot', thigh.
'not', amethyst.
'not (capable of being) cut or split',
  insect.
'not holy', profanity.
'notification', tariff.
'notify', tariff.

'not in control of one's mind', giddy.
'not to know', nice.
'nouns', vernacular.
nov-, noon.
novem, noon.
November, 167.
November, September; noon.
novus, noon.
'nuisance', pester.
num-, nemesis.
'number', algorism.
'number-manipulating', algebra.
'numbness', torpedo.
numismatics, nemesis.
nun, 133.
nun, nun.
nunch, noon.
nuncheon, noon.
nunne, nun.
nurus, bridal.

O

o, nest; pain; person.
'obedient', buxom; xxi.
'obligatory labor (in lieu of monetary
  payment)', task.
'obligatory labor or piece of work',
  task.
'obligatory payment', tribute.
'obliging', xxi.
'obscene behavior', harlot.
'obscene sexual behavior', harlot.
'obscene woman', harlot.
obsequious, xxi.
'observe', auspices.
'obstinate', restive; xx.
'obtained by theft', furtive.
Occam's rasor, dunce.
occident, solar.
Ockham's rasor, dunce.
October, 167.
October, September.
'odds and ends', lumber.
ōdĕ̄, tragedy.
'ode; song', tragedy.
odont-, solar.

oe, pain.
'offer a suggestion', hint.
'offer a thing to be seized', hint.
'office of', senate.
'officer in a royal or noble household',
  groom.
'officer in charge of a group of 100',
  censor.
'officer of the peace', shamus.
'office seeker', candidate.
'office seekers', xxix.
officius, xxi.
'offspring of sisters', sister.
'offspring of those who sewed
  together', sister.
'off-white', auburn.
'of himself', felon.
'old', senate; shanty.
'old, broken-down woman', harridan.
'old, worn-out woman', harridan.
'older', puny; senate; xxvii.
'Old Grog', grog.
'Old Grogram Cloak', grog.
'old house', senate.
'old-looking', hag.
'old maid', spinster.
'old men', senate.
Old Nick, nickel.
'old retainer', senate.
'old roof', senate.
'old (storm) house', shanty.
'old whore', harridan.
'ominous', sinister.
-on, electric.
-one, atone.
one, atone; eleven.
'one', eleven; man.
'one eye', man.
'one nucleus', man.
'one saved by others', serf.
'one who', sister.
'one who bears something off',
  furtive.
'one who betrays his country', xxix.
'one who feeds at another's expense',
  parasite.
'one who goes on foot', pedigree.
'one who goes with another',
  constable.

'one who inhabits the *hæþ*', heathen.
'one who is on a trip abroad or a
  journey away from home', pilgrim.
'one who likes everything sweet',
  persuade.
'one who lives for pleasure',
  persuade.
'one who makes heat', chauffeur.
'one who pays a *fare*', fare.
'one who saves others', serf.
'one who shares the (same) stream or
  brook', rival.
'one who sits near the food',
  parasite.
'one who spins', spinster.
'one who takes care of horses',
  henchman.
'one who travels through fields or
  territories', pilgrim.
'one who travels to a religious shrine
  or holy place', pilgrim.
'one with four feet', swastika.
on loof, aloof.
'on the bearer's left side', sinister.
'on (the) rudder', aloof.
-(o)on, cannon.
-ō; -ōnis, picayune.
'open', frank.
'open air', serenade.
'open air cantata', serenade.
open-face sandwich, sandwich.
'opportunity', hint.
ōrang, orang-utan.
orange, map.
orang-outang, 135.
orang-utan, 135.
ōrang-ūtan, orang-utan.
orang-utan, orang-utan.
orang-utang, 135.
'ordained minister', cleric.
'order', task; tire.
'ordinary', average.
ordrj/ordru, Tartar.
'ore or metal from Cyprus', copper.
orient, solar.
'ornament', shroud; smock.
-os, nest; sarcophagus.
ostracism, 135.

ostracized, **ostracism**.
ostrakismós, **ostracism**.
óstrakon, **ostracism**.
otchek, **woodchuck**.
-oþa, **tithe**.
'other', **alibi**.
otter, **winter**.
'outer top garment worn (primarily)
   by men', **shirt**.
'outfit', **equip**.
'outfit a ship', **equip**.
'outline portrait in black', **silhouette**.
'overly righteous person', **prowess**.
'overshoe (often made of a rubberized
   material)', **galosh**.
'overused', **hackney**.
'owner', **heir**.
'ox', **bugle**.
'ox-goad', **center**.
'oxhide sack', **mail**.

P

p, **pain**.
*p, **pumpkin**.
p-, **pain**.
pā-*, **companion.
'paddle', **poodle**.
'paddle or rudder used for steering a
   ship', **aloof**.
pagan, 137.
pagan, **pagan**.
pāgānus, **pagan**.
pāgus, **pagan**.
pai, **pajamas**.
pain, 137.
pain, **pain**.
'pain', **pain**.
pains, **pain**.
'*pains* and penalties', **pain**.
'painting on canvas', **canvas**.
pajamas, 139.
pakkā, **pumpkin**.
palace, 139.
palace, **palace**.
Palātium, **palace**.
Pales, **palace**.
palisade, **palace**.

'palm of the hand', **aloof**.
'palm sap', **toddy**.
'palm tree', **toddy**.
'palsy or paralysis', **left**.
'paltry', **picayune**.
pālus, **palace**.
pân, **pandemonium**.
pan, **companion**.
Pan, **panic**.
'Pan', **panic**.
Pandaemonium, **pandemonium**.
pandar, **pander**.
Pandare, **pander**.
Pandaro, **pander**.
Pandarus, **pander**.
pandemonium, 140.
pandemonium, **pandemonium**.
pander, 141.
pander, **pander**; xix.
panderer, **pander**.
pane, 141.
pane, **pane**.
panel, 142.
panel, **panel**.
panel discussion, **panel**.
paneled wall, **panel**.
panellus, **panel**.
panel of a door, **panel**.
pane of a nut, **pane**.
pane of a quadrangle, **pane**.
pane of a stone, **pane**.
panic, 143.
panic, **panic**; xix.
panic fears, **panic**.
panic terrors, **panic**.
pānis, **companion**.
'Panish fear', **panic**.
pannus, **pane**; **panel**.
pant, **pants**.
Pantalone, **pants**.
Pantaloon, **pants**.
pantaloons, **pants**.
panties, **pants**.
pants, 143.
pants, **pants**.
papiliō, **pavilion**.
papiliōnis, **pavilion**.
para-, **parasite**.

parabolāre, **parlor**.
parabolḗ, **parlor**.
parade marshals, **marshal**.
Paradise Lost, **pandemonium**.
paṛai, **pariah**.
Paraiyar, **pariah**.
parasite, 143.
parasite, **parasite**.
parásitos, **parasite**.
'parch', **toast**.
par Dieu, **jingo**.
Pareah; Piriawe; Bareier, **pariah**.
pariah, 144.
pariah, **pariah**.
parlor, 145.
parlor, **parlor**.
'part', **meretricious**.
PARTIAL FADING, 260.
'particular burnt color', **phlegmatic**.
'partner', **rival**.
'pass', **fare**.
'passage money', **fare**.
'passenger', **fare**.
'passion for food', **parasite**.
'password', **shibboleth**.
'pastoral form of verse', **madrigal**.
pastōri(um), **pester**.
pasture, xxx.
'pasture', **pester**.
pater familias, **heir**.
Patience, **lace**.
'patronage', **auspices**.
'paved', **street**.
'paved road', **street**.
pavilion, 146.
pavilion, **pavilion**.
'payment extorted by threat of force or harm', **blackmail**.
'payment for damage or loss', **average**.
'payment from an inferior to a superior', **tribute**.
'peace', **belfry**.
peach, 146.
peach, **peach**.
peachy, **peach**.
peasant, 137.
peasant, **pagan**; xxi.
'peasant', **villain**.

pec, **peach**.
pech(e), **peach**.
'peculiarity of pronunciation', **shibboleth**.
pecūnia, **picayune**.
pecuniary, **picayune**.
'pecuniary value', **worship**.
pecus, **picayune**; xvii.
pedegrue; pedegrewe, **pedigree**.
pedem, **pedigree**.
pedestrian, **pedigree**.
pedigree, 147.
pedigrue, **pedigree**.
'pedlar', **chap**.
'peel', **tart**[1].
PEJORATION, 260; xx; xxx.
PEJORATIVE SPECIALIZATION, 261.
*pek^w, **pumpkin**.
pelegrīnus, **glamour; pilgrim**.
'pelican', **Alcatraz**.
pen, 148.
pen, xxii; xxix.
'penalty', **pain**.
'penalty or fine levied for commission of a crime', **pain**.
pen chi, **shantung; tussah**.
'penis (as the instrument of marital 'service')', **shamus**.
penna, **pen**.
'pennes of ye pecok', **pen**.
pens, **pen**.
'people', **gorilla; lewd**.
'people (named on a list)', **panel**.
'people who produce silk', **silk**.
pepō, **pumpkin**.
pépōn, **pumpkin**.
pepsin, **pumpkin**.
peptic, **pumpkin**.
pequeñiño, **pickaninny**.
pequenino, **pickaninny**.
pequeñiños, **pickaninny**.
pequeninos, **pickaninny**.
pequeño, **picayune; pickaninny**.
pequeno, **pickaninny**.
*per, **fare**.
per-, **person; persuade; pilgrim**.
pereger, **pilgrim**.
peregrination, **pilgrim**.

peregrīnus, **glamour; pilgrim.**
'perform an evaluation', **test.**
'perform fellation', **felon.**
'perform one's marital duties',
  shamus.
pericarp, **carpet.**
periodontist, **solar.**
'perish of cold', **starve.**
'permanent mark on the okin', **mail.**
Persai, **peach.**
Perseus, **peach.**
Persia, **peach.**
'Persian', **peach.**
persic, **peach.**
persica, **peach.**
persicum mālum, **peach.**
persikòn mâlon, Mâlon, **peach.**
persikós, **peach.**
person, 148.
person, **person.**
-person, **person.**
'person', **chap.**
persōna, **person.**
'personal and obligatory heirs', **heir.**
'person apt to swoon', **swindle.**
'person belonging to a country
  household', **villain.**
'person convicted of a serious crime',
  felon.
'person from Mongolia', **Tartar.**
'personification of divine retribution',
  nemesis.
'person looking for a fight', **spaniel.**
person of average ability, **average.**
'person of distinguished character',
  man.
'person of low breeding or
  disreputable habits', **cadet.**
'person of succinct speech habits',
  laconic.
'person's lot with regard to his parents
  estate', **cleric.**
'person under Roman jurisdiction',
  pagan.
'person under the jurisdiction of
  Christ', **pagan.**
'person wearing the mask', **person.**
'person who caters to another's baser',
  pander.

'person who engages in any
  transaction', **chap.**
'person who has committed a serious
  (capital) offense', **felon.**
'person who lives in the countryside',
  pagan.
'person whose antics border on the
  insane', **zany.**
'person whose health is drunk', **toast.**
'person who works the land', **pagan.**
'person who works the land for a
  living', **pagan.**
'person with a single obsession',
  man.
'person with whom food is shared',
  meat.
persuade, 149.
persuade, **persuade.**
persuādēre, **persuade.**
'pertaining to', **pilgrim.**
'pertains to harlots or prostitutes',
  meretricious.
pēs, **pedigree.**
pesc, **peach.**
pessic, **peach.**
pest, **pester; xxii.**
peste, **pester.**
pester, 149.
pester, **pester; xxx.**
pestered, **pester.**
pestilence, **xxx.**
'pestilence', **pester.**
pestis, **pester.**
petit, **picayune.**
petticoats, **shirt.**
'petty', **picayune.**
'petty sophistry', **dunce.**
pʰ, **fanatic.**
'phallic staff carried by Dionysus',
  torso.
phaneîn, **sycophant.**
phantasm, **sycophant.**
-phe-, **profanity.**
-phēm-, **fanatic.**
phenomenon, **sycophant.**
phersu, **person.**
phleg-, **phlegmatic.**
phlegm, **phlegmatic.**

placid,   placebo.
'placing side by side',   **parlor.**
plaga,   plagiarism.
plagiarism,   153.
plagiarius,   plagiarism.
plagiary,   plagiarism.
plagium,   153.
plagium,   plagiarism.
'plague',   **pester;** xxx.
'plague or annoy',   xxx.
plánēs,   planet.
planet,   154.
planet,   xxiii.
plánētes astéres,   planet.
*plánēt-s,   planet.
plankton,   planet.
'plant that tolerates salty soil',   **salary.**
'platform extending from one side of
a vessel to the other',   **thug.**
'platitude',   **bromide.**
'play',   **hobby.**
'play a part',   **hypocrite.**
'playing piece in the game of
dominoes',   **domino.**
'plaything',   **hobby.**
'plaything in general',   **hobby.**
plea,   placebo.
*ple12salk-,   placebo.
pleasant,   placebo.
please,   placebo.
'please',   **placebo.**
'pleasing',   **placebo.**
'pleasure trip masquerading as
business',   **junk.**
plēg-,   stroke.
'pliable',   **buxom.**
'pliable (bendable) earth',   **buxom.**
'pluck',   **carpet.**
'plucked',   **carpet.**
'pluck the day',   **carpet.**
'plump',   **buxom.**
'plunder',   **rout.**
pocket handkerchief,   handkerchief.
pod,   galosh.
podiatrist,   pedigree.
poen-,   pain.
poena,   pain.
'poet',   **scold.**
'poet-lampooner',   **scold.**

poinē̆,   pain.
'point',   **stigma.**
'pointed implement',   **broach.**
'pointed pin',   **broach.**
'pointed rod',   **broach.**
'point of intersection',   **gable.**
'pole',   **palace.**
'policeman',   **shamus.**
'police officer',   **constable;** cop.
'Pollyanna Hypothesis',   xxi.
'poltergeist',   **hobby.**
polymer,   meretricious.
pompeon,   pumpkin.
pompion,   pumpkin.
pompon,   pumpkin.
pongee,   173.
pon gee,   shantung; tussah.
pongee,   shantung; tussah.
Pongee,   tussah.
poodle,   154.
poodle,   poodle.
'pool financial resources',   **club.**
'pool resources',   **club.**
'poor wretch',   **wretch.**
popon,   pumpkin.
port,   fare.
portāre,   fare.
'porter',   **cadet.**
'porter for a golfer',   **cadet.**
'portion',   **cleric;** meat; meretricious.
'portion of something to eat',   **meat.**
'possessed by a god or spirit',   **giddy.**
post,   puisne.
'postal matter',   **mail.**
'pot',   **test.**
potamos,   hippopotamus.
potassium,   bromide.
'pot for boiling',   **chowder.**
'pouch',   **mail.**
'pouch containing correspondence',
mail.
pounce,   meerschaum.
'pounce',   **meerschaum.**
'pound',   **delirium.**
'pour',   **alchemy.**
'powder',   **alcohol.**
'powder used as eye make-up',
alcohol.

'power', virtue.
'powerful', xxi.
'practice of plucking at bedclothes',
  carpet.
praetor peregrīnus, pilgrim.
'prayer', bead; xxiii.
'precise', mathematic.
preserve, serf.
'preserve or save', serf.
press, xviii.
'press', shampoo.
pressȝre, xviii.
'pressure', shampoo.
'pretend', feint.
'pretense', feint.
pr(e)u, prowess.
pr(e)u de femme, prowess.
Pr(e)u de femme, xxii.
pr(e)u d'homme, prowess.
'price', pain.
'price list', tariff.
'prick', center.
*priH, belfry.
'prince', tycoon.
'princeling', basilisk.
printing press, xviii.
prō, prowess.
pro-, profanity.
'process of dressing or grooming
  oneself', toilet.
'procurer', pander.
prōde, proud; prowess.
prōdesse, prowess.
'product to be used in washing the
  hair', shampoo.
profānitās, profanity.
profānitātem, profanity.
profanity, 155.
profanity, profanity.
profānus, profanity.
'prohibited', taboo.
'prohibition', taboo.
'projecting teeth of animals', broach;
  brooch.
'prone to do evil', villain.
'proof', alibi.
PROREPTION, 261.
'prosperous', silly.

'prostitute', fornication; hackney;
  meretricious; tart[1]; tart[2].
'prostitutes', harlot.
'protect', meat.
'protection', belfry.
'protective tower', xxii.
proud, 155.
proud, prowess; prude.
pro(u)esce, proud; prowess.
'prove himself alibi', alibi.
'providing pleasure', peach.
'province', pagan.
provost marshal, marshal.
prowess, 155.
prowess, proud; prowess.
prude, 155.
prude, prowess; xxii.
prud/prod, prowess.
p'tuksit, tuxedo.
'public assembly', xix.
puddel, poodle.
puddle, poodle.
Pudel, poodle.
Pudelhund, poodle.
puis, puisne; puny.
puisne, 157.
puisnė, puny.
puisne, puny.
puis nhe, puny.
pukka, pumpkin.
'pull out', carpet.
pumpion, pumpkin.
pumpkin, 156.
pumpkin, pumpkin.
Pumpkins, pumpkin.
Pumpkinshire, pumpkin.
PUN, 261.
'punctuation mark', stigma.
'puncture', stigma.
'puncture mark', stigma.
punish, pain.
punishment, pain.
puny, 157.
puny, puny.
'put a person in a good mood',
  cheer.
'putting things together', algebra.
'put to sleep', cemetery.
pyre, bonfire.

Q

qabbālāh, cabal.
qandi, candy.
qobba, alcove.
'quality', virtue.
'quality or trait that evokes
  admiration', charm.
'quarrelsome', scold.
quean, 159.
quean, queen; xxiii.
queen, 159.
queen, queen; xxiii.
'querulous', sour.
quick, 159.
quick, quick.
quick and the dead, quick.
'quilt-', street.
quint-, ether.
'*quint*-essence, ether.
'quintessential element', ether.
quisling, xxix.

R

r, cancel; cancer; charm; delirium;
  glamour; macabre; peach; pilgrim;
  sister; vernacular.
RADIATION, 261; xviii; xxx.
radish, licorice.
rādix, licorice.
'rafter', shanty.
'rag', pane.
'railing', cancel.
railroad tariff, tariff.
rainbow, buxom.
'raining', dreary.
ram-, shack.
Ramnes, tribute.
ramshackle(d), shack.
'ram's horn', jubilee.
'rank', pedigree.
rāp, stirrup.
'rapid sweeping movement', whisker.
*rast-, restive.
re, furtive; gamut.
rē-, restive.
'reach one's destination', arrive.

'reach shore', arrive.
real, picayune.
'real *mensch*', man.
recausāre, junk.
'received', cabal.
'recess in the coastline', cove.
Recke, wretch.
'recompense', pain.
'reddish yellow', peach.
'redintegration', algebra.
'Red, White, and Blue Rosette',
  chauvinist.
'reed', cannon; junk.
'reed or reedlike stem', cannon.
'reeds', junk.
'refreshing snack', noon.
refuge', xx.
'regular payment for services', salary.
'regular payments made for professional or white-collar services',
  salary.
regurgitate, gargoyle.
'relief from activity', restive.
'reluctant to move', xx.
'remain', restive.
'remainder', restive.
'Remarks by the Chorasmian on the
  Indian Art of Reckoning',
  algorithm.
*Remarks on the Art of Reckoning
  with Indian Numerals—Algoritmi*,
  algorism.
'remembrance', money.
'render void by drawing lines through
  it', cancel.
'renown', worship.
'renowned', slogan.
'rent', blackmail.
rep-, serpent.
'repose', restive.
'reprieve, or general favor', thigh.
reptile, serpent.
'reptile', serpent.
'reputation', fanatic; worship.
'request', bead.
'resembling', grotesque; iodine.
'residence of a ruler', palace.
'resound', lumber.

rest, restive.
'rest', Sabbath.
restāre, restive.
rester, restive.
restif, xx.
restive, 161.
restive, restive; xx.
'restive', restive.
restīvus, restive.
restless, xx.
'restoration', algebra.
'restrain', chignon; xxx.
'restrain within the bounds of a
  pasture', xxx.
RESTRUCTURING BY FOLK ETYMOLOGY,
  262.
'result', stigma.
'result of', broach; charm.
'result of the point', stigma.
'result of the speech', fanatic.
rétif, restive.
*reup, rout.
revert, worship.
revolve', xxx.
'reward', pain.
rhiza, licorice.
rhizome, licorice.
'riding chaps', pants.
right, left; sinister.
'right', sinister.
'rights and place of the deceased',
  heir.
'rigorous', mathematic.
ring, circus.
'ring', circus.
Ring, circus.
rip, rout.
'rip', rout.
rīpa, arrive.
rīpārius, arrive.
'ripe', pumpkin.
'rip off', rout.
'rising', solar.
rival, 162.
rival, rival.
rīvālis, rival.
river, arrive.
'river', hippopotamus.
'river horse', hippopotamus.

rīvus, rival.
'road', street.
rob, rout.
'robber', thug.
'robber-murderer', thug.
Robby, hobby.
Robert, hobby.
robin, hobby.
Robin, hobby.
'rod', rout.
'rôle one plays in the world', person.
'Roman clan', pagan.
'roof', thug.
'roof beam', shanty.
'room', timber.
'room in which to receive guests',
  parlor.
'room servant', xxi.
'room set aside for talking', parlor.
root, licorice.
'root', licorice.
rope, stirrup.
'rope', lace; stirrup.
'rope made from reeds (or hemp)',
  junk.
'rope too worn ', junk.
'rope used to bind a furled sail to a
  boom', gasket.
'rough-cut timber', lumber.
rout, 162.
rout, rout.
'rout', check; chess.
route, rout.
rover, rout.
'rude', lewd; shanty.
'rude woman', hussy.
'rule by those who value honor',
  pain.
'rule by those with a certain amount
  of wealth', pain.
rule of thumb, thigh.
'ruler', palace; tycoon.
'rumor-mongering', gossip.
'rump', bumpkin.
rumpere, rout.
'rump of a horse', chagrin.
'runner', dromedary.
'running', dromedary.

'running place for horses',
   hippopotamus.
'run-of-the-mill', average.
-*rup*, stirrup.
rupta, rout.
rush, junk.
'rush', junk.
'rushlike plant with yellow flowers',
   junk.
'rustic', bumpkin; pagan; villain.
'rut', delirium.

S

s, delirium; hulk; nausea; nest;
   peach; puny; sister; solar; torpedo.
-*s*, mathematic.
s-, salary; serf; serpent.
sábado, samedi, Sabbath.
sab(b)at, Sabbath.
sabbath, 163.
Sabbath, Sabbath.
sabbatical, 163.
sabbatical, Sabbath.
sabbatum, Sabbath.
'sack', mail.
'sacrifice', God.
sad, 164.
sad, sad.
'sad', dreary; forlorn hope.
sad bread, sad.
'saddle (made of a rough pad of
   cloth)', panel.
sadian, sad.
sad-iron, sad.
'sad or desperate wish', forlorn hope.
sæd, sad.
sælig, silly.
'sail', canvas; equip.
'sailor', nausea.
'sailor's condition', nausea.
sal-, salary.
sal, salary.
sal ammoniac, ammonia.
sāl ammoniācum, ammonia.
salary, 164.
salary, salary; xvii.
'sale', auction.

salesperson, person.
'salesperson', cleric.
salt, salary.
'salt', salary.
'salt money', salary.
salty, sour.
'salty', sour.
Samstag, Sabbath.
'sanctify', bless.
'sanctuary', fanatic; profanity.
'sand', arena; xx.
'sandstone', arena.
sandwich, 165.
sandwich, sandwich.
Sandwich, sandwich.
sandwiched, sandwich.
sandwiches, sandwich.
'sandy', arena.
'sandy beach or shore', arena.
'sandy desert', arena.
'sandy place', arena.
sanguine, 165.
sanguine, phlegmatic.
Sanguine, sanguine.
sanguineus, sanguine.
sarcophágos, sarcophagus.
sarcophagus, 166.
'sash worn around the waist',
   cummerbund.
sate, sad.
'sated', jade; sad.
satis, sad.
'satisfy', placebo; sad.
'Saturday', Sabbath.
'sauce', catsup.
'sausage', botulism.
'saviour', serf.
saw, frank.
scaccarium, check.
scaccum, check; chess.
'scale of eleven notes', eleven.
scalh, marshal.
scamellum, shambles.
scamnum, shambles.
scamol, shambles.
'scamp', nickel.
scenc, noon.
sceptre, shambles.

Schaum, meerschaum.
'schedule of customs duties', tariff.
Schemel, shambles.
schipper, equip.
schmuck, smock.
'scholar', cleric.
Schwindler/Swindler, swindle.
'science that deals with reptiles',
serpent.
scissors, shirt.
scold, 166.
scold, scold.
'scorch around', bust.
'scorching', serenade.
Scotism, dunce.
Scotist, 59.
Scotist, dunce.
Scotists, dunce.
'Scotland', dunce.
Scotus, dunce.
'scratch', sour.
'screen', shroud.
scum, meerschaum.
scyrte, shirt.
scythe, frank.
*sd, nest.
*seA-, sad.
'sea', marshmallow; meerschaum;
shanghai.
'seafaring vessel', junk.
'sea foam', meerschaum.
'seafood', catsup.
'seal', gasket.
'seaman', nausea.
'seamstress', sister.
Séamus, shamus.
sean, shanty.
Séan, shamus.
'seasickness', nausea.
sebolech, shibboleth.
'secretarial', cleric.
'(secret) society', club.
section, frank.
'section of window glass', pane.
'secular', madrigal.
'security', belfry.
sedentary, nest.
'sedge', hassock.
'seduce; entrap', lace.

'see', specious.
'seeds of edible cereals', corn.
'seeks to please', placebo.
'seemingly attractive ', specious.
seirios, serenade.
'seize', hag; hint.
'seized by humans', hag.
'select or sift', garble.
selenium, solar.
'self-disciplined', laconic.
'self-satisfied manner', smirk.
selig, silly.
šelkŭ, silk.
'sell', cheap.
'seller', chap.
'sell something by incremental bid',
auction.
SEMANTIC LOCALIZATION, 262.
SEMANTIC RESHAPING BY FOLK
ETYMOLOGY, 262.
SEMANTIC RESTRUCTURING BY FOLK
ETYMOLOGY, 262.
sememe, xxvii.
semi-, megrim.
sen-, senate.
senate, 167.
senate, senate.
senator, senate.
senātus, senate.
senep, mustard.
senēs, senate.
seneschal, senate.
senior, senate.
'senior member of the religious order',
nun.
seoluc, silk.
sēowian, sister.
'separate the ideas accurately',
garble.
sepiolite, meerschaum.
'sepiolite', meerschaum.
sēpion, meerschaum.
September, 167.
September, September.
serēn-, serenade.
serenade, 168.
sérénade, serenade.
serenade, serenade.

serenata, serenade.
serene, serenade.
serēnum, serenade.
serēnus, serenade.
sḗres, silk.
serf, 169.
serf, sergeant.
'serf', villain.
serge, 178.
serge, silk.
sergeant, 170.
sergeant, sergeant.
sergeant-at-arms, sergeant.
sergeant major, sergeant.
sērica, silk.
sērica lāna, silk.
sērikós, silk.
'serious', sad.
*serp-, serpent.
serp-, serpent.
serpent, 170.
serpent, serpent.
'serpent-dragon with lethal breath and
   glance', basilisk.
'serpents', torpedo.
'servant', marshal; sergeant; shamus;
   slogan; zany.
'servant of a knight', sergeant.
servāre, serf.
'serve', sergeant.
'service', shamus.
serviēns, sergeant.
servile, serf.
servire, sergeant.
servum, serf.
servus, serf; sergeant.
set at one assent, atone.
'setting', solar.
'seventh day', Sabbath.
'seventh day of the week', Sabbath.
'seventh day of the week (on which
   rest is appropriate)', Sabbath.
sew, sister.
'sew', sister.
sexta hōra, siesta.
'sexual purity', virtue.
sh, shibboleth.
-sh, galosh.
shabat, Sabbath.

shabatu, Sabbath.
shack, 171.
shack, shack.
shacks, shack.
'shadow', silhouette.
'shadow of a career', silhouette.
'shadow pictures', silhouette.
'shadows of the departed', indri.
'shaft', torso.
shagreen, chagrin.
shagri, chagrin.
shāh, check; chess.
shāh māt, check.
shake, shack.
'shake', shack.
shaky, shack.
'shaman', jumbo.
shambles, 171.
shambles, shambles; xix.
shammash, shamus.
shammes, shamus.
shammesh, shamus.
shampoo, 172.
shampoo, shampoo.
shamus, 172.
shamus, shamus.
shan-, senate.
shan, shantung.
shang, shanghai.
shanghai, 173.
Shanghai, shanghai.
shantung, 173.
shantung, shantung.
Shantung pongee silk, shantung.
shanty, 174.
shanty, senate; shanty; thug.
sharāb, syrup.
sharab, sherbet; syrup.
'share', cleric; meretricious.
'share expenses', club.
shariba, syrup.
sharkskin, chagrin.
'sharp', stigma; tart[1].
'sharp or bitter to the taste', tart[1].
'sharp-pointed implement', broach.
'sharp pointed thing', center.
'sharp wine', mustard.
'shaving', spoon.

*sHd, nest.
'sheepfold', madrigal.
'shell', test; testicle.
'shellfish', catsup.
shemch, noon.
sherab, syrup.
sherbet, 192.
sherbet, syrup.
shibboleth, 175.
shibboleth, shibboleth; xxx.
'shift', smoch.
SHIFT OF SEMANTIC FAME, 263.
'shine', ether.
'shingles', serpent.
'shining', blanket; electric.
'shining forth', phlegmatic.
'shining sun', electric.
ship, equip.
'ship', equip.
shirt, 176.
shirt, shirt.
'shirt', shirt; smock.
'shirt or shift worn over the clothes ',
    smock.
shirt/skirt, shirt.
shirt, shroud.
'shock or clump of hair', hassock.
'shoddy', cheap.
shoe, lace.
'shoe', galosh.
'shoemaker's last', galosh.
'shoe money', salary.
'shopkeeper', chap.
'shore', arrive.
short; shear, shirt.
'shout for joy', cheer.
'show', sycophant.
'showed figs', sycophant.
shrab, 192.
Shrab, syrup.
sh-r-b, syrup.
shred, shroud.
shrew, shroud.
shrewd, xxi.
shroud, 176.
shroud, shroud.
shrub, 192.
shrub, syrup.
'shy', nice.

sib, gossip.
sibboleth, shibboleth.
'sibboleth', shibboleth.
sickle, frank.
'siege tower', belfry.
siesta, 177.
siesta, siesta.
'sieve', garble.
'sign of the fig', sycophant.
'sign or omen', auspices.
silhouette, 177.
silhouette, silhouette.
silk, 178.
'silk', silk.
'silken', silk.
silly, 178.
silly, silly; xxi.
'silly', nice.
'silly old man', hobby.
'silver', salary; solar.
'simpering', smirk.
simple, xxi.
'simple person', bumpkin.
'simulated', feint.
'simulated attack', faint.
'simulation', feint.
sināpsis, mustard.
'sing', cant; charm; hen.
'singer', charm.
'singing', cant; slogan.
'singing of a group of finches',
    slogan.
'single link', mail.
sinister, 179.
sinister, sinister.
sion, shanty.
sion tig, shanty.
sir, senate.
Sirius, serenade.
sir-kek, silk.
sister, 179.
sister, sister.
'sisters', nun.
sīt-, parasite.
sit, nest.
'sit', nest.
'sit down', nest.
'site in which the seeds develop',
    nest.

'site of conflict', **arena.**
sitology, **parasite.**
sitomania, **parasite.**
sitosterol, **parasite.**
'sixth hour', **siesta.**
skāld, **scold.**
skāldskapr, **scold.**
*skǎp-, **shambles.**
*skap-, **shambles.**
*skapnom, **shambles.**
skǎp-tron, **shambles.**
skêptron, **shambles.**
*(s)ker, **circus.**
*sker, **shirt; shroud.**
skiff, **equip.**
'skin', **tart¹.**
'skin disease', **serpent.**
'skinflintish', **cheap.**
*skip-, **equip.**
skip-, **equip.**
skipper, **equip.**
skirt, 176.
skirt, **shirt; shroud.**
skirts, **shirt.**
skruð, **shroud.**
skyrta, **shirt.**
'slanderer', **sycophant.**
'slander in verse form', **scold.**
'slaughter', **decimate.**
'slaughterhouse', **shambles; xix.**
Slav, **slew; slogan.**
slave, **slew; slogan.**
'slave', **serf; sergeant.**
'slave born in the house of his
   master', **vernacular.**
'sleep', **cemetery.**
'sleepy', **lethargic.**
slew, 180.
slew, **slew; slogan.**
'slew of children', **slogan.**
'slice of ham', **noon.**
'slippery', **smock.**
slóg, **slogan.**
slogan, 180.
slogan, **slogan.**
'slovenly', **harlot.**
slow, **quick.**
slúagh, **slogan.**
Slúagh, **slew.**

slue, **slew; slogan.**
sluga, **slew; slogan.**
sluggard, **hag.**
'sly', **smirk.**
'small', **picayune; pickaninny.**
'small amount', **tithe.**
'small ball threaded on string', **xxiii.**
'small coats', **shirt.**
'small copper coin of relatively little
   value', **picayune.**
'Smaller Bear', **cynosure.**
'small group of secret plotters',
   cabal.
'small horse', **hobby.**
'small lattice', **cancel.**
'small object of little value',
   picayune.
'small or worn-down thing', **corn.**
'small ribs', **jade.**
'small room', **cove.**
'small value', **insect.**
smearcian, **smirk.**
*smer-, **meretricious.**
*(s)meug, **smock.**
smile, **smirk.**
'smile', **smirk.**
smirk, 181.
smirk, **smirk.**
's *mobile*', **torpedo.**
smock, 181.
smock, **smock.**
smocking, 181.
smocking, **smock.**
'smoke', **buccaneer.**
'snake', **serpent.**
'snare', **lace.**
'snare with a rope or noose', **lace.**
So, **gamut.**
'social outcast', **pariah.**
sodium bromide, **bromide.**
sōl, **solar.**
sol, **solar.**
solar, 182.
solar, **solar.**
'Soldier of Christ', **pagan.**
solea gallica, **galosh.**
'solid', **sad.**
'(solo) actor', **hypocrite.**

spoon, spoon.
'spot', mail; stigma.
'spot on the sun', mail.
'spotted', mail.
'spread fertilizer', manure.
'spread out', street.
'sprightly', quick.
'spring', vernacular.
'spur', center.
spy, specious.
'stable attendant', xxx.
stadium, furlong.
'staff employed as a symbol of
    authority', shambles.
'stain', mail.
'stake', palace.
'staked out', pagan.
'stallion', henchman.
'stamp', shampoo.
'stand', restive.
'stand back', restive.
'star', comet; planet.
stāre, restive.
starve, 187.
starve, starve; torpedo.
'starved of education', starve.
'starved of love', starve.
'star with long hair', comet.
'state or quality of manliness', virtue.
'state or quality of wickedness',
    profanity.
'stationary point of a compass',
    center.
'statue', bust.
St. Audrey's laces, tawdry.
'steal', rout.
'stealthily or secretly', furtive.
'stealthy', furtive.
'steed', henchman.
steer, torpedo.
stella, comet.
steorfan, starve.
'step', pedigree; shambles.
'step down', pedigree.
-st(e)r, spinster.
-ster, spinster.
sterben, starve.
'stern critic', bumpkin.
sternere, street.

*sterp-, torpedo.
sthag, thug.
stick, stigma.
'stick', club.
'stick (with something sharp and
    pointed)', center.
'stiffness', torpedo.
*stig-, stigma.
stig-, stigma; stirrup.
stīgan, stirrup.
stigma, 187.
stigma, stigma.
stigmata, stigma.
stigos, stigma.
stigrāp, stirrup.
'stink', bromide.
stirrup, 188.
stirrup, stirrup.
stirrups, stirrup.
'stitching', broach.
'stock', torso.
'stock (of a plant)', torso.
'stock or clan', tribute.
'stolen', furtive.
'stolen goods', cheat.
'stool', shambles.
'stop', check.
'stoppage', check.
'stopping to examine', check.
'stop to examine', check.
'storehouse', magazine.
'storehouse of (published or publisha-
    ble) information', magazine.
'storm', shanty.
'story', zany.
strǣt, street.
'stranger', pilgrim; wretch.
'strangler', sphinx.
Strasse, street.
strāta, street.
strāta via, street.
strātum, street.
straw, street; xxii.
stre, spinster.
'stream', rival; shibboleth.
street, 188.
street, street.
-stress, spinster.

'stretch', **thing.**
strew, **street.**
'string', **lace; yarn.**
'stringed musical instrument',
  cithara.
'string made of gut', **yarn.**
'string of rules', **sister.**
stroke, 189.
stroke, **stroke.**
'stroke', **stroke.**
stroma;, **street.**
'structure of any sort', **machine.**
'stud', **broach.**
'studded with nails', **broach.**
'study of food or nutrition', **parasite.**
'study of fruit', **carpet.**
'study of insects', **insect.**
'study of man's life', **quick.**
'stunned', xxi.
stupid, xxi.
'stupid', **nice.**
'stupid or ignorant person', **dunce.**
style, xx.
su, **swastika.**
*su-, **sister.**
-suād-, **persuade.**
'submarine', **torpedo.**
SUBREPTION, 266; xxii; xxix.
'subtle', **nice.**
'suburban residence', **villain.**
'suck', **felon.**
'suckling', xxx.
'sudden fear', **panic.**
'suffer a deprivation of', **starve.**
'suffering', **pain.**
'sufficient', **sad.**
'sugar', **candy.**
sugar candy, **candy.**
'sugared', **candy.**
'suggestion', **hint.**
'suicide', **felon.**
sui juris, **heir.**
'suitable for wearing', **shroud.**
sulcate, 93.
sulcate, **hulk.**
sulciform, **hulk.**
sulculus, **hulk.**
sulcus, **hulk.**
summer, **gossamer.**

summer-gauze, **gossamer.**
summer-goose, **gossamer.**
sun, 182.
sun, **solar.**
'sun', **solar.**
'sung', **cant.**
sunne, **solar.**
*sunth, **solar.**
'superior ability', **prowess.**
'superiority in battle', **prowess.**
'superstition', **taboo.**
'supplies (for a journey)', **fare.**
'supply with necessities', **equip.**
'support', **shambles.**
'supporter', **henchman.**
'surf', xxi.
'surface for counting out money',
  shambles.
'surgical treatment of fractures',
  algebra.
suster, **sister.**
sūtra, **sister.**
suture, **sister.**
svastika, **swastika.**
*sw-, **sister.**
'swallow', **gargoyle.**
swastika, 190.
swastika, **swastika.**
sweet, **persuade.**
'sweet', **licorice; persuade.**
'sweet alcoholic beverage', **syrup.**
'sweet beverage', **syrup.**
'sweet confection', **junk.**
'sweet cooling drink', **syrup.**
'sweet drink made from sugar',
  syrup.
sweetie pie, **tart[1].**
sweet-meat, **meat.**
sweetmeat, **meat.**
'sweetness', **tart[1].**
'sweet wine', **syrup.**
'swelling', **cancer; thigh.**
swestor, **sister.**
swindle, 190.
swindle, **swindle.**
swindler, **swindle.**
swintan, **swindle.**
swintilōn, **swindle.**

'swollen finger', **thigh.**
'swollen hundred', **thigh.**
'swollen part of the leg', **thigh.**
'swoon', **swindle.**
'sword', **frank.**
sycophant, 191.
sycophant, **sycophant.**
'sycophant', **placebo.**
sŷkon, **sycophant.**
sykophántēs, **sycophant.**
syndactylism, **dactyl.**
SYNONYMY, xxiii.
syphilis, 192.
Syphilis, **syphilis.**
'Syphilis ('Pig-lover')', **syphilis.**
Syringa, **lilac.**
Syringa vulgaris, **lilac.**
syrup, 192.
syrup;, **syrup.**
szĕ, **silk.**
szŭ, **silk.**

T

t, **botulism; dactyl; money; nausea;**
nest; stigma.
-t-, **censor; nausea.**
t-, **pain.**
ta, **taboo.**
'table', **shambles.**
'tablecloth', **map.**
'table companion', **parasite.**
'table for displaying materials up for
sale', **shambles.**
taboo, 195.
'taboo', **Sabbath.**
tabu, 195.
'tack', **broach.**
tāh, **dactyl.**
Tah-dzû, **Tartar.**
tai, **tycoon.**
'take', **nemesis.**
'taken illegally', **furtive.**
'take *pains*', **pain.**
take the Dutch route, **bumpkin.**
'taksa', **task.**
tāla, **toddy.**
'tale', **zany.**

'tale-teller', **gossip.**
'tale-telling', **gossip.**
'talk', **blackmail; parlor.**
'talkative', **slogan.**
'talking', **parlor.**
'tall grass', **hassock.**
Talmud, **cabal.**
tam, **tandem.**
tá mathēmatiká, **mathematic.**
tambu, **taboo.**
tandem, 195.
tandem, **tandem; xxix.**
tangere, **tax.**
tap, **tattoo.**
'tapered stick used for hitting', **club.**
'tapping', **broach.**
taps, **tattoo.**
tap toe, **tattoo.**
tap to(o), **tattoo.**
tap too, **tattoo.**
Tap Too, **tattoo.**
tapu, **taboo.**
tārī, **toddy.**
taʾrif, **tariff.**
tarifa, **tariff.**
tariff, 196.
tariff, **tariff.**
'tariff', **taxi.**
tart¹; tart², 196.
tart, **tart¹.**
Tart¹, **tart¹.**
Tart², **tart².**
Tartar, 197.
Tartare, **Tartar.**
Tartars, **Tartar.**
Tartarus, **Tartar.**
Tarter, **Tartar.**
tart up, **tart¹; tart².**
tasca, **tax.**
task, 198.
task, **task.**
Tatler, **toast.**
tattoo, 199.
tattoo, **tattoo; xxix.**
taurus, **torpedo.**
tawdry, 200.
tawdry, **tawdry; xxx.**
tax, 198.

tax, tax.
'tax', tribute.
taxa, task.
taxameter, taxi.
taxe, taxi.
taxe/taxa, taxi.
taxi, 200.
taxi-, taxi.
taxi, taxi.
taxi-(cab), taxi.
taxi-cab, taxi.
'taxicab', hackney.
'taxicab driver', hackney.
taximeter, taxi.
taximeter-cab, taxi.
taxi-mètre, taxi.
taxing labor, task.
taxing task, task.
táxis, taxi.
'tax or levy', tithe.
taxrare, task.
tax the imagination, task.
'teachings', cabal.
tear (apart), tart[1].
'tear', rout.
-tect, thug.
Te Deum, placebo.
'tell a story', yarn.
'telling (i.e. counting) ones beads',
    xxiii.
'tell the truth', soothe.
'temple', fanatic; profanity.
'temple sexton or beadle', shamus.
ten, tithe.
'ten', eleven; tithe.
*ten-, thing.
tenēre, thing.
'tent', canvas.
tenth, tithe.
'tenth', decimate; tithe.
'tenth part of something', tithe.
'tent without walls', pavilion.
*terk^w, tart[1].
terra, toast.
terribly, xxii.
'territory', pilgrim.
'terror', panic.
*ters, toast.
'terse', laconic.

test, 201.
test, test.
testa, noggin; test.
testa/testum/testū, test; testicle.
testicle, 202.
testicles, testicle.
'testimony', martyr.
testū, test.
testum, test.
tête, noggin; test.
'tether (an animal)', pester.
teu(H), thigh.
th-, tandem.
th, gamut; solar.
ṭhag, thug.
thassein/thattein, task.
thatch, thug.
'thatched cabin', shack.
'that which has been poured forth',
    God.
'that which one deserves',
    meretricious.
the, gamut.
'theater auditorium', cave.
then, gamut.
thĕr, treacle.
there, gamut; tandem; tart.
thēriakà, treacle.
thēriakà phármaka, treacle.
thēriakḗ, treacle.
thēriakós, treacle.
thermometer, fornication.
thermonuclear, fornication.
thermós, fornication.
the; this; then, tandem.
'they stopped and examined a motel',
    check.
'they stopped and registered at a
    motel', check.
'thick, sweet liquid', syrup.
'thick, sweet medicinal liquid', syrup.
'thief', furtive.
thigh, 202.
thigh, thigh.
'thin board', panel.
'thin board within a frame', panel.
thing, 203.
thing, thing; xix;

'thing', thing.
thingamajig, thing.
'thing said against something',
   fanatic.
'things decreed', fanatic.
'thing sung', cant.
'thing to be seized (and used to
   advantage)', hint.
thingumbob, thing.
thingummy, thing.
'thing which is bent', buxom.
thirst, toast.
this, gamut.
Thomism, dunce.
Thomist, dunce.
'thorax', cithara.
'thorn', center.
thousand, thigh.
'thrash', canvas.
'thread', sister; yarn.
three, testicle; tribute.
'three', tribute.
'throat', gargoyle.
'throne', shambles.
'through', person; pilgrim.
thug, 203.
thugs, thug.
Thugs, thug.
thumb, 202.
thumb, thigh.
thumb a ride, thigh.
thumbs down, thigh.
thumbs up, thigh.
thumb through, thigh.
thumb your nose, thigh.
'thus', tandem.
thyrse, torso.
thýrsos, torso.
thyrsus, torso.
'tie up with string', lace.
tig, shanty.
tiga, stigma.
'tighten', sphinx.
'tilling the land', manure.
timber, 204.
timber, pane; timber; xix.
tīmē, pain.
'time for napping', siesta.
timocracy, pain.

tīmokratia, pain.
tincture of iodine, iodine.
ting, thing.
-tion, auction.
tire, 205.
'tissue bed or framework', street.
tithe, 205.
tithe, tithe.
'tithe', decimate.
tithing, tithe.
Tities, tribute.
'to', arrive.
'toady', parasite.
toast, 206.
toast, toast.
'toast', toast.
'toast of the town', toast.
tobacco, nicotine.
toddy, 207.
toddy, toddy.
toe, dactyl.
'toe', dactyl.
'toe of an animal', dactyl.
'together', sister.
toile, toilet.
toilet, 207.
toilet, toilet; xxi.
toilet(te), toilet.
toilette, toilet.
-tom-, insect.
'tomb', bust.
-tomy, insect.
tonsillectomy, insect.
'too obliging', xxi.
tooth, solar.
'toper', bevy.
'topic', thing.
'top story of a house', attic.
Torah, cabal.
'torment', pain.
torpedo, 208.
torpedo, torpedo.
torpēre, torpedo.
'torpid', lethargic.
torque, tart[1].
torrēre, toast.
torso, 209.
torso, torso.

torte, **tart**[1].
tostāre;, **toast.**
toster;, **toast.**
tostus, **toast.**
'touch', **feint; task.**
'touch again and again', **task.**
'tough guy', **thug.**
'toward', **arrive.**
'towel', **map.**
'tower', **torso.**
'tower of protection', **belfry.**
'towns of importance', **worship.**
'tow or drag', **hulk.**
-tr-, **meretricious.**
'track', **delirium.**
'tracker', **cockatrice.**
'tracks', **cockatrice.**
tractus, **train.**
'trading vessel or merchantman',
   hulk.
trag-, **tragedy.**
tragedy, 209.
tragedy, **tragedy.**
tragere,* **train.
tragināre, **train.**
tragōidia, **tragedy.**
trahere, **train.**
train, 210.
train, **train.**
trained, **train.**
TRANSFERENCE, 266; xx; xxviii.
TRANSMISSIONAL FILTERING, 276.
'trash', **junk.**
Tratrar, **Tartar.**
traurig, **dreary.**
'travel', **fare.**
'travel along a runway before take-off
   or after landing', **taxi.**
'travel by (*taxi-*)*cab*', **taxi.**
'traveler', **pilgrim.**
'traveling bag', **mail**[2].
treacle, 210.
treacle, **treacle;** xviii.
'tree', **bumpkin.**
'trees', **timber.**
trèfle, **club.**
'trefoil', **club.**
trethan, **gable.**
tri-, **tribute.**

triacle., **treacle.**
'tribe', **tribute.**
tribus, **tribute.**
tribute, 211.
'tribute or rent', **blackmail.**
tributum, **tribute.**
Tributus, **tribute.**
'trifling talk', **gossip.**
'trite expression', **hackney.**
Triton, **gable.**
triubhas, **pants.**
Troglodytes gorilla, **gorilla.**
Troilus and Cressida, **pander.**
'troop', **slogan.**
'trouble', **pain.**
trousers, **pants; pajamas.**
'trousers', **pants.**
'true and original meaning', xvii.
'true meaning', xvii.
'trumpet', **jubilee.**
TRUNCATION, 276.
trunk, **torso.**
'trunk', **torso.**
'truth', **soothe.**
tsiap, **catsup.**
'tube for the conduction of bodily
   fluids', **cannon.**
'tube used for the conduction of
   fluid', **cannon.**
'tumbledown house', **shanty.**
tumor, **thigh.**
'tumult', **harlequin.**
tung, **shantung.**
'tunic', **shirt.**
Turdus migratorius, **hobby.**
turn, **giddy.**
'turn', **circus; worship.**
'turned into', **worship.**
turngiddiness, **giddy.**
turngiddy, **giddy.**
'turn into', **worship.**
turris, **torso.**
tussah, 173.
tussah, **shantung.**
tusser, **shantung.**
tussor, **shantung.**
tussur, **shantung.**
tussure, **shantung.**

-tut, virtue.
-tūt, virtue.
Tut-Ånkh-Åmen, ammonia.
tuxedo, 212.
tuxedo, tuxedo.
Tuxedo Lake, tuxedo.
Tuxedo Park Country Club, tuxedo.
twelve, 63.
twelve, eleven.
'twelve-sided figure', eleven.
'twist', cancel; tart[1].
'two', eleven.
'two-headed axe', labyrinth.
'two left', eleven.
'two-wheeled coach drawn by a single horse', taxi.
tycoon, 212.
tyrós, thigh.
týrsis, torso.

U

u, giddy; pain; sister.
'ugly', grotesque.
uisquebaugh, winter.
-ulus, circus.
-um, peach; solar.
'unattractive', dreary.
'unbeliever', heathen.
'unblemished', mail.
unchecked, check.
'uncivilized warrior', Tartar.
'uncle', nun.
'uncontrolled uproar', pandemonium.
'uncontrolled uproarious behavior', pandemonium.
'unconventional', bizarre.
'uncovered', sycophant.
'uncultivated land', heathen.
unda, winter.
under a person's thumb, thigh.
'undergarment', smock.
'under his own legal jurisdiction', heir.
'underpants', pants.
'under Roman jurisdiction', pagan.
'understood', hint.
under the auspices of, auspices.

'under the influence of grog', grog.
undine, winter.
'undivided unit of food', bread.
undulate, winter.
'unfortunate', silly.
'unhappy', sad.
'unhappy or unfortunate person', wretch.
'unisex undergarment', shirt.
'unite', atone.
'unit made up of such links', mail.
'unlettered', lewd.
'unmarried', spinster.
'unmarried woman', spinster.
'unpleasant', grotesque.
'unpleasantly gloomy', dreary.
'unpleasant-tasting', sour.
'unravel', carpet.
'unravelled', carpet.
'(unruly) crowd of people', rout.
'upholstered stools', hassock.
'upper air', ether.
'upper body (without head and arms) of a statue', torso.
'upper leg', thigh.
'uproar or riot', rout.
Urdu, Tartar.
ūrere, bust.
Ursa Major, cynosure.
Ursa Minor, cynosure.
-us, sarcophagus.
'useful', prowess.
'Useful', prowess.
'useful in battle', prowess.
'useless odds and ends', lumber.
Ut, gamut.
'utter defeat', rout.
'utter defeat on the field of battle', rout.

V

v, quick.
v-, botulism; bugle; serf; tart.
vacca-, bugle.
'vagabond', harlot; planet.
'vainglorious', prowess.
'valiant', bizarre.

W

'warning', check.
'washing place', xxi.
'waste', heathen.
'waste away', corn.
'watch', auspices.
'watchman', shamus.
'watch-tower', belfry.
water, winter.
'water', winter.
'water animal', winter.
'water-carrier', Alcatraz.
'water closet', toilet.
'wave', winter.
Waverley, henchman.
'way', street.
'w.c.', toilet.
'weak', beriberi; feint; left.
'weaken', lewd.
'weakened', lewd.
WEAKENING, 268; xxii.
'weak in body', silly.
'weakness disease', left.
'weak or feeble', puny.
'weak sound', feint.
'wealth', picayune.
'wear down', corn.
'wearer of whitened clothing', xxvii.
'wearing long hair', comet.
'wear out', jade.
'weary', sad.
weather, ether.
'wedding or marriage', bridal.
'weepily sentimental', maudlin.
*weH, ether.
welfare, fare.
'well', swastika.
well groomed, groom.
wenćel, wench.
wench, 215.
wench(e), wench.
*weng, wench.
'went with', constable.
weorðoan, worship.
weorðoscip, worship.
wera, canter.
were-, canter; virtue.
'were-gild', pain.
werewolf, canter; virtue.
wet, winter.

'wet', smock; winter.
'wet season', winter.
What cheer, cheer.
'whim', migraine.
whisk, whisker.
whiskbroom, whisker.
whisker, 215.
whisker, whisker.
whisker pole, whisker.
whiskey, winter.
'whiskey', corn.
whistlepig, woodchuck.
'white', Alcatraz; auburn; blackmail; blanket.
'whiten', xxix.
'white of an egg', auburn.
'white or gray horse', blanket.
'whitish', auburn.
'whole', pandemonium.
'whore', queen; xxiii.
'wicked', profanity.
'wicked or blasphemous language', profanity.
'wicked person', felon.
'wicker (*caned*) basket', cannon.
'widow', heir.
'widower', heir.
'wife', bridal.
'wife of a king', queen.
'wild', hag.
'wild animal', xix.
'wild beast', treacle.
'wild hawk', hag.
'wild-looking', hag.
'wild man', orang-utan.
'wild people with hair all over their bodies', gorilla.
'wild; venomous beast', treacle.
wind, ether.
'wind', ether.
'winding sheet', shroud.
'windpipe', gargoyle.
'wine', amethyst; syrup.
'wineskin', mail.
winter, 216.
winter, winter.
'wise', xxi.
'wispy', gossamer.

X

Y

'youthful university hanger-on',
  cadet.
yovel, jubilee.
ypocrite, hypocrite.

Z

z, delirium; quick.
Zan(n)i, zany.
zany, 221.
žárna, yarn.

Zeus, jovial.
Zimmer, timber.
zither, 46.
zither, cithara.
zithera, cithara.
zoo, quick.
zoological garden, quick.
zoology, quick.
zôon, quick.
zôós, quick.